FORGED
BY
COAL

FORGED
BY
COAL

A Family's Story

TERRY BAILEY

Gooney Otter Press

Cover design by Alitia Riddle. Book design by the author. All photos and illustrations are by the author unless otherwise indicated. Font is Georgia 12 pt., printed on 60# bright white offset paper.

Library of Congress Cataloging-in-Publication Data has been applied for.

ISBN 979-8-9861332-0-1 (cloth)
ISBN 979-8-9861332-1-8 (paper)

FIRST EDITION (2022)

Printed in the United States of America

Progressive Printing
Greenville, South Carolina

1927 - 1989   1923 - 2002

To my parents, Vergie Ellen Terry Bailey and Lowell Douglas Bailey. This is their story of living and raising their family in the coal mining town of Covel, in southern West Virginia. They provided for, supported, and loved my brothers, Rick, and Jeff, and me. Dad set the highest standards for a work ethic and expected us to always do what was right. Mom nourished and guided us to succeed in whatever we choose to do and showed us the intrinsic value of education.

To the miners that I have known who had commitment and virtues as enduring as the mountains that overlie the West Virginia coal seams.

.

CONTENTS

- Continued -

INTRODUCTION

After nearly a decade of contemplating my childhood in Covel, West Virginia, I finally decided it was time to put my reflections onto paper. This is my personal testament of the last years of coal camp life in West Virginia. I am a member of the last generation of Americans able to give a firsthand account of life in a coal camp, also known as America's twentieth century feudal system. You didn't just live in a small town built by a coal company; as a child, you were at the bottom rung of the system. Your entire life – food, clothing, housing, medical, schooling, the money you had in your pocket – was controlled by the Coal Company because coal, "Black Gold," was your life.

As the late Tennessee Ernie Ford sang in *16 Tons*, "...I owe my soul to the company store." This is my firsthand account of growing up as the son of a coal miner, living in a coal camp – Covel, West Virginia. Theodore Roosevelt referred to the living conditions of coal miners as worse than the serfdom of the Middle Ages. I hope this story accurately reflects the Appalachian region of my youth, when Coal was King, and based on my firsthand experiences, refutes Roosevelt's reference. This was the last decade in which coal companies maintained full ownership. The life of my family is an accurate depiction of that of the other miners and their families living in the Covel coal camp through sometimes tragic but often joyful times.

On April 10, 1946, I came into this world during the first quarter of the first year of the official "Baby Boomer" generation. I was born at home in a log cabin at the foot of the Appalachian Mountain Chain. I like to tell the story of my birth in a log cabin since it makes people want to compare me with President Abraham Lincoln. But that's probably one of the few things we have in common. I have spent a life of work in service, but I was never a contender for President of the United States. For forty-five years, I was an educator because from an early age my parents encouraged me to do anything but coal mining. The story that you are about to read is not meant to be about me, specifically, but rather my entire family.

Part I of this story deals with the Bailey family of Rock, West Virginia, and the Terry family of Littlesburg, West Virginia, and how these families became intertwined with the meeting of Vergie and Doug, and the tragedy that occurs when my mother is expecting her first child, me.

Part II covers the decision and the struggle to settle in a coal camp.

Part III is the major portion of the story and covers our family's life in Covel, the coal camp of my youth. How the experiences of the 1950's with my extended family, other miners' children, and the culture of the coal camp helped shaped me for my life's journey.

This is my family's story as it unfolded in the "coal camp." I feel that it is important for the reader to understand why it was a unique community experience that was developed, owned, and operated by the coal companies. As Robert Munn wrote in 1979, "The coal industry's involvement in the housing and social welfare of its labor force was the result of historical accident rather than conscious choice." I hope the reader will have a better understanding of this involvement through the experiences of my family which were instrumental in shaping our lives during the last years of the company town.

The events, family names, locations, and dates are factual in *Forged by Coal: A Family's Story*. However, some names and activities were created to provide transition and continuity as a composite to represent actual outcomes.

My wife, Margaret Ann, says I might have a John Steinbeck in me, and says she might have a Cézanne in her, because she is always wanting to go paint somewhere. She says she can paint while I write my book about the coal camp kid. A John Steinbeck or James Still, I am not but I still want to tell you what it was like. So, you can know how it was. Why? As F. Scott Fitzgerald wrote, "You don't write because you want to say something: you write because you've got something to say."

PART I – Before the Coal Camp

Chapter 1 – New Beginning: Vergie & Doug

Vergie met Doug in October of 1944. She and two of her high school girlfriends had gotten a ride from Princeton, West Virginia to the roller-skating rink that sat in the outskirts of Oakvale, a small town to the east. Oakvale was not much more than a spot in the road, but it did have a post office and a rural school that served the county from there to the Virginia state line. The teenagers had graduated from high school in May and on the following Monday started work together on the production line at the Maiden Form factory in Princeton. The factory was one of the largest employers in the area, outside of coal mining. It employed more women than any other business, mainly because running the sewing equipment was considered a feminine pursuit. When they weren't working, the young women hung out together, but they all still lived at home.

The skating rink was a favorite spot for the trio. They loved the lights and the loud swing music, but most of all, it gave them a chance to be away from the factory and the day-to-day family routine. As she skated around the rink, Vergie noticed a tall, thin but muscular man wearing thick glasses with a cigarette hanging from his lips. She had not seen this fellow around the rink before. With the war on, most skaters were females because most of the men were in Europe or the Pacific. It was unusual to see a new man, but there was something about his smiling face that also caught Vergie's attention. None of her girlfriends knew him either. Vergie gave him a quick glance more than a couple of times. She smiled slightly when he noticed her and shot her a sheepish grin.

Doug skated over and introduced himself. "Hi, my name's Doug. and who do we have here?" He waited for a response with a broad smile as the light from the string of incandescent lamps reflected off his forehead and glasses.

Bev, the most talkative of the trio, was first to respond, "Hi to you too! I am Bev, and these gals are my dearest friends, Vergie, and Peggy. Peggy is the best skater, Vergie's the smartest and I am the prettiest, what can I say?"

Doug responded with a big grin and said, "Glad to meet you gals. Let's skate." The girls all skated around Doug for the rest of the evening. When they stopped for a coke, the rink managers eyed them to be sure they didn't bring their bottles into the rink. It was obvious that Doug was sizing the girls up for a possible future date. Bev caught his attention first. She was 5' 10" and a flirt. Peggy seemed too quiet, but she was a good skater. Vergie had the nicest smile, but a little short from his vantage point at 6' 2". Doug became more enchanted with Vergie as the evening continued. It was obvious that she spoke only when she had something to say, unlike Bev, who seem to talk whenever there was a lull in the conversation.

As the skating rink closed on that Saturday, Doug offered the girls a ride back to Princeton. Looking directly at Vergie with his smile across his 5 o'clock shadow, he announced, "I've got a couple of fresh peaches, so whoever likes peaches can ride up front with me." He held the peaches up, and Vergie lengthened her 5 feet 1-inch frame as much as she could and pulled the fruit from Doug's hand. She rode in the front seat of the Model A Ford, which Doug had borrowed from his dad, and they headed back to Princeton on US 460 with Bev and Peggy in the backseat. The foursome started chattering as Doug pulled out of the parking lot.

Referring to their work in the Maiden Form Plant, "So you girls are contributing to the war effort by making brassieres and girdles," Doug joked.

"No!" Vergie responded. "With war needs, we are sewing undergarments for the Women's Army Corp, including heavy underwear for the cold in Europe." Vergie responded. Bev chimed in, "Some days the line does go into production of brassieres. We had a run-in khaki as well as white just this week. What are you doing to win the war?"

Doug responded, with a slight apologetic tone, "I am welding down at Norfolk, Virginia to help with ship building. We are turning them out faster than ever. I tried joining the Navy but didn't make it because of my eyes. My three older brothers are all in the Army."

Doug had gone to work in Norfolk because it was good money and because he wanted to contribute to the war effort. He had dropped out of school in the ninth grade, instead of working on the family farm and doing other odd jobs in the Rock, West Virginia community where he grew up. When the country went to war, though, he knew he had to do more. His older brothers, Wallace, Orville, and Junior were all in the Army. They enlisted within weeks of the Pearl Harbor attack. Only his youngest brother, Melvin, was still in school. Doug wanted to serve his country too. Seven days after the attack on Pearl Harbor, he had turned 18 and tried to join the Navy, but he was rejected due to his poor vision. He had undergone cataract surgery when he was a boy for what was likely a congenital condition. When he was later drafted, he again failed the physical for the same vision condition.

Doug, Lowell Douglas, used the shorten version of his name. Only his mother, called him Loel when she needed something or wanted to know where his younger brother or sisters were. His Mother thought that she had named him Loel Douglas but somehow the birth certificate would have Noel on it. Maybe because he was a December 14th arrival. Doug thought his name was spelled Lowell and wrote it that way. Decades later he would have it legally changed to Lowell to satisfy a Social Security Office inquiry.

Aside from the chance to contribute to the war effort, Doug was also grateful for the job in the shipbuilding yard, because he wasn't keen to work "in a hole in the ground", as he liked to call the ubiquitous coal mines of West Virginia. In southern West Virginia, the best paying jobs were in the mines, but his vision would make it difficult for him to work in the low light of the mines. The thick glasses he wore would be covered quickly with coal and rock dust.

As they neared the Princeton city limits, Bev and Peggy told Doug he could drop them off first. Vergie, who did not want to lengthen Doug's drive any farther, announced to Doug, "I can get a ride from here, or I will stay with Bev tonight and ride the bus home tomorrow."

Doug straightened his shoulders and said with his now familiar grin, "No I can take you right to your doorstep, young lady." Vergie looked at Bev and Peggy for a few seconds, then turned back to Doug and spoke. "Okay, then, take me home. I live on the Littlesburg Road from here."

Vergie told Doug to take the Littlesburg Road—State Route 20—toward the courthouse. Doug continued his smile and said in a lower voice. "Glad we have some time, just the two of us." Vergie responded only with her smile and a slight giggle. Over the next 3 miles at 35 mph, Doug learned that Vergie Ellen Terry, at 19 years old, was the youngest daughter of Edward and Laura Terry. All her four sisters—Mildred, Helen, Marie and Carrie—were already married. She would be the last of the girls to be "hitched" as her dad would say. She had three brothers. Her oldest brother, Kenneth, was still single and "just waiting for the right one." He was in the Army and had seen combat, pushing toward Berlin and victory in Germany. Kenneth did not write home often, but the family knew he had not been injured. Her other two brothers were Clarence and Donald, 16 and 12, respectively. They still lived at home and attended the local school. Clarence was the serious one and a terrific student. Donald, the youngest of the Terry clan, was full of energy, and as the baby of the family, spoiled. At least according to Terry siblings.

"Is it okay to come and see you tomorrow?" Doug asked as he opened the passenger door for Vergie. "We go to church—the one we just passed—at ten in the morning. Services let out around noon, depending on if anyone comes to the alter for prayer requests, that can take some more time before the minister dismisses us." Vergie responded. "So that's an answer of yes. Around 1?"

"I have to catch the 7 o'clock train back to Norfolk. So, we will have time to go to Princeton, see a movie and eat before that." Doug responded.

Doug borrowed his brother's truck, which Junior had left at the homeplace when he shipped out. Doug's Mother was the church organist, so his dad would need his own car to take her and Doug's youngest brother and two sisters to the

Rock Methodist Church. Feeling anxious, Doug started earlier than necessary to arrive at the Terry home. In fact, it wasn't but 11:10 when he passed the church on the Littlesburg Road. He turned around and parked in the church lot, then he decided to go into the church. From the back, he couldn't tell where Vergie was seated.

The service ended with prayer requests, but no one felt the need to come down to the alter. As the organist played "Until We Meet Again", Doug spotted Vergie. The light from the window struck her light blue dress as she pulled her arms into the sleeves of her heavy wool coat. Doug thought, "She is prettier today in the sunlight than she was last night at the roller-skating rink."

When Vergie turned to walk back up the center aisle, she was surprised to see her tall, skinny date, standing with a grin on his face at the back of the church. She had only just told her mother on the way to church that she had a date and now here he stood. With some embarrassment, Vergie stammered, "This is Doug. I mean…Doug…this is my mother, Mrs. Terry. Mother, this is the man I told you was coming by today, Doug…Douglas Bailey from Rock."

As they walked toward the church door, Doug said, "Very nice to meet you, Mrs. Terry. I enjoyed talking with Vergie last evening. You have got a very nice family, from what she tells me."

Despite being a little flushed, Vergie was able to introduce the rest of the family that was present. "These are my brothers, Clarence, and Donald. My sisters are all married and live away. It just us and Papa. Papa couldn't get out this morning. He had to meet somebody about some cattle."

"I told him that it wasn't a good idea to do business on Sunday," Mrs. Terry noted, "But he said, 'You got get it when you can.'"

"Doug, we walked to church." Vergie said as they came down the steps.

She was about to suggest they meet at the Terry home when Doug said, "Let me give you all a ride. If the boys can ride in the back of the truck, you and your mother can ride up with me."

"That's not necessary, we can walk home." Mrs. Terry responded.

"Please let me give you a ride. It is still a little chilly today." Doug stated.

Mrs. Terry smiled as the boys acknowledged that they would like a ride. "Thank you. I think the boys would enjoy the ride. They don't get in vehicles too often." Clarence and Donald hopped into the back of the truck while Vergie rode in the middle between Doug and her mother. This was the first time that they touched each other as they sat close in the front seat.

The ride lasted only a couple of minutes. Mrs. Terry invited Doug to come in for lunch. "It is ready. Ham, green beans, stewed tomatoes, and mashed potatoes. We have apple pie for dessert. It's a little tart since we can't use as much sugar." Referring to the sugar rationing for the war effort. At first, Vergie felt a little uncomfortable with her mother's invitation but on second thought, she knew it was the best thing to do. She had seen this with her brothers-in-law as they courted her sisters. She knew her Mother wanted to get to know this young man before he took her youngest daughter out alone in a pick-up truck.

Vergie turned to Doug. "Please come on in. We will still have time to get to the picture show. Mother is a fine cook. I know you haven't eaten yet, since your folks go to church too." Vergie indicated.

"I would be pleased to have lunch and to meet Mr. Terry," Doug said with a reassuring tone.

Doug thought Vergie was right. "This is fine cooking. Almost as good as my mom's." Mr. Terry didn't say a lot when he met Doug. He did ask him if his dad had a herd of cattle. Doug told him they only had two cows for milk, butter, and cheese.

"Your dad and you both do public work?" Mr. Terry asked. Doug knew that public work was meaning that you worked for someone or a company and not for yourself. He tried to make a good impression as Mr. Terry sized him up.

"Yes, pretty much. Dad is a carpenter for Pocahontas Coal Company at McComas. He and a partner repair and build around the mines and in the coal camps. He also does some work for folks on their houses or outbuildings in Rock, but that's more to help them out. They usually pay him back with crops or chickens. Sometimes they come over and return the favor if he needs an extra hand. With all his sons gone except my youngest brother, Melvin, he sometimes needs the help on the farm."

Mrs. Terry graciously asked all about Doug's work and Norfolk, Virginia. "I haven't had many train rides. I think it would be interesting to see the Virginia countryside by train," Mrs. Terry stated.

Doug hit it off with Clarence and Donald since they also liked to hear about fishing and hunting. This was a topic of their brothers-in-law and Doug had plenty to share with the river and woods around his homeplace. He started fishing with his brothers almost from the first day that he could hold a pole. He loved to fish and hunt. The boys were most interested, however, in hearing about Doug's brothers and where they were stationed. They were proud that their big brother, Kenneth, was in the Army.

As they finished the last of their pie, Mrs. Terry told Vergie, "You go on. The boys can help with the dishes."

Doug thanked Mrs. Terry for the dinner, saying, "The meal was delicious, and the pie was just the way I like it – not too sweet." Doug said his goodbyes and shook hands with Mr. Terry. Doug didn't get a great feeling as he walked away from Mr. Terry. He enjoyed lunch and appreciated the reception he received from Mrs. Terry and Vergie's brothers, but he was glad to escape Mr. Terry's scrutiny and be alone with Vergie.

"I really enjoyed meeting your family" Doug told Vergie as they pulled out onto the Littlesburg Road and headed west toward Bluefield. "They seem nice. And the meal was terrific." Doug added.

"You haven't met the rest of my sisters or my older brother yet." Vergie stated.

"Well, that's about like my family except, I have three older brothers, and two younger sisters." Doug replied.

Vergie suddenly realized they were headed toward Bluefield and not Princeton, "Oh, why are we headed this way?"

"Better movie choice in Bluefield. I figure you would like to see a movie in color and with music. How about *State Fair*?" Doug responded.

"I heard from Peggy that it was great. Good choice." Vergie declared with a smile.

"Glad you like the idea."

They did enjoy the movie. When the characters Mangy and Pat met on a Ferris wheel, Doug took Vergie's hand and held it for the rest of the film.

After the movie, they didn't have time to go to dinner before Doug's train left. He drove Vergie home. He surprised her when he opened her car door and tentatively kissed her right on the lips. She had thought he might kiss her when they reached the door. But then, maybe out of the sight of her parents and brothers was best. She reached up and returned his kiss perhaps with a little more exuberance.

Vergie and Doug saw each other every weekend after that. Doug came up from Norfolk on either the N&W or the Virginian train. He borrowed his dad's car or that of one of his buddies away in the service and headed to Littlesburg to visit Vergie. They went to the skating rink, on picnics, fished on the Bluestone or saw picture shows in Bluefield or Princeton. On Sunday evenings, he caught the last train back to Norfolk. Between visits, he worked long hours welding on ships while Vergie was sewing bras at the plant in Princeton.

Doug asked Vergie to marry him on New Year's Day 1945, just before he boarded the train back to Norfolk. This wasn't a surprise to anyone, because these two were crazy about each other. Besides it was their turn. His older brothers were married, and her older sisters were married.

Two huge obstacles stood in the way of their marriage. First, Vergie had only known Mercer County, West Virginia, and she refused to uproot her life to live in Norfolk, Virginia. She wanted to be near her mother, sisters, and her brothers. Her sister, Carrie, had moved off and rarely visited her family, and Vergie did not want to live like that. Doug told her, "I can't just quit my job and come back here. This is defense work and the war effort depend on us. I could be imprisoned or fined or kept from other work if I just leave."

One late evening after a long day at the shipyard, it dawned on Doug on what he should do. He asked his dad to write a letter to the Draft Board, requesting that his son could come back home to help on the farm since his three oldest sons were all away in the Army. The letter worked. He was given the permission to leave his work as a welder and return to Rock, West Virginia to help on his dad's farm.

The second obstacle was finding a paying job in Rock once he returned to West Virginia permanently. The only work in the area that paid to support a family was coal mining. Doug still wasn't keen on "working in a hole", but he was in love and wanted more than anything to marry Vergie Ellen Terry. Doug's Father, Lake, told him that they might be hiring at the Crane Creek Mine at McComas.

Lake was a carpenter with the coal company at McComas, working as one half of a two-man team with his partner Curt Parcell. They did some construction and repair work around the mine operation, but they spent most of their time repairing structures in the company owned town, McComas, where most of the miners lived. Lake was an exception. He and his wife, Cora Lee, lived on a knoll overlooking the Bluestone River at Rock. Their 88 acres was a very small parcel of the 8000 acres that Richard Bailey, Jr., Lake's great grandfather, had acquired in the early 1800s.

The Baileys of Rock could trace their ancestry to England with William Bailey who came to Jamestown in 1610 on the Prosperous. His wife, Mary joined him, seven years later. They had a son, Henry whose son James and his wife,

Lucy had five children. Their son, Richard and his wife, Elizabeth had ten children. Their son Richard, Jr., was the one that settled in the most western region of Virginia in present day, Tazewell County, Virginia and Mercer County, West Virginia.

Lake and Cora Lee raised their family of six boys and two girls on this farm. They had cows, pigs, and chickens. There were fruit trees and berry bushes. They canned their produce crops for winter. For the most part, the family was self-sufficient on the top of this knoll.

Doug went to McComas with his dad at the start of a shift. McComas, one of the oldest coal operations opened by the Pocahontas Fuel company, had been operating since 1902. The company had constructed coal camps at McComas and the nearby Crane Creek and Sagamore mines. With the need for war production, all the mines were in full operation. Doug checked in with the Foreman and was hired the same day. Now on the coal company payroll, he was partnered with an experienced miner for training and shadowing. Of course, he was also required to join the United Mine Workers of America (UMWA). He was eligible for coal company benefits as defined by the UMWA contract, including housing in the coal camp of McComas. The only problem, there were no vacant homes, and there was a waiting list.

He and Vergie could marry, but where would they live? All of Doug's brothers had left home when they married. All of Vergie's sisters had done likewise. So, they weren't going to be the first to start their marriage in their childhood homes either at Rock or Littlesburg.

On several of their rides in a borrowed car, the couple passed the Rock View Swimming Pool which was located between the Bailey homeplace and Littlesburg. Having grown up within sight of a good flowing river, the Bluestone River, he and all of the Bailey kids loved swimming. He promised Vergie they would go to the pool either here, at Rock View or Lake Shawnee Pool. She had never been in the pool water at either place. On one of their trips, traveling between Rock and Littlesburg, Doug stopped the car suddenly at the Rock View Pool. There was a For Rent sign in front of Mrs. Linkous's house. Everyone knew the Linkous log home, one of the oldest in town, on the road adjacent to the swimming pool property. Mrs. Linkous had been a widow for almost ten years. Her husband had died in a mining accident.

Doug and Vergie knocked at the door and the 60+ year old Mrs. Linkous opened the door. She knew Doug, and she told them, "Yes, my renters got a house over at the Tralee coal camp. They are moving this weekend." The threesome climbed the steps to the second floor to view the three-room apartment. You could tell that originally, there had been three bedrooms and a small storage area on the second floor. The spaces had been converted to a bathroom, kitchen, living room and a bedroom at the front of the house. Vergie thought it was cozy and she could see how they could start with some limited furniture. They agreed to rent it and Doug gave her a $10 deposit toward the first month's rent. Doug thought as they left the Linkous house, "we're going to get married. Wow!" Vergie said, "Doug when can we see the preacher?" Doug responded, "I think we have to go to the courthouse and get a license first. We are ready!"

Having overcome all the obstacles to their marriage, they were now free to wed. On May 28, 1945, twenty days after Germany surrendered in World War II, Lowell Douglas Bailey and Vergie Ellen Terry exchanged vows in the Methodist Parsonage in Littlesburg, only a couple of miles from where Vergie had been born and where she grew up. They went directly to their first home, the little apartment over Mrs. Linkous's house. Mrs. Linkous was very kind and kept to herself allowing the newlyweds their privacy.

Fortunately, Vergie's older, married sisters had forewarned her about what to expect on her wedding night. Within months, they were expecting their first child, a boy who would be a coal camp kid. He would spend most of his first 18 years of life living next door to other coal miners' kids. He was the first of four babies and the one to remember the way it really was in the coal camp. He would play cowboys and Indians, attend a three-room elementary school, become a big brother, deliver newspapers, become a Boy Scout and be the part of the last generation to grow up in the company's coal camp.

Vergie woke up from a quick morning nap around 9. It was good to catch a little extra sleep. She and Doug enjoyed listening to the radio in the evenings and some of the best programs came on at 9. They loved the Lone Ranger and the Lux Theater.

Doug, who, by now, she had been married to for almost six months, had caught his ride to the mines a little after 7 AM on this chilly November morning. As had become her routine, she got up when he got up, prepared his breakfast, then packed his lunch box, two lunch meat sandwiches with butter pickles from her mother-in-law's pantry along with two apples, also from his home place. She filled a thermos of coffee and a jug of water, both staples for miners. The aroma of strong coffee still filled the air. The smell didn't bother Vergie like it did a few weeks ago, in her earlier stages of pregnancy. She was looking forward to having her first baby due in April. She was almost giddy about having a baby. Doug was hoping for a boy. It really didn't matter to Vergie, but deep down she thought a girl would be nice. They had already picked out names: if it was a boy, they would call him Terry Douglas, and if it was a girl, Pamela Kay.

Vergie was starting to think about what she would fix for dinner when she heard Mrs. Linkous exclaim, "Oh my, how terrible!"

Forged by Coal

Chapter 2 – Tragedy at Littlesburg

Vergie slowly opened the door at the top of the steps that lead to Mrs. Linkous's home, downstairs. "Is everything all right, Mrs. Linkous?"

"Can you come down here, Vergie?" Mrs. Linkous responded. At the bottom of the steps just inside the front door, Mrs. Linkous stood with a Mercer County Deputy Sheriff.

"Are you Vergie Terry?" the deputy asked.

"I am Vergie Bailey, married to Douglas Bailey, but I am a Terry."

"I'm Deputy Bird—Bob Bird—with the Sheriff's Department. I have some bad news for you. Could we sit down?" Mrs. Linkous motioned them into the parlor. She sat beside Vergie on the couch while the Deputy pulled up a chair.

At that moment, the only thought running through Vergie's mind was that something must have happened to her husband. She knew that Doug didn't care for working in the mines. Something awful had happened. Vergie mustered just enough strength to ask in a barely audible whisper, "What has happened to Doug?" With a gasp, she leaned toward the Deputy.

"No, it is not your husband, Mrs. Bailey," replied Deputy Bird. "I'm sorry to tell you that your mother and your brother died this morning." As Vergie reeled from the unexpected news, Mrs. Linkous put her arm around Vergie's shoulder. The Deputy continued, "We are not sure exactly what happened but they both appear to have died from gun shots." Vergie could not begin to understand what the Deputy was saying.

"What are you telling me? Who shot them? Which brother? Clarence, Donald. Is Kenneth back?" Her breathing became labored as she listened to the Deputy. Her questions came out rapidly and disjointed as she tried to make sense of his words.

"I am sorry. Let me start with what we know. Your sister," he glanced down at a notebook, "Mrs. Mildred Tabor, called from a neighbor's home to tell us that your dad discovered your mother dead in the kitchen when he returned from feeding the hogs this morning. He ran to his daughter's home—that's Mildred Tabor's—to tell her about your mother, and Mildred came back to the house with him. They first thought your mother had died of a heart attack. Then, they discovered your brother," again he referenced his notebook page for a forgotten name, "Donald, was dead in his bed from a gunshot"

As Vergie slumped with shock, Mrs. Linkous held on to her with both hands to support her from a total collapse. "Get a glass of water from the kitchen, Deputy." Deputy Bird followed Mrs. Linkous command and returned to the parlor with a glass of water. "Vergie, drink this slowly," commanded Mrs. Linkous.

Suddenly scores of questions rushed into Vergie's head. Who would do this? Why was Donald home? It was a school day. How could they both be dead?

"It seems that your brother, Donald, may have accidentally shot his...your...mother. After he saw what happened he used the gun on himself, we think." Deputy Bird used a slower, more deliberate but nervous tone.

More questions immediately came to mind. Where did Donald get a gun? Why would he have it in the house? How

18

did this happen? How could he kill himself? Where is Doug? I need my husband.

"Mildred has provided addresses and phone numbers for everyone in the family. The Sheriff has sent another deputy to Piedmont to tell your other sisters, Marie, and Helen. He also called your sister in New Jersey and spoke to her himself. The Sheriff will be calling the Red Cross to get word to your brother, Kenneth. Mildred told us he is in the Army stationed in Germany." Hating to leave Vergie with the tragic news, the Deputy then turned to Mrs. Linkous, "Will you be here until Mrs. Bailey's husband gets in from work?" Mrs. Linkous nodded in the affirmative.

"Ok. I have to get back to the house to help with the investigation. I must pick up Dr. Peters, the county medical examiner to take him to Littlesburg. We have a lot to look at and hopefully get the facts together for us and your family. Doc may be able to give us more details about how they died. I am very sorry." Deputy Bob Bird put his hat on and slowly retreated, closing the front door in a deliberate, slow manner.

Vergie sat dazed on the sofa, thinking, "Mom and Donald dead. Mom and Donald dead?"

"I wish Doug was here. I wish I was back home with Mom, Papa and Donald. I wish I was with Mildred." Conflicting thoughts swirled through Vergie's head.

At that moment, Doug was deep in the number Two Mine at McComas. Digging coal in the dark with only the miner's light on his cap was every bit as tough as Doug had imagined before he took the job. It wasn't the hard work that bothered him. He was used to long hours and hard work, having grown up doing chores on the family farm and then building ships at the Norfolk Naval Yard for World War II. No,

Doug was nervous by nature. He didn't like the darkness, and the dust-filled air made it even more difficult to see.

Before the attack on Pearl Harbor, Doug had gone down to see about employment at the Norfolk Naval Yard. They offered a vocational training program for welders. He was thinking about this opportunity at Thanksgiving in 1941, and his folks encouraged him. His dad, Lake Erie Bailey told him that he didn't think Doug would care much for the mines, since he liked the outdoors. Besides, it would be a problem for Doug to work in the darkness of the mine. Doug had a vision problem. A major vision problem. He was the only one of his parents' six boys and two girls to develop cataracts at an early age. He underwent cataract surgery, which removed his natural lens and provided him no ability to focus naturally. This would later be determined to be congenital cataracts, a condition that would be passed on to the next three generations of the Doug Bailey family.

Fortunately, Lake was a union member, working for Pocahontas Coal, under the union contract all children under 18 were covered for doctors, hospital stays and surgeries. Most farmers had no insurance to cover medical expenses. Lake was thankful to have the benefit of the UMWA contract.

Once the United States entered the War, though, Doug thought he would follow his three older brothers into the service. Orville, Wally, and Junior were all in the U.S. Army by the first year of the conflict. Doug didn't wait for his Draft Notice. He thumbed a ride to the Navy Recruiting Station in Bluefield and signed up. With the other boys in the Army, he thought he'd like to be different and see the world from the ocean. He had not spent much time at the ocean but had been to Virginia Beach several times. Doug liked the water. He loved the beach, the waves and the feel of the saltwater.

Doug was called for his Navy physical. All went well until it came to the vision test. All the services required a minimum of 20/100 vision in each eye without glasses and corrected with glasses to 20/40 in each eye. Without glasses, Doug's vision was 20/400 in each eye.

A disappointed Doug left Rock on a train to Norfolk to seek training and employment as a welder. Despite failing the Navy physical, Doug later received a draft notice and, hoping for different results, he returned to the Bluefield Armed Services Induction Center. Once again, he was rejected based on the vision test. Resigned to his fate, Doug headed back to Norfolk, Virginia. Doug was quick to catch on to welding. He was a visual learner, and he was experienced with his hands, thanks to his dad and the farm responsibilities.

Norfolk and especially the beach were a popular place for service men on leave and the huge number of defense workers, men, and women. He was boarding just outside the Naval Yard. It was easy to get to the beach and into downtown, Norfolk, Virginia's largest city. He also liked welding and felt that he was contributing to the war effort, but all this took second place when he fell for Vergie Ellen Terry.

As he dug his pickaxe into the seam of coal for the thousandth time that day, Doug made up his mind to go to the mine foreman at the end of the shift and make a serious request. He got off the rail car that carried the men in and out of the mine, the man trip, and asked the foreman, Joe Lusk, if he could talk with him.

"What's on your mind, Doug," Joe asked. "I wanted to know if there is any outside work available?" replied Doug.

"What do you want to do, Doug? You know the money is in mining inside. The tipple work and clean up don't pay as much scale. You are catching on and look like you are doing a good job." "I know," said Doug, "but I don't like working inside the dark tunnel. With my vision and all, the darkness makes it tough to see my work. You know last week I had a close call. The crew was setting the blasting charges at the mine face. I wasn't told or didn't hear them, that they were setting off the blast. The blow back from the blast knocked me on my rear and almost took my helmet off. If I had been closer, I would have been out cold."

"Yea, sometimes that happens. You have to be alert, pay attention. Sorry, but we ain't got anything here outside. All the jobs are taken and men waiting for any openings, inside or out," Joe responded. He thought for a moment, "You know American Coal is increasing their mines in Deerfield, over the mountain in Wyoming County. I hear that some of the tipple crew is going inside, and they are expanding the outside work. If you want to go try for it, I will get you the name of the foreman." Doug thanked him and said, "Yes, I'd like to look into it."

Doug hurried to catch up with his ride. Chet Smith had a Ford coup with five good-sized men waiting for Doug to ride back toward Matoaka. Doug's house was the first stop, about a five-minute drive from the mine, and the rest of the men were home in another 15 minutes on a dry day. The heavy coal trucks caused rutting and rain, or snow would double the driving time because of the poor road conditions caused by the heavy coal trucks.

When he opened the door and saw his bride of six months flushed, eyes swollen and at the side of Mrs. Linkous, he immediately thought of the baby. Something had gone wrong with the baby.

Forged by Coal

Chapter 3 – Family Changed Forever

"Vergie, do you feel okay? Is the baby all right?", Doug rushed to her side.

Mrs. Linkous blurted, "Doug, there's terrible news from Vergie's family. Her Mother and brother—the young one—died today. They were shot." In disbelief, Doug reached for his bride and embraced her almost forcefully.

"What do you mean 'dead'? Shot?" he asked.

"Doug, it's terrible. Mom and Donald are gone. They think Donald shot mom and then killed himself!" Vergie's voice cracked as she broke down in tears again.

Except for her sobs, the room was silent for a moment, which felt like an hour. Mrs. Linkous broke the silence to relay what Deputy Bob Bird had told them earlier. When she finished, she said, "I can leave you alone to talk," and she stood up. "Let me fix you some dinner," she offered.

"Mrs. Linkous, it's okay. Vergie and I need to talk. I don't think we can eat now," Doug softly muttered. Then he turned to his wife, "Vergie, let's go upstairs. Vergie nodded, and Doug helped her up the steps.

Vergie whispered, "I am glad and relieved that you are here. We ought to go over to my parents' home and see what's happened."

"Okay, let me get us a ride. Will you be okay while I go up to the store and call Chet? His neighbor has a phone. I will ask if he can take us, or can I borrow his Ford."

"I'll be okay. I'm going to pack a suitcase so we can stay at Mil's if we need to or decide to. What do you think?"

"Yep, we ought to plan for that," Doug replied.

Doug walked the couple hundred yards to the store at the crossroads. You could see it from the Linkous house. It was almost closing time on a Monday evening, and as Doug rushed to use the phone before they closed, he noticed that the weather had turned cooler. Junior Boyles, the owner's son, was starting to sweep up. Doug asked, "Can I use your phone to call Matoaka?"

"Sure, the cost is ten cents since it is Matoaka. Just lay the dime on the counter." Junior replied.

Doug picked up the receiver and in seconds, he heard the operator's crisp voice come on the line, "Number please."

"I need Russell Shrewsbury in Matoaka," Doug replied.

"One moment and I will connect you. The number is 87 W 11. I will ring it." The operator stated.

Doug heard the ring—in a pattern of one long, one short—repeat three times before a young, high-pitched voice came on. "Hello, this is Jane. Mom's taking in the clothes."

"Can I speak to your daddy?" Doug replied. Doug could hear Jane yell, "Daddy, someone wants you on the telephone."

In less than a minute, Russell came on the line. "Yep, this is Russell," Doug heard. Doug told him who he was and why he was calling Chet Smith. He told Russell of the sad news of the unexpected deaths of his Mother-in-Law and his young Brother-In- Law.

"Sure, sorry to hear about your woman's loss. That's pretty bad. I will send Jane over to get Chet. Just hold on."

"Thanks," Doug muttered. Doug could hear Russell telling his daughter to go fetch Chet.

While waiting for Chet over a silent line, Doug remembered the last time someone spoke to him about his "loss". It was twelve years ago. His brother, Ralph, had died in a car accident less than a mile from their homeplace. Doug was only 12 and Ralph was 17. He remembered that day as if it happened last week. Ralph and his friend, Everett Underwood, went out that evening to celebrate their entry into the Civilian Conservation Corps. They were going to take the train the next day to Camp Preston in Kingwood, West Virginia. As they neared the Bailey's home, Ralph veered off the road and into a tree. Everett wasn't injured in the crash and ran to Ralph's house to tell the Baileys that Ralph was hurt bad and was out cold. Doug remembered that the whole family ran down the hill and into the road to find Ralph's lifeless body pinned between the vehicle and a tree.

He remembered the funeral and how sad his mother had been when Ralph was gone. Ralph had been active in the Epworth League of the Methodist Church and was well known in the Rock Community. More than a hundred attended the funeral.

Doug recalled his decision to be baptized about a month after Ralph's death. His Mother and Father were so glad. Doug knew that he and his siblings had been christened but with the death of Ralph, he was thinking about the afterlife for the first time. It was the right thing to do in the church where the family had always worshiped. His Dad was a Sunday School Teacher and his mother played the pump organ and they brought the family to church every Sunday.

As he heard Chet approaching on the other end of the line, his thoughts returned to his wife. Doug wondered if Vergie was strong enough to cope with all of this and stay strong for the baby.

Chet came on the line, "Doug what do you need? Are you working tomorrow?" Doug explained the situation with the unexpected family deaths and asked for a ride or to borrow Chet's car. Chet said, "My goodness, that is terrible to hear. You must tend to your wife. This has got to be a big shock to her. It's probably best to take you and your Mrs. over." Doug replied that would be fine. He and Vergie had already thought about staying with Mil. Chet told Doug he would be over within the hour.

When Chet pulled up, Doug put the oversize suitcase in the trunk of the Chet's 1935 Ford. Chet was proud of this vehicle. He had purchased it from the Widow Blankenship after her husband passed in '41. She didn't drive, and, even before he died, they hardly went anywhere except church. Her boys were in the service and headed to the Pacific, so the widow had decided that it didn't seem right just to leave a perfectly good car moldering by the barn.

Vergie sat between her husband and Chet on the bench seat. When Chet arrived, he had offered a quiet, reverent condolence to Vergie. They did not know each other well, as he'd only met her on the couple of occasions that he saw them at the Rock View Swimming pool during the summer. After the initial greeting, there was dead silence during the 20-minute ride to Littlesburg. Vergie started to tell Chet about the tragedy, but she thought better of it when she realized she wasn't anywhere clear about the details. Vergie was probably in shock and still not able to comprehend the tragedy.

On seeing her sister, Mildred, the two women embraced tightly. Vergie broke into an outburst of tears unlike any Doug had ever witnessed, Mildred glanced at Doug and shook her head as if to say, "I don't know how this happened or what are we going to do?" Papa Terry and Clarence were seated on the sofa motionless, seeming to be waiting for their turn to console Vergie. The pair stood and entered the embrace of Mildred and Vergie.

After a moment, Papa Terry said, "Vergie, you better sit down. Mil, can we get her a glass of water?" Papa Terry and Vergie sat on the sofa while Clarence stood at the end of the sofa.

Clarence said, "I will get sis a glass of water." He headed to the kitchen.

Mildred's husband, Nathan Tabor—Nat for short—was holding their daughters, Ruth and Louise, by the hands Nat's bewildered expression indicated that he was at a loss as to what to say. The Tabor sisters, who had never seen their mother or Aunt Vergie cry, held on tight to their dad.

Vergie had questions for her dad. As she started asking him about the mornings' events, he shook his head. His almost inaudible responses where about the same each time. "I don't know. Not sure. I told the sheriff, but he didn't understand." For the most part, Papa Terry could not provide Vergie with more clarification. Vergie could still not understand how her brother could accidentally shoot her mother and then turn the gun on himself.

A silence fell over the room. Nat took the girls to his and Mildred's bedroom. The girls were sleeping in their room for the night while Doug and Vergie would take the girls' room. Mil had prepared another bedroom for Carrie and Larry. She and her one-year-old son were living in New Jersey with her widowed Mother-In-Law, Mom Teel. Larry had just been discharged from the Army. Housing was a problem since little construction had been done during the war. They had been looking for a place for several months. They would be here by morning. They were driving down during the night to make better time with less traffic. Larry was known for his "aggressive" driving.

Clarence and Papa Terry returned to their house where Papa Terry's brother Joseph Cleveland Terry and his wife waited. They had come over from McDowell County to help. They were waiting at the homeplace. "Tell Aunt Molly and Uncle Joe that we will see them in the morning, and we appreciate them coming," Mildred managed to tell Papa Terry as he was leaving. When everyone was settled around the Tabors' living room, Mildred explained that their brother, Clarence was with his dad and their sister Helen and her husband, George. They had left their two children Lois and Lowell with neighbors in Piedmont. George didn't think it was a good idea to have the kids here just now.

Vergie, Doug, Mildred, and Nat had just settled in the living room when the front door opened. Vergie and Mildred's other sister, Marie, and her husband Robert entered. Their two-year-old daughter, Donna, had fallen asleep on the trip from Piedmont, so Robert carried her. The scene of sobbing and uncontrollable crying was renewed.

"We are not going to spend the night," Robert said. "I have to check on my mother back in Piedmont in the morning. Dad's away up in Ohio on a Moose Convention. We can be back tomorrow evening after work." It was apparent that Marie was also expecting a child when she sat down in one of the dining rooms' chairs that Nat had pulled into the living room. She and Vergie both had due dates for April, as best they and the doctors could figure.

Having received unsatisfactory answers from Papa Terry, the family prodded Mildred for information about the deaths. The room was intently silent as Mil answered their questions with her characteristic stoicism. "Papa burst through the back door into the kitchen here about 9:30 this morning and said, 'Laura has had a heart attack!' I told the girls to stay in the house and I was going with Papa Terry to check on Grandma. When we got there, Mama was sitting in a chair in the kitchen. I could see blood coming down from her shoulder." Mil paused as her mind visualized the morning events. She resumed, "I told Papa it wasn't a heart attack, but she did look dead. I asked him what happened. He said that's how he found her when he came from feeding the hogs. I told him that we should call the Sheriff's office and go get the boys from school. That is when he said, 'Donald is here. He still has a case of pneumonia and stayed home today.' I shouted to Donald and heard no answer. So, I went into his room and found him." She hesitated and began with a lower voice. "... with Kenneth's shot gun. His chest was covered in blood, and the bed sheets were soaked. The Sheriff and his men came after we called from the Harmons'. The Sheriff thinks Donald must have accidentally fired the gun and when he saw that it hit Mama, he killed himself."

Everyone sat in silence until Nat spoke, "It's good that Mil had everyone's address written down. She told the Sheriff everything he asked for. You know, Mil doesn't miss much."

Doug asked the question everyone was thinking, "Mil, I don't see how your dad would not have seen the blood on your Mother and why didn't he look for Donald before he came to get you?"

Mil shook her head and softly muttered "I just don't know."

Chapter 4 – Gathering for the Good-Bye

Mildred Terry Tabor awakened before anyone. It was a little after 5 and the rest of the house remained asleep. Mil changed from her nightgown into a worn but neat, well-pressed housedress. She would change into Sunday clothes in the afternoon, but for now, she had to fix breakfast for eight.

When she went downstairs, she saw that some of her neighbors had already visited and left ham biscuits, stewed apples and a couple dozen eggs. It was the Appalachian tradition: in mourning, feed the body to soothe the grief. Neighbors started bringing food to the Terry and Tabor residences as word got out about the tragedy. The first covered dish arrived while Mil was changing the bed linens. Mil expected that there would be plenty more to eat, since the community universally liked Laura who had always been active in the local Methodist church since she was a child. She had passed her sweet disposition on to all of their daughters.

Mil had almost single-handedly made the arrangements for the funeral service. As the oldest daughter of Edward and Laura Terry, Mil had helped raise her sisters and brothers. She was prepared by experience and necessity to be the matriarch of her family. At his best, Papa wasn't much at making plans or organizing. He had depended on his wife and his oldest daughter. But in the face of this tragedy, he became even more lethargic and distant in responding to Mil's questions or suggestions.

"Whatever you think, Mil." Was his slow, consistent reply.

In planning the funeral, Mil had provided all the details to the funeral director at Mercer Funeral Home in Bluefield. He would bring the bodies of her mother and brother back to the Terry home this afternoon in preparation for the wake this evening.

Mil put on a pot of coffee. Since rationing had ended the year before, they were fortunate to have plenty of Maxwell House coffee. With the joint funerals planned for the following day, she anticipated that the next two days would be the longest and saddest.

As Mil finished scrambling a full pan of eggs, Doug entered the kitchen. "Vergie is still asleep, I think expecting is harder on her than she thought it was going to be", Doug stated directly. "Your Mother had Vergie as her sixth child before she was expecting Clarence. I guess she didn't let on like there was much to it with Vergie. Of course, I don't know much about expecting a baby. My Mother didn't share a lot with us either."

"Having your first child is full of surprises and new experiences, Doug," Mildred responded.

Doug picked up his cup of hot coffee and sipped it slowly and then said, "Mil, your mother was a nice, kind, and gentle woman. In some ways, she has...had a sweeter way about her than my mother."

Mil smiled, "Yes she was very special." Her voice dropped off as she said, "Just the opposite of the old man," in reference to her father.

Edward—Papa Terry—had a matter-of-fact disposition and few real friends. He preferred the company of his livestock to church services. He was consistent and steady to his daily routine. He dressed the same except for an occasional trip to church, you would find him in his starched bib overalls. Laura always made sure they were crisp and pressed. Maybe because, Papa Terry had come through the Great Depression mainly on his wits in making a living, he may have lost the values of his childhood.

"Yes," Doug responded without hesitation. He remembered how each responded when he and Vergie talked to them about getting married.

"Well just as Vergie is working and making money at the Maiden Form factory, you come along and ask her to get married and start with raising kids, huh?" Papa Terry expressed under his breath to the couple when they told them of their engagement.

Looking at Papa Terry with a slight stare, Laura had exclaimed with a pleasant, sweet tone, "I know you two are head over heels for each other. You make a precious couple. We wish you all the happiness."

Laura Terry's other four daughters had already left home. They all got out as soon as they could. Of course, marriage is expected for the girls. She had only seen her oldest, Mildred, get married. The others had married in simple ceremonies away from home, though most local daughters married in their local church. She anticipated that Vergie and Douglas would do the same as her sisters, which they did at the Littlesburg Methodist Church parsonage about a month later on May 28, 1945. The Rev. L.W. Rudy married the couple, and he would preach the funeral tomorrow.

"Doug, I guess we had better have breakfast. Folks...especially Mother's sisters and their families...will be coming by early this afternoon. The funeral directors will be at the homestead by 3." Doug stifled the questions he had for

Mil. He thought there must be more to the events of that fatal morning, but he knew there would be time to talk later.

At the Terry home, Clarence was awake before daylight. He had not had much time to reflect about his brother and his mother's death. He just could not believe it. He could not understand how this could happen. He barely remembered the events of yesterday at school. He was in math class with Mr. Sauder explaining an equation on the board when Mr. Murdock Mackenzie, the principal, came to the door and ask to see Clarence Terry. Clarence racked his brain and thought, "I ain't done nothing lately."

As if reading his thoughts, Mr. McKenzie said, "Bring your books and come with me. Don't worry, you are not in trouble. I just need to talk with you."

Clarence recalled as they walked down the hall, Mr. Mackenzie told him that there had been an accident and he needed to go home. "I'll drive you."

Mr. Mackenzie started his '38 Plymouth and lit his worn pipe. He and Clarence did not say a word until about half-way from Glenwood Park to the house. "I am afraid I have bad news for you, Clarence. There has been a terrible accident at your home." As he pulled off the road to park in the yard beside the two sheriffs' car. Clarence didn't recall much of the rest of that day. He said later, "it seems like a fog settled over me, and I still have trouble trying to remember all that happened."

Clarence was moving toward the kitchen where he saw his dad sitting at the table as if he was waiting to be served his morning coffee before breakfast. "Pop, what are we going to do?" came from Clarence to his dad in an uncertain voice.

Papa Terry looked up at his son and in almost inaudible reply said. "I don't know, we will ask Mil."

The day continued as in slow motion. Sister Carrie and her husband, Larry Teel, were the next to join Doug and Mil in the kitchen. They had arrived at the Tabor home around 3 a.m. Mil had left the front door unlocked for them to make their way into the spare bedroom. They came through the house quietly, so as not to wake the others. They had left their son, Jimmy, with Larry's mother.

Vergie was last to join the family for breakfast. The Tabor daughters, Ruth, the oldest and Louise had finished their breakfast of biscuits, eggs, sausage and of course, fresh milk from Bertie, the family's cow.

"Vergie, how are you doing this morning?" Nat inquired. "Did you sleep okay?" India added. Vergie replied in the positive to both. She was still numb from the tragic events, and she kept wondering how it could have happened. She started to cope by ignoring her feelings and attempting to block out the events of yesterday. This would become her coping mechanism for the years ahead. After the services, she would rarely speak of the events that changed her and the family forever. In fact, Vergie never discussed the tragedy even with her own children.

The Tabors and the Baileys got ready to go to the Terry home to meet the family and friends who would pay their respects to Laura and Donald. Mil's family required her attention. Nat was used to wearing his white shirt for church and owned three neckties. His favorite one was from his wedding almost fourteen years ago, a dark blue one. Mil told him to wear that tie and said she would iron his shirt before the funeral since it was the best one he had. His only suit was a dark wool one that hung from his thin frame. Some people said, "he has to stand in the same place twice to make a shadow."

Nat's work as a roofer was picking up now that the war had ended and building materials were becoming more readily available. The Terrys had been raised to be as self-sufficient as possible. They kept a cow, raised pigs, and had a family garden that provided vegetables for canning to get them through the winter months. This carried over into Mil and the other daughters' married life. Doug and Vergie didn't have a place to have a garden or livestock. Vergie had been spoiled by her older sisters and brother. They along with her parents, didn't put as many chores on her list. Mil had the most to handle. She took charge of most all of the home responsibilities into her marriage and carried this on into her marriage.

Except for PFC Kenneth Terry, the whole of the Terry family was present when the funeral directors arrived at 2. Mil and Nat Tabor, their daughters Ruth and Louise, and Nat's mother, India Tabor. Helen and George Davis and their children Lowell, Lindell, Lois, Connie. Carrie and Larry Teel. Marie and Robert Gilley and their daughter, Donna. Vergie and Douglas Bailey and the youngest remaining brother, Clarence. Papa Terry, sitting in the corner, seemed to be in another world as the funeral directors carried the caskets into his parlor. The family spoke not a single word as they set up the caskets side by side and wall to wall in the living room. A deeper still came over the family members as the funeral directors opened the caskets.

The undertaker had applied rouge to Laura and Donald's faces, lending an artificial quality to their skin. Not a single hair was out of place, which was unnatural for Donald but very correct for his mother. Laura was wearing her newest Sunday dress, a dark blue, A-Line with long sleeves and white trim at the neckline. Carrie placed in the right sleeve of her mother's dress a dainty, white handkerchief with an "L" monogrammed on it. Carrie had sent it as a gift from New Jersey on her mother's last birthday in August and had retrieved it this morning from her mother's bedroom dresser. Donald had been dressed in his only white shirt, which was crisp from extra starch. He had never owned a necktie, so he now wore a black tie that the funeral home had provided. Before they left, Mil thanked the directors and asked when they would return to move the caskets from the Terry home to the Methodist church.

The two-story timber frame farmhouse became crowded at the stroke of 3 o'clock. The smell of chicken, ham, cooked vegetables, and pots of forever strong coffee mixed in the air with the aroma of flowers.

The Rev. Rudy arrived early and greeted the family. When he reached Vergie and Doug, he said, "I see you folks have been busy since I married you" with a big grin, referring to the young bride's swollen belly.

Doug with a slight grin replied, "Nature takes its course with young couples." Vergie was not listening, she felt like she was in a different place and time. She did not acknowledge the Reverend or Doug's comments.

Doug said, "Reverend, I know the family appreciates you being here and conducting the service tomorrow. It is going to be a tough day."

Rev. Rudy replied, "It is a tragedy. I don't know how to make sense of what happened, but we all know that the Lord prepares us to handle whatever comes." Vergie wished the Lord would tell her why this happened. The reverend started around the room to shake hands with every person present. He stayed for the next five hours making sure to speak with every mourner. He only paused for fried chicken, apple pie and a few cups of strong coffee.

The local women, farmers and self-employed neighbors arrived early to pay their respects, along with Papa Terry's sisters. As the working men completed their day shifts, the house nearly overflowed. All the visitors wore their Sunday best. Many would not be able to attend the funeral the next day due to work, but they wanted to make a show of support to the family—especially the sisters. Visitors stayed as late as 10 PM.

Vergie felt like the wake lasted much longer than seven hours. When Vergie's best friend, Betty Thomas, arrived, Vergie burst into uncontrollable tears. The two hugged each other, as Betty began weeping too. She managed to say, "I am so sorry." But mostly, she held on to Vergie or clasped her hand. Vergie seemed more at ease with her friend by her side.

For the most part, the visitors offered Papa Terry short greetings of condolence. Still sitting dazed in the corner, he seemed comfortable with this. Ever practical, he had briefly expressed his worries to Mil. He needed someone to care for Clarence who still attended school. Papa Terry recognized that he needed as much or more care than Clarence. He was not prepared to cook and perform household duties in addition to carrying on his outside work. He had neither the domestic skills nor the inclination to learn. It was woman's work. He would need to address these worries sooner rather than later.

The night became chillier as the last of the visitors left. The sudden quiet amplified the loneliness of a family missing two of its members. They closed the casket lids, conscious that they would be opened only one more time for their final good-bye.

On the morning of the funeral, Wednesday, November 21, the adults drank coffee, but nobody had much of an appetite. Sausage, gravy, and biscuits sat uneaten on the kitchen table. There was also chicken and pie left from the wake and there would be more food brought in throughout the day.

The funeral directors arrived at half past noon to move the caskets to the Littlesburg Methodist Church. The white frame country church building sat less than two miles from the Terry and Tabor homes. A dozen local folks standing outside of the church watched as the black hearse slowly backed up the gravel driveway to the front of the church. The directors instructed the pallbearers to carry the caskets to the front of the sanctuary and place them in front of the altar.

For the last time, the two lids were opened by the Funeral Home Directors for the attendees to file by and say one final good-bye to mother and son. The church was filled as relatives and community members had filed in as early as an hour before the service was to begin. When all the mourners had taken their seats, the family approached the caskets. Laura's daughters sobbed and their spouses held them. Their children didn't understand the events. They had never seen their mothers like this. They only knew their mothers were very sad.

The only member of the family not present was brother, Kenneth, in the Army stationed in Germany. The Red

Cross had communicated to him the terrible news, but the distance and time frame made it impossible for Kenneth to obtain leave to be home for the service. Kenneth had no dependents; his discharge would be later based on the Army's criteria of having head of households muster out as soon as possible.

When the family settled into their seats, the funeral directors closed the casket lids, and the service began. It was the saddest and most solemn service. The community had lost young men in battle during the war. In wartime, the community had expected soldiers' deaths, but this double death of a young boy and his mother shocked them. It was very rare for two members of a family to have their final rites at the same time. And what can be said for a youngster just starting to understand life and a mother just reaching middle age? The long, good life platitudes invoked at the traditional funeral, had no meaning in these tragic, unexpected departures.

Donald had a lot of friends, so there were more children present than usual for a country church funeral. He and his pals loved to play out of doors, and they often explored along the creek and over the rolling fields that made up most of the Littlesburg area. There was plenty of room for the youngsters to exercise their imaginations, pretending to be soldiers defeating the Japanese and the Germans. They did not know real death until Donald's funeral. Now they knew their friend was gone. Some had older brothers, uncles and fathers that had been in the war but losing their buddy was a new experience that each was handling in their own way.

The girls were more outwardly emotional, some crying softly while others dramatically sobbed. At this age the girls

42

were starting to think about boys and had from tradition and family experiences of a loved one dying, a set of expectations as to how they should show emotion and react to death.

Vergie and Doug watched the service in a daze. Doug worried about how his wife was doing during the hour that the two ministers preached and read scriptures, and the congregation sang hymns. When it was all over, the attendees stood as the pallbearers carried the caskets from the church to the hearse. Mercer County Sheriff, Perry Dye, led the procession with the red dome light rotating as he solemnly drove his vehicle in front of the hearse that had two coffins, side by side. A procession of automobiles with their headlights on followed the hearse as they arrived at the foot of the steep slope to the Sandlick Cemetery. The mourners, wearing their winter coats, walked steadily up the hill to the graves that lay side by side. Next to Laura's final resting place, the gravedigger had left a space in the earth for Papa Terry.

The sisters, hand-in-hand with their spouses and children, stood around the open graves as the cold November wind blew across the hillside. Sobs broke the sad silence as each family member spoke his or her farewell. Mildred held Papa Terry by one arm to support him, and he looked frozen in the moment.

The graveside service lasted only minutes before the family stepped back and began the labored walk down the hill. Only Laura and Donald Terry remained on the hillside, overlooking the countryside where they had been born and lived. Their lives' journey had taken them no more than five miles from where each had come into this world.

At the service, Vergie and Marie carried two yet to be named grandchildren: future grandsons, Terry Douglas Bailey and Robert Lane Gilley. Both would be born in April, and both would be coal camp kids. Unlike their grandmother and uncle, Terry and Robert would travel thousands of miles from their West Virginia birthplace

Laura Belle Hendrick Terry
About 1939
1897 - 1945

Bluefield Daily Telegraph, Bluefield, WV – Front Page November 20, 1945

Mercer Youth Is Believed Suicide After Accidentally Slaying Mother

A 48-year-old mother was accidentally shot fatally and her 12-year-old son c o m m i t t e d suicide yesterday morning between 8 and 9 o'clock, county and state officers said after investigating the deaths of Mrs. Edward P. Terry and her son, Donald Gene Terry, at the Terry Home on the New Hope Road.

Officers found Mrs. Terry, seated in a chair in the kitchen of their home, near Smith's chapel. First belief was that she had died of a heart attack and it was not until a physician arrived to make an examination that they discovered she had been shot by the blast of a 20-guage Remington shotgun.

Body Found

The boy's body was found on the floor between two beds in the bedroom. After investigating, the officers decided that an inquest would not be necessary.

Reconstructing the scene, officers concluded that the boy, Donald, recently recovered from an attack of pneumonia and kept home from school yesterday because he was suffering the preliminary effects of a head cold, had been playing with the shotgun. He was in bed and his mother had just given him a dose of medicine and returned to the kitchen, where she sat in a chair.

Charge Strikes Mother

The gun accidentally went off, the blast traveling through the open bedroom doorway to the kitchen, where it struck his mother under the right shoulder blade. Shocked by what he had done, the boy then shot himself through the chest, officers concluded.

The father was feeding the pigs half a mile away from his house when the accident occurred. When he returned to the house he found Mrs. Terry dead in the kitchen and did not notice that she had been shot. He thought at the time that

Turn to Page 2 – Column 4

45

MERCER YOUTH IS

(Continued From Page One)

she had died of a heart attack. Failing to notice the boy, he ran to his daughter's home nearby and the two returned to the Terry home.

They then discovered the body of the boy but still thought Mrs. Terry had died of a heart attack, probably when she saw that the boy had been shot. Police officers, called to investigate, had the same opinion until they went back to Princeton for a physician and returned a second time for the examination.

The boy's bed was just 18 feet and four inches away from the chair in the kitchen, where the mother was killed.

Active Church Member

Mrs. Laura Belle Terry was born August 15, 1897, at Littlesburg, W. Va. a daughter of the late Robert W. and Biddie LaRue Hedrick. She was an Active member of the Littlesburg Methodist church.

Besides her husband she is survived by seven children Clarence and Kenneth, the latter in the army and the owner of the shotgun; Mrs. Robert Gilley and Mrs. George Davis, both of Matoaka; Mrs. C. N. Tabor, of New Hope, Mrs. Larry Teel, of Lambertsville, N. J. and Mrs. Douglas Bailey, of Rock.

Mrs. Terry is also survived by five sisters, Mrs. Mary Broyles, Mrs. G. J. Taylor, Mrs. J. W. Bogle, all of Littlesburg; Mrs. Will Hall, of Northfork and Mrs. Ellen Hambrick, of Princeton; Five brothers, T. J. Hedrick, of Abney, W. Va.; C. W. Hedrick, of Pocahontas, Va.; Arthur Hedrick, of Portsmouth, Va., and eight grandchildren.

Donald Gene was born July 19, 1933 at Littlesburg. He was a pupil in the sixth grade at the Central school at Littlesburg.

Double funeral services will be held Wednesday afternoon at 2 o'clock at the Littlesburg Methodist church. The L. W. Rhudy, pastor, will officiate, assisted by the Rev. Eugene Kahle and the Rev. Garnett Tiller. Interment Will follow in the Sandlick cemetery.

The bodies will be removed From the Mercer Funeral home here to the Terry residence this afternoon.

Investigating officers were; Magistrate E. Dale Bailey, acting as ex-officio coroner; Sgt. W. E. DeMoss and Cpl. Jim Childers of the Princeton detachment of state police; Sheriff Perry L. Dye; Deputy Sheriff Bob Bird; Constable Walter Fielder, and Dr. I. T. Peters, of Princeton, who made the medical examination.

PART II – Moving to the Coal Camp

Chapter 5 – Spring – A New Beginning

"I wish we could get a house. We are going to need the room when the baby gets here, and it would be nice to have a yard," Vergie said to Doug on an April morning in 1946.

"My pay envelope is better than most of the men's since we don't trade much at the company store and don't have company house rent," Doug responded.

The mining companies ran coal camps as a secondary business, but a practical one. When coal mines opened in remote, rural areas of Kentucky, Virginia, and West Virginia in the 1890s and early twentieth century, no housing existed for the newly employed miners. The housing had to be close to the mines due to the lack of transportation, and miners could not be expected to stay with an operation that didn't have a place for their wives and kids. The companies had no choice but to provide housing. The miners rented the houses with the monthly rent deducted from their pay. Miners received their pay on Fridays in envelopes containing company issued script instead of US dollars. Script functioned like money but could only be used at the company store or with local stores that had a prior arrangement with the coal company. Script was also issued as credit against the miner's work. Each miner had an employee number on a card that could be presented to secure an advance before the end of the pay period. Outside of the immediate area of the coal camps, the script was worthless.

By the 1940s, the war effort had slowed house construction at the camps and company reached capacity as the war came to an end. With growing automation resulting in less need for labor, the companies avoided expanding or building new coal camps. The aging clapboard frame homes with tar paper roves required frequent repair.

Doug's dad, Lake Bailey, also worked for American Coal. He and his partner, Greg Parcell, were skilled carpenters and members of the United Mine Workers of America (UMWA). They always worked as a team. They went into the mines on occasion to build a wall or cabinet around the mining operations, but for the most part, they worked outside maintaining company buildings and miners' homes in the coal camps at McComas, Crane Creek, Pinnacle and Sagamore.

Doug and Vergie were saving the pay envelopes in a coffee tin in the kitchen cupboard. They knew they could exchange it for cash currency with some of their kin and possibly with some merchants who would probably give them eighty cents on the dollar. They wanted to buy a car.

"Vergie, I think we are saving, planning, and doing all we can for now. I just wish I could get an outside job, then we will know where we will be and get a house there." Doug stated with a firm sense of commitment.

Vergie smiled and looked at her husband saying. " You are right we are planning ahead. Once the baby is here and you get the work you want, we will move on to getting our own place. We will have neighbors and the baby will have some playmates later, too."

The Terrys had been raised to be as self-sufficient as possible. They kept a cow, raised pigs and had a family garden that provided vegetables for canning to get them through the winter months. This carried over into Mil and the other daughters' married life. Doug and Vergie didn't have a place to have a garden or livestock. Vergie had been spoiled by her older sisters and brother. They along with her parents, didn't put as many chores on her list. Mil had the most to handle. She took charge of most all of the home responsibilities into her marriage and carried this on into her marriage

Vergie knew they were lucky to receive meat and canned vegetables from Doug's parents and her sister Mildred. The Baileys also had an apple orchard that provided fruit throughout the year since the family stored the apples in the cellar. What they didn't store, the family cooked and placed in canning jars. They provided a delicacy, especially when Vergie fried them for breakfast. Wild blackberries and strawberries were plentiful in West Virginia. Vergie had learned from her mother and sisters at an early age how to make them into jam and preserves. They had all grown accustomed to less sweetness in the berries since sugar rationing began. Gooseberries—ground cherries to locals—grew wild and were sweeter than blackberries and strawberries. The ground cherries tasted good raw and would keep for five or six weeks in a cool place, or industrious families could make them into a tasty jam.

Doug continued to be anxious about working underground but this was the best paying job he could have and stay in the state of his birth and raising. Vergie wasn't going to leave her sisters who all lived within 15 miles except for Carrie. They also wanted a place of their own. Living above Mrs. Linkous was okay, and she was the nicest landlady, but they wanted privacy and with their child coming, they needed more room. With only one bedroom it would not be possible to get more than a few hours' sleep at a stretch with a newborn. Vergie and Doug had their name in for company housing but that didn't seem likely. They were very unsettled about their living situation.

Since the funeral, Doug had been focused on getting an outside job and procuring company housing at the McComas coal camp. Each day Doug would say to his foreman. "Any possibility of outside work?" Each time, the foreman responded with a negative shake of the head. It did not look promising since the McComas mine was slowing down and there was no expansion of the work outside.

One afternoon, as Doug was getting off the man-trip from the mines, his foreman let him know. "Doug, American Coal Company is expanding their operations over in Wyoming County. You ought to check it out. They are building a new tipple. You could apply to work there." In the tipple, workers sorted coal by size and rinsed it with water to remove dirt before being loading it into coal hoppers that trains would transport all over the country.

Vergie hoped that Doug could get the outside job he wanted. She knew it was generally safer but just as hard, necessitating that he works outside in all kinds of weather. She remembered that the West Virginia winter cold and wind could cause temperatures well below zero for several days each year. Inside the mine, he could count on a cool 58 degrees year around. A lot of miners liked that condition and looked forward to going inside for "nature's air conditioning."

Food rationing had largely ended since the Japanese surrendered in August 1945, but sugar remained at a two-pound limit per month per individual. Vergie's morning coffee had slightly less than a teaspoon of sugar on this April morning. This was her second cup after seeing Doug off to work. His ride picked him up at 6:30 sharp for the 15-minute commute to the mine entrance at McComas.

She re-read for the third time the letter she received from Carrie. Her sister had married the dashing air army corpsman, Larry Teel, right after college and moved with him to New Jersey. Carrie and Larry had met while she was studying to be a home economics teacher at Concord College. He was there for pre-flight instruction.

Vergie missed her sister. They had been close growing up since they were less than two years apart in age. Carrie was smart and ambitious. She jumped a couple of grades in school and entered college at 16. Vergie had thought about following Carrie to Concord, but she didn't think she was as smart as her sister. And anyway, she'd been offered work in the Maiden Form Plant immediately after high school graduation. Then she met Doug, and now she was going to be a mother. It was reassuring, to hear that motherhood agreed with Carrie whose son, Jimmy, would soon be two.

Since the funeral, Carrie had taken on the role of mother to their younger brother, Clarence. They lived with Larry's widowed mother in his childhood home. Mrs. Teel had kept Jimmy during the funeral and realized that Papa Terry did not have the skills to care for Clarence. She took Carrie aside and told her, "I want you to bring Clarence back with you. He can stay with us and take the extra bedroom." Carrie was relieved because she did not know how Clarence and his father could manage without her mother. Carrie and Larry did not hesitate to invite Clarence to live with them in New Jersey.

Carrie wrote in her letter that Clarence was adjusting to his new home. Some of his classmates made fun of his West Virginia drawl, but his size and strength kept the boys from picking on him. Carrie also wrote that Clarence was good to watch Jimmy. He had learned by playing with his younger brother Donald.

Papa Terry moved in with the Tabors, making him the sixth person in the household. He joined Mildred and Nat, their daughters, Ruth and Louise and Nat's Mother, India Tabor. India had lived with Nat and Mildred from the start of their marriage. Her husband had deserted her years ago. No one really knew the story, and Nat and his mother never talked about it.

India was reluctant about Papa Terry joining the household. "I don't want to be here with him alone. I don't want people to get any ideas about me and Mr. Terry," she declared to Nat.

Nat replied, "Mom, I don't think you need to worry."

India did not want the neighbors' tongues wagging, but she also missed being the sole focus of her granddaughters' attention. Papa Terry did not have an affinity toward grandchildren as their Nana, but the children felt sorry for him knowing that he had lost his wife and son.

None of the other adult, married daughters had the room or the desire to have their father join them. It was customary for the oldest to take in the father. "Men can't cook, wash clothes or do house chores, so they have to be taken care of by someone – mother or wife," Mildred stated in her matter-of-fact manner.

Finishing the letter and folding it to place back in the envelope for storing with her other keepsake letters, Vergie realized the baby felt more active this morning. Or maybe it was the second cup of coffee? Vergie felt different today like something was going to change. She had not had morning sickness for some months. She made the bed and then washed the breakfast dishes.

Recently, Vergie had taken to spending the morning downstairs and talking with Mrs. Linkous until lunch. They would listen to the news from the Bluefield radio station on the hour. Mrs. Linkous had three adult sons. She enjoyed telling Vergie about them. The two oldest served in the Army during the war. One went to the Pacific and the other went to Europe. They were both discharged in time to be home for Christmas 1945 with their wives and children. They had settled back into civilian life. One drove a truck hauling goods for Sears from Greensboro to Roanoke, Virginia, and Bluefield and the other worked at a bank in Bluefield. The youngest graduated from high school and landed a job at the Celanese Fiber plant in Narrows, Virginia. He lived near Narrows and was sweet on a girl he had met at work.

"I just hope if I have a son, he doesn't have to go to war," Vergie had shared with Mrs. Linkous on more than a dozen occasions.

Mrs. Linkous always replied, "I sure hope not."

This morning Vergie decided, instead, to read the Saturday Evening Post that she had purchased at the company store in McComas last Saturday when they were getting the week's groceries. Orville, Doug's oldest brother worked in the American Coal operation at McComas mine as well, so he had driven them to the company store.

Duvall, Orville's wife, and their five-year-old son, Bobby Lee, went along to pick out new clothes for Bobby Lee. Duvall said, "This boy is outgrowing his clothes so fast, I think he may be a basketball player."

Vergie replied. "It will be good for our child to have an older Bailey cousin. They can be some company to each other when we are there on Sundays and the holidays. You know my sisters all have kids. In fact, Marie will be delivering again about the same time that this one is due."

Orville joined in the conversation in his usual low, steady, monotone "With Junior and Wallace off to war almost as soon as they got married, they didn't have time to have kids. I have a feeling they will make up for lost time. Bobby Lee and your all's child will have a lot of cousins in the next few years."

Duvall gave birth to Bobby Lee the year before Pearl Harbor. Junior and Wallace got married just before they shipped out to Europe and the Pacific. On his return, Junior re-united with his childhood sweetheart and bride, Opal. They lived in Rock, just a mile from Doug and Vergie. Junior was working at the Rock Cliff Bottling Plant, a short walk from where he lived. Rock Cliff made the best ginger ale, Vergie's favorite drink to settle her stomach during the pregnancy.

Wallace--"Wally" to the family—had not been able to locate his wife, Alice, since he arrived home in December. None of the neighbors knew where she had gone. Wally had not been in contact with Alice for more than six months before his discharge. His assignment in the Pacific had top secret classification. There was no "soldier mail" delivery to or from his island location. He had been directed to keep his mission a secret, even after returning home and, in fact, may not have been given a lot of details about the assignment to begin with. The family speculated that he served on the island from which the planes took off with the atomic bombs that destroyed the Japanese cities of Hiroshima and Nagasaki, contributing to the surrender of Japan and ending the war.

Spring – A New Beginning

Coming home to find Alice missing had shocked Wally. Moreover, it was beginning to look like she had left on her own, according to some of their friends. Wally kept trying to contact her and confided to Doug, "I can't understand why she left. I want to know where she is and that she is ok."

Doug replied, "You know, Alice was not too serious about anything. We both knew her in school, and you know I had a couple of dates with her before you. I think maybe she got swept away and thought it was the thing to do, to marry a solider headed off to war and all. Then when you left, and she had time to think about it...maybe it scared her some."

Wally shook his head. "I would just like to know."

***

Vergie came back to the present as she focused on her reading of the "Post" for the next couple of pages then she dozed off. She fell soundly asleep on the worn sofa that had long since seen its best years. They had received it as a hand-me-down from Doug's Aunt Ocie, his mother's sister. When she awoke, she wasn't sure how long she had been asleep, but the baby was kicking more and seem to be much more active than the last few weeks.

Vergie had some idea about child birthing. Her mother gave birth to two younger brothers at home when Vergie was five and seven years old. She had also seen the movie *Gone with the Wind* and remembered the birthing scene where Scarlett assists Melanie with her delivery. She had laughed out loud in the theater when Prissy said in a high pitched, strained voice. "Oh, Miss Scarlet, I's don't know nothing about birthing no baby."

"It is going to be okay," Vergie thought as she went to get a Rock Cliff ginger ale from the refrigerator. As she reached for the bottle opener in the drawer, she felt a big burp rising. She thought, "That's odd, I haven't had a drink of the ginger ale yet."

Chapter 6 – Birthing is Not Easy

In a few minutes, Vergie suspected that her labor had started. She could feel the baby moving with more vigor than she had ever noticed. It felt as though the baby had stretched out its arms and legs in opposing directions—one last stretch before joining the world.

"I am going to have the baby!" she shouted. Mrs. Linkous rushed up the steps.

"You should go to bed," Mrs. Linkous directed. "I am going to tell John to call the doctor."

Mrs. Linkous rushed next door and asked their neighbor, John Greenway, to call the Dr. Bilger in McComas and tell him Mrs. Douglas Bailey was going into labor. Doug and Vergie had enlisted John early on when Mrs. Linkous suggested that they make a plan for when Vergie went into labor. Doug had known John's older brother, Steve. They had all fished together on the Bluestone around the bend at the Bailey farm, then both brothers had enlisted in the service. John lost an arm during the Battle of the Bulge and was waiting to be fitted for a prosthesis at the Veterans Hospital in Salem, Virginia. His brother, who served as a guard for German prisoners, had made it out of service without a scratch.

After getting the message from Mrs. Linkous, John walked swiftly to the store at the crossroads to make the call.

Mrs. Linkous sat in a chair beside the bed and reassured Vergie that it was going to be fine. "Babies are born every day, and this is going to be over in just a little while." Vergie appreciated Mrs. Linkous being there but she really wanted her sister Mildred and her husband to be nearby.

Since Mildred did not have a telephone, they could not easily get word to her. In any case, she and Nat did not own a car and neither of them could drive.

John knocked on the front door and then entered to yell up the stairs, "The doc said he would be on his way, probably half hour."

"Did you tell him that she is in labor?" Mrs. Linkous shouted back.

"Yep, he said there is time, but he would come straight on."

Vergie was starting to feel anxious without the doctor or Doug, but she did not want to betray her nerves to Mrs. Linkous. She took a deep breath and began to repeat in her mind, "It's going to be ok. All is fine."

Vergie remembered that her sisters all welcomed the news when she had told them she was expecting. Their kid sister was going to join them in motherhood. Vergie also remembered that each one of them said the same thing, "Vergie, you will do fine. Terry women make good mothers." She felt that her sisters were holding back on the details of their actual birthing experience. It seemed to her that most women gave the same pat statement that, "You will do fine," but their body language suggested there was more to the story.

Dr. Bilger arrived with his nurse, Vergie Cooper and ascended the stairs to check Vergie. As he completed his exam, he confirmed, "Labor has started, but it is going to be a little while unless something changes quickly. I haven't had any lunch, so I am going home and will be back in an hour or so. Nurse Cooper is going to stay with you. You remember her, you both are Vergies." Dr. Bilger spoke with a little smile. Vergie, who by this time could not hide her anxiety, thought the doctor a bit too casual as he exited the room and descended the stairs again. She looks at the nurse and said. "I'm glad you are here."

"Don't worry, I have three of my own. It is going to be okay." Vergie the nurse indicated.

Just then, Chet's Plymouth pulled up and Doug jumped out as he saw the doctor's car parked in front. With his long stride of his six-foot two frame, he rushed up the steps. "Everything okay, doc? Has she had the baby?" Doug said breathlessly.

"Your missus is doing fine. It is going to be a little longer labor...usually is with the first one. I will be back shortly. Just tell her to be calm and think good thoughts, Nurse Cooper is here with her." Doc said.

Chet, whose wife had already given birth four times, yelled to Doug as he walked quickly to the doorway, "It will be fine. Good luck. Look forward to seeing you and hearing about the baby tomorrow morning!"

"Okay," Doug shouted back.

"How are you doing, Honey?" Doug asked.

Vergie replied, "So far, not too bad, but I wish the doctor had stayed. Good to have you here." Suddenly she felt a sharp pain unlike any before. She winced, gave out a loud, "Ohh!" that seemed to resonate throughout the house.

As the contractions continued and the pain became more intense, Vergie wanted the doctor back. Her eyes widened as she suddenly felt water go down her legs. With a knowing look, Nurse Cooper kindly used a clean towel to dry Vergie's legs, and she placed a clean, dry towel under. She took Vergie's hand in her own and encouraged Vergie to squeeze when she had a contraction.

When Dr. Bilger returned about an hour later, he told the couple that she shouldn't be too much longer. It had been about 8 hours since her first contraction, and based on the doctor's estimation of her dilation, it looked like maybe a couple of hours remained.

"You folks might want to go downstairs and have some coffee," Dr. Bilger suggested.

Mrs. Linkous motioned to Doug, "I guess we might be in the way. Let's get some coffee. I can start a fresh pot. Doc and nurse, do you want a cup?"

Doc shook his head to the negative at the same time the nurse did likewise. Doug gave his bride a gentle kiss on the forehead and said, "See you and the kid real soon." He smiled and hesitated before he backed out of the bedroom.

The swirl of pain and sweat and contractions became much more intense. She felt annoyed as she had the flashback of her sisters saying, "You will do fine." Tired from the labor, Vergie's mild-mannered nature gave way to impatience. She planned to tell them that they should have been more honest about this birthing business.

Dr. Bilger spoke in a deliberate and reassuring tone. "Mrs. Bailey, you are doing fine. The baby is coming along nicely. I can see the crown of the head. Looks like we are almost there."

Vergie continued inhaling and exhaling at a notable pace, along with pained exclamations of "ohhh". Dr. Bilger continued to praise and encourage her. "This baby is strong. It is not going to be long. Almost there, Vergie. Then you and Doug and this child will be ready to get on with life." At that very moment the doctor reached for the emerging baby and

Vergie felt that although her baby was leaving, her child would always be a part of her.

The doctor lifted the baby up with his right hand and with his left, gave a slight smack to the buttocks. The baby, having just emerged from his cozy den, gave an immediate distress cry.

Vergie, with a renewed energy and focus wanted to see her child's face. She could not wait to meet this new addition to the family that she and Doug had brought into the world.

"Well, Mrs. Bailey, you have a good size boy here. Congratulations!" the doctor said in a voice infused with fanfare as he handed the newborn to Nurse Vergie.

Vergie and the doctor heard footsteps coming up the stairs and Doug burst through the doorway. "Everything okay? I heard cries." Doug asked.

"It sure is. Say hello to your son." Dr. Bilger responded.

Doug's face lit up with excitement and relief. They had a family, a son. The nurse wrapped the baby boy in a new lightweight cotton blanket and laid him next to his mother. As she held her child for the first time, she looked at him directly in the eyes. She glanced at Doug and with pride and tenderness she stated, "Say hello to Terry Douglas Bailey."

Doug replies, "Boy. Hello Terry Douglas!"

Doc says, "So it's Terry Douglas Bailey, Junior." As the Nurse Cooper was writing in the full name on the application for a birth certificate. "Your son just made it in for April 10, you know it's almost midnight. I saw 11:25 pm on my watch. Doctor is that okay by you?" the nurse Vergie Cooper stated matter factorially. Dr. Bilger nodded in agreement.

"No, not quite. He isn't a Junior," Doug chimed in, "Just Terry Douglas Bailey." He looks to Vergie, "That's what we talked about, right honey?"

She nods. "Yes, doctor, Doug and I agreed on Terry for my maiden name. And Doug for his middle name."

"Okay, fill out the birth certificate. No junior," The Doctor indicated as he looked toward the nurse.

"Are you doing, okay?" Doug asks Vergie.

"She did really well," Dr. Bilger stated before Vergie could respond. "I think she is a natural mother."

In almost whisper, Vergie says, "I am fine but really very tired."

Nurse Cooper had gone out to the doctor's car to get the scale to weigh the newborn. When she returned, she placed Terry in the scale's pan and held the spring measure up to read, 8 pounds and 4 ounces.

The doctor promised to check on mother and the boy in about six weeks but implored them to let him know of any problems or if the baby wouldn't take the mother's milk.

Terry did take his mother's milk. He gained weight and soon, he was able to turn over on his own in the loaned crib from his Aunt Mildred in which his two cousins Ruth and Louise, had slept before him.

Vergie and Douglas Bailey with their six-week-old,
Terry as they visit the Bailey Grandparents, Lake and
Lee at the homeplace in Rock, May 1946.

Chapter 7 – Got to Get Outside

Perhaps housing would be easier to obtain in camps near the Deerfield operation.

Doug's leg bounced up and down as he watched Joe Murphy look over the coal dust covered application the Doug had completed in pencil. The Superintendent of the Deerfield operation had come over the mountain to the McComas mine looking for experienced miners for the expanding Deerfield operation. "Doug, you know it gets cold and wet outside. It requires a lot of walking and standing. Most men would say it takes more than working inside."

"Yes, sir, I know all that."

"And the contract calls for less pay than you get mining." Joe Murphy told him. Doug had figured the difference in pay, which was about $2 a day, but he thought that it would be worth it to get outside

"I understand, sir."

"Okay, Doug, we can take you on the third shift as a car dropper at Deerfield." Murphy was anxious to get his full crews for each shift and he thought it would be a boon to have an enthusiastic young man on the tough third shift. Demand for coal had kept the mines running five days a week, twenty-four hours a day. Some weeks they would also work on Saturday to keep up with orders from the steel manufacturers.

Having waited for months for a chance to get out of the mines, Doug felt relief at this good news. He wanted to jump at the opportunity, but he knew he should discuss the change with his young wife

"Can I let you know at the end of next week?" Doug replied.

"Sure Doug. Just remember we have men wanting your job here in McComas, so you probably can't come back." The Deerfield tipple was under construction, but operations would not begin for a month

That afternoon, Doug broached the subject with Vergie while she was nursing Terry. She didn't respond with the same excitement Doug had shown. "What's the matter, honey?" Doug asked.

"Where are we going to live over there? I have never even been across that mountain," was Vergie's response as she wiped the baby's mouth with a small washcloth. "What am I going to do in the evenings and at night while you are working? The evening shift is the worst. You come home, eat breakfast and go to bed for most of the day." Vergie sputtered.

"I know you would be alone with Terry. I would rather be with you both in the evenings too. But you know I just got to get out of the mines, and this is my best chance," Doug shrugged his shoulders as he sat down in the kitchen.

Beside the terrible hours, Vergie worried they'd be utterly without support in Deerfield. Nearly her whole family lived nearby, and Doug's parents lived only three miles up the road. Mrs. Bailey, as Vergie referred to Doug's mother, had already been a great help with Terry. She had raised six boys and two girls. She knew what to expect. "Your Mother is not going to cross the mountain to help like she does here. I have learned from how to manage what Terry needs and what I need to do for myself and the housework" Vergie pointedly informed Doug.

"I know, honey but we will manage. I know it will be okay," Doug responded before continuing, "I will see if I can borrow a car this Sunday and we will drive over the mountain and look it over, maybe we can find a place until an opening from the company comes available," Doug hopefully suggested.

Vergie sighed. "Let's go over. It can't hurt to see the place. I bet it's dirty, and you know the houses are built right on top of each other in those coal camps."

On Sunday, Vergie, Doug and Terry piled into Junior's car for the drive over Arista Mountain. Vergie had visited her sisters in Matoaka and Piedmont, but that was as close to Wyoming County as she had been.

Vergie based her opinion of coal towns on Piedmont-- the only coal camp that she had ever visited. She didn't care much for it. The Piedmont tipple sat at the head of the hollow, upwind from the housing. The dust from the tipple blanketed everything in town. The railroad tracks that had been put in place to carry coal out of town sat as close to the housing that at times the windows would shake if the train got up speed before it left the camp. Remembering the dingy town, Vergie grew anxious, but she knew that she had to check things out for Doug's sake and to find more room before Terry started walking.

With six-month-old Terry in her arms, Vergie sat in the passenger side of the '39 Ford as Doug shifted gears and they pulled out onto the Rock Road toward Matoaka. As they passed the turn off for Piedmont, she though they would not have time to stop and see Helen and Marie on this trip. They made their way around the many curves of the winding mountain road. At the top of the mountain, a weathered sign reminded her that they were leaving Mercer County and entering Wyoming County. It was the farthest she had ever ventured from her birth county, and it dawned on her that she was thinking of living somewhere else for the first time in her life.

Doug had to shift down to keep the car from going too fast around the switchback turns as they descended the mountain, which had had a new name on the other side: Herndon Mountain, elevation 3200 feet. One thing Vergie noticed, there was no housing on either side of the mountain just lots of trees and a thick undergrowth of rhododendron, the official West Virginia flower.

As they reached the base of the mountain, Garwood, the first coal camp on that side of the mountain, emerged, and on the hillside in the center of the camp sat the two-story company store. They continued west, and within a half-mile on West Virginia Route 10 they started through a series of coal camps, beginning with Covel and followed by Herndon, Monticello, Bud, Alpoca and Deerfield. Deerfield was nothing but a clearing on both sides of Route 10. The mine entrance loomed to the left and on the right, they saw--under construction—a three story tipple with a façade of shiny tin.

The color had drained from Vergie's face as they made the harrowing drive across the mountain pass. She paled further as she realized there were no houses near the Deerfield mining operation. "Where would we live?" she asked.

"I don't know. Maybe back up the road in one of the coal camps we passed," Doug replied.

He pulled the car over next to the tipple. They felt relieved to stretch their legs after the long drive. A locomotive pulling a long line of empty coal hoppers came down the tracks headed to the lower end of the county or on to McDowell or Logan Counties. The Virginian Railway served the two Virginias thus the name; from Norfolk, Virginia to

Huntington, West Virginia through this southern end of the state.

Doug surveyed the tipple. The bright reflection of the sun off the new tin siding made it appear more impressive than the tipples at the Mercer County mines that had been in operation for more than twenty years. The sun reflected starkly off of it today, but Doug knew it would become dull with a layer of coal dust once it became operational. In his mind's eye, he could see himself working there, climbing onto the ladder of the coal hopper car, releasing the brake with the hand wheel, and bringing the empties to the tipple and taking the loaded cars down the track for hopefully a smooth, connection to a locomotive. He could see himself walking up the tracks, climbing the steps up into the tipple and most of all looking out into the distance and breathing air that was not being driven by a ventilation fan with limestone particles being pushed into the air you breath while coal dust is being stirred by the constant mining equipment. He just needed to convince Vergie.

"Vergie, we need to find a place to live." Doug stated with a sense of determination. For a couple of seconds, Vergie looked at Doug but did not respond. She nor any other woman had ever worked in a coal mine in West Virginia. She could not begin to imagine what it would be like, but she knew her young husband had the strongest resolve to get out of the mines. At that moment she accepted and understood what Doug needed to continue to work for the coal company.

"I need to use the bathroom, Doug." Vergie announced after a beat. "We will go on toward Mullens, less than three miles and find a place that is open," Doug responded.

The family got back in the car. Doug pulled onto the pavement and continued west on Route 10. Just around the curve they came upon Tralee with its traditional wood frame coal camp houses and a large tipple parallel with the railroad. Unlike the Deerfield Tipple, this one was black as coal.

As they entered Elmore, Doug pointed out the Virginian Railway train yard. In the yard sat long lines of empty coal hopper cars waiting to be taken to the tipples and filled. Cars full of coal awaited the locomotives that would transport them east to be distributed up and down the east coast or to foreign ports. The Virginian also had a major maintenance operation for its electric engines just at the north Mullens city limits.

They crossed over the Guyandotte River on a one lane bridge. "I guess you have to wait if another car was coming across from the other side," Doug quipped. He turned right toward Mullens and spotted an Esso station at the city limit. While he waited for Vergie to finish up in the bathroom, Doug approached the store's lone clerk. "It's Sunday, so I guess I will order two pops since I can't get a beer," Doug smirked at the clerk.

"What kind of pop?" he replied without acknowledging the joke.

"A Coca Cola and do you have ginger ale?"

"Yep, we have Rock Cliff."

"Good. That's my wife's favorite."

Mullens wasn't a coal camp. It was the largest town in the county. It reminded Vergie of Princeton where she went to high school. It had two movie theaters, an A&P and a Kroger supermarket, a bank, and a variety of stores. There was even a bowling alley. She thought maybe they could live here. It would be a good place to live with everything within walking distance. Doug pulled the car into a metered parking space and while he inspected at the parking meter, a teenager offered, "Mister, you don't have to pay on Sundays." Doug smiled back and dropped his quarter back into his pocket.

Doug approached a couple of men leaned against the G.C. Murphy Five & Dime Store, puffing Camel cigarettes. On Sunday, all the retail outlets were closed. Doug engaged the men in small talk. After a few minutes, he asked them about housing in the area, explaining that he was taking a job at Deerfield. They were not very encouraging. It seemed there were mining operations opening and the Virginian Railway had added more employees at their Elmore and Mullens operations. They didn't know of anything for rent in Mullens. Taking a long draw on his cigarette, one of the men added, "Besides, most miners live in the coal camps. Rent's cheaper and you are around your own kind. Here in town, most people work for the railroad or are business folks."

The other man said he worked at Tralee, and he knew some folks who were headed to Kentucky to be near family. The company planned to tear down their house to make way for an enclosed conveyer belt from a new mine entrance, but maybe it could be available until fall. Doug thought it was worth looking into as a stopgap measure while the family worked its way up the waiting list for housing in the coal camps owned by American Coal.

Doug thanked the men and turned to Vergie, "Let's head back and stop in Tralee." The couple got back in the Ford and drove through town. As Doug had suspected, they had to wait their turn at the single lane bridge.

Doug made a sharp left and crossed the four sets of railroad tracks that intersected the dirt road up toward the hollow where the Tralee community was located. This was the couple's and Terry's first visit in a coal camp in Wyoming County.

The homes sat close together with small yards of grass clumps. The miners had smaller houses usually with outdoor toilets but with inside water facets. The ubiquitous coal dust had settled on the houses. It came from the Tralee tipple operation and the passing, long trains carrying the coal out of the county. Vergie was almost mesmerized as she watched a train traveled east bound with full coal loads in the hoppers. She could see the fine continuous mist of the black dust. There were no covers over the hoppers and the dust was free to be whipped into the mountain air.

Vergie pointed out a couple sitting on their front porch. Doug stopped the car in front of the house close. The man and woman were swayed in a porch swing hung from the rafters by two heavy chains. Doug rolled down the window and spoke to the couple. "Hi, we are looking for a place to live. I am starting up at the Deerfield Tipple. My wife and I trying to find a spot. We live over in Mercer County now."

The woman sitting in the swing replied, "Come on up. Bring your wife and your young one."

The couple introduced themselves as Abby and Glen Rhodes. They made a fuss over the baby, "What a fine looking young one," Abby remarked. Vergie smiled broadly and said. "He is one of the reasons we are looking for new housing." Doug got back to the point of housing in a few minutes. Glen said, "Yes the house as you start up the hill behind us will be empty soon. Those folks are going to Kentucky. I know the company plans to tear down all the homes up that road to make way for the new conveyor. That will save them money on trucks and drivers carrying the coal to the tipple. You know the company: if they can find a way to cut man out, they save money."

Doug asked, "Do you think the company might rent to us until they need to tear it down?"

"I don't know, Doug. The company's bookkeeper would, though. Knowing him, he would like to get the rent money." Glen indicated with a knowing grin. "His name is Mr. Shrewsbury. He lives in the third big house up the road on the left. He is probably home, and it wouldn't hurt to check with him. Tell him I sent you. We would like you as neighbors. Nice to have young folks around."

Doug and Vergie thanked the Rhodes' and made their way to the front of the third big house. The superintendent, foreman, and the bookkeeper lived in each of the three largest homes in the camp--two-story homes with indoor bathrooms.

Vergie stayed in the car while Doug walked across the nicely kept wide front porch and knocked on the front door. A portly man in his 50s came to the door. "I am looking for Mr. Shrewsbury," Doug announced.

"You've got him. What do you need?"

Doug explained his need and asked about the house that was about to be vacated. Mr. Shrewsbury responded bluntly, "No, it's going to be torn down."

Doug responded pensively, "Well, that's what Glen Rhodes told me, but he thought you might let us rent the place until you were ready to tear it down."

Mr. Shrewsbury hesitated and then moved his bottom lip to the left for a couple of seconds as if he was thinking about what to add to his "no" response. "How do you know Glen?" Shrewsbury inquired.

Doug explained that he and his wife had just met them as they were driving into Tralee. "They were really nice folks. They liked our baby boy. They told us to check with you and tell you that Glen sent us." Doug explained.

Again, Shrewsbury paused for a couple of seconds and then responded. "Since Glen vouched for you and you have a young one...and so long as you understand that you have to move if we give you a week's notice, we could let you move in. We will probably be ready to tear the houses down as early as October, but it may not be until November or December. That your wife in the car? Tell her to come on in. How about a glass of iced tea?" Mr. Shrewsbury's tone had warmed substantially.

Doug motioned for Vergie to come up to the porch with Terry. They followed Mr. Shrewsbury into the beautifully furnished house. Vergie noticed the upright piano set against the wall. It was certainly furnished better than the farmhouses in Littlesburg. Mrs. Jean Shrewsbury brought out tall glasses of very sweet, iced tea as her husband explained that Glen had sent the couple up to see them. As it turned out, Glen and Abby had been a great source of comfort to the Shrewsburys after their son, Harry Junior, was killed in the Pacific. A Japanese plane dove into the ship carrying Harry Junior and his fellow Marines. Mr. Shrewsbury would always be grateful for the kindness and support from the Rhodes, especially Abby, who stayed with Jean during the daytime while Mr. Shrewsbury was at the office.

"Harry was the piano player. We have kept the piano. Neither one of us can play but we just can't let it go, knowing

Harry enjoyed it so much," Mrs. Shrewsbury confided in a sad but proud voice.

The room became silent until Doug spoke in a lower tone for him, "Very sorry about your son. We all are grateful for the men who went to war. I tried to enlist and was drafted but each time I failed the physical because of my eyes." Doug had felt a need to explain his lack of military service since most of his age had served. He was about to tell them that he had helped built ships when Vergie spoke.

"Doug was working at the Norfolk Naval Yard when I met him. He was a welder. I think a lot of men and women were able to help even if they were not allowed to fight." Vergie's voice trailed off as if she was providing a justification for Doug's absence from military service. She cleared her throat and shifted Terry from her right shoulder to her left one. "I think this young one is needing a diaper change. May we use the bathroom?" Jean pointed out the entrance to the bathroom in the hall.

Vergie was surprised at the large bathroom with a bit claw foot tub. The sink and the toilet were made of the whitest porcelain Vergie had ever seen. This was the nicest bathroom compared to the one she shared with her sisters and brothers and the small one at the Linkous apartment.

"You could actually walk up the tracks to the new tipple at Deerfield from here. It is shorter than the highway." Shrewsbury indicated. Doug acknowledged he may need to do that since he didn't normally have a car. Most of the miners liked being close to their work, since automobiles were not as available because of the auto factories had been producing vehicles and other equipment for the war effort. When vehicles would again be in mass production, miners would be able to purchase them. Miner's wages had increased, thanks to the UMWA negotiations.

It was about twenty miles to the new mines, but it would take an hour commute due to the mountain to cross and general road conditions. Housing was still a problem. American Coal owned several camps in the county but there was a waiting list for the housing. Soldiers returning to their jobs had priority. In some cases, the wives had moved back to their parents' home while their husbands were deployed. There was a great number of young single men who had entered the service for their country that was ready to start their new family life. Everyone was anxious to get back together in their own house and continue life before it was interrupted by the war.

Miners and their wives were no different than the rest of their fellow Americans, they were ready to settle into their own family life. Terry was part of the first quarter of the first year of what the Census Bureau would label as the Baby Boomer generation – a spike in the birth rate starting in 1946 and continuing until 1964.

Doug had less seniority since he had joined the union with his first job in the mines only a year ago. That put him at the bottom of the wait list for housing and the day shift positions.

After leaving the Shrewsburys and starting back east on Route 10, the couple looked at each other with a smile of relief. It was beginning to look like things would work out for the young Bailey family to make a home in a new county and the coal camp life would begin at Tralee.

Chapter 8 – Tralee, this is not Ireland

Mrs. Linkous had tears in her eyes as she kissed Terry's forehead. She handed the one-year-old back over to his mother. "I am going to miss all of you but especially this one. He is growing fast. You have to bring him back to see me," Mrs. Linkous said softly.

"Now you know we will. We are going to miss you too. I think I am also going to miss the bathroom here. You know I am trading it for an outhouse about 50 feet from our new back door," Vergie responded with a tinge of regret.

Mrs. Linkous had kindly watched Terry while his parents packed their belongings and moved their few household furnishings down the stairs and into the farm truck they had borrowed from Rudy McKinney, a neighbor who lived down the Rock Road near Doug's parents. Vergie, Doug and Terry were moving out of the upstairs apartment to their four-room coal camp house in Tralee today.

Doug's brothers, Junior, and Wally, planned to follow Doug over the mountain to Tralee. Wally would drive McKinney's truck back to Rock.

Doug gave Mrs. Linkous an extended hug and told her. "You know I appreciate all you done for us. You treated us like kin. You helped Vergie so much when her mom died. I think Terry thinks you are his second mom. We will be seeing you."

Mrs. Linkous choked a little as she responded, "You be careful in that new job. You know there is danger outside too. Take good care of Vergie and that little one. That boy will grow up quicker than you think. I know. Come back soon."

The couple sat in silence as they drove out of Rock. Each one reminisced about their courtship and their first couple years of marriage. Doug thought how he would miss the Rock Swimming Pool this summer. He remembered teasing his bride to be the first time they had been at the pool. He was an experienced swimmer, having grown up on the farm that had the Bluestone River as its property line. All his brothers and sisters enjoyed the "swimming hole"—a bend in the river with a deep, still channel, the perfect antidote to the hot West Virginia summer months.   So, when he finally convinced Vergie—who had never learned to swim—to take a dip with him in the Rock Swimming Pool, he encouraged her toward the deeper end of the pool so that he could support her. He welcomed the chance to put his arms around her and be playful.

Vergie was thinking about giving birth in the apartment and her sisters' first visits to meet their new nephew. Would they cross the mountain to visit? Would Doug get a car so they could visit on Sundays at the Baileys or at Mil and Nat's place? She was already missing the connection with her home county.

As they approached the mountain, Vergie's thoughts shifted to their new home. After they visited Tralee, she had been curious about the town's name. Mrs. Linkous had a set of Funk and Wagnalls Encyclopedia that she purchased from a door-to-door salesman in 1928, so Vergie asked to use it. After some searching, she found that Tralee was the largest town in Kerry County Ireland. The encyclopedia article also indicated that Tralee meant the strand or the stream of the Lee River. She found out later that the mother of the coal miner's owner had immigrated from Tralee, Ireland. Their Tralee was near a smaller body of water too: Barker's Creek. The creek received it's main source when the Gooney Otter flowed in from Covel as it ran parallel with West Virginia Route 10. until it dumped into the Barker's Creek about three miles west of Herndon.

Glen and Abby stood on their porch watching the truck and the Ford coupe come up the dusty road. The Rhodes walked over to greet them as Doug backed the truck up to the front porch of their temporary home. Abby held out her hands to each of them and said, "Welcome to Tralee. Let me take the young'un while you folks' unload."

Doug introduced his brothers to the couple while Junior and Wally started unloading the truck. With Glen's help, the unloading took less than a half-hour. Junior worked at the Rock Cliff Beverage plant, so he was accustomed to handling heavy crates of glass bottled soda. Wally was in excellent shape too, having handled heavy loads of equipment while in the army as ground support for the air corps. He was usually one of the most talkative of the Bailey boys but he, Orville, and Junior didn't say much about their war experience. They preferred to talk about the present and make plans. When they finished unloading, Wally remarked, "Doug looks like you are going to need more furniture. I am sure they will let you order at the company store. Probably be glad to do it." Wally was the salesman of the family.

"We will start back, Doug," Junior said. Vergie interrupted, "No, you should eat some lunch first! Abby fried chicken for all of us."

Everyone went to the Rhodes' home and had a full plate of fried chicken, canned green beans from the Rhodes' hillside garden, mashed potatoes, and big buttermilk biscuits. The potatoes had also been grown in the garden and stored under the house in a makeshift root cellar. Many of the coal miners had farming backgrounds and looked for a place to have a vegetable garden.

"Really good meal. Thank you so much Abby." Wally said and Junior nodded in agreement.

"Yes, great cooking!" Doug added. "I hope we can raise a garden when we finally get settled. I will miss getting my own food from the ground. Getting everything out of cans just isn't as tasty." Doug concluded.

Terry had slept during the drive over the mountain and was just getting restless and hungry. Vergie left the table and picked him up from the blanket on the floor. She took him into the living room and sat on the couch to nurse the boy for the first time in his new town. Afterward, she opened a jar of Gerber's apple sauce, one of Terry's favorites. "You do like to eat. You must follow after the Terrys," Vergie said to her son.

Wally overheard Vergie and quipped, "The Baileys can hold their own at the table too. We just burn it off faster." The Bailey children did take after their mother, each maintaining a slim frame.

After saying good-bye to his brothers and promising to get over to the Rock homeplace soon, Doug arranged their limited furniture under Vergie's direction. With their belongings settled, the couple, with baby in tow, ventured up the road to check out the camp. Tralee was the first of the coal camps built up Route 10 east of Mullens at the beginning of the twentieth century. The houses and the company store were about 25 years old after the Virginian Railway had made it into Mullens in 1906 and opened transportation of coal out to the electric power plants, steel mills and for sales for heating.

American Coal Company was expanding with new mines in the county and preparing the coal for shipment. The operations in the surrounding counties of Mercer, Logan, McDowell, and Raleigh were not expanding as rapidly as the Wyoming County operations. The Wyoming mines had coal seams that were wider, making the mining operation more profitable. Starting Monday, Doug would walk up the railroad tracks about a mile to the new Deerfield Tipple.

The couple had brought over the mountain canned goods in Mason jars from Doug's mother and Mildred. Vergie planned to get some flour, coffee, sugar and other basics from the company store, which opened at 6 each morning and closed at 6 each evening, Monday through Saturday. With Doug working the evening shift, they could go together. "It is convenient to have the store close by. I think we need to get Terry one of those red Radio Flyer wagons. I can take Terry with me and bring the groceries back in the wagon," Vergie suggested.

"Sure, go ahead and order one from the store." Vergie did just that at a cost of ten dollars, though later she would see one in the Sears catalog for $8.50. Company stores had a greater markup probably due to the captive market and credit convenience given to the miners.

Sunday evening, Vergie had packed Doug's lunch as she had done every working day since they had been married. The only exception had been the week after Terry's birth, when Doug's father had dropped his mother off at their home each day on his way to work. The black metal lunch box contained the same items every day – a thermos of strong coffee with cream, two sandwiches—usually bologna or country ham on a biscuit or store-bought sliced bread—an apple and a piece of pie or cake. On Sundays, she included left over chicken from their Sunday dinner. Per the terms of the union contract, the company provided drinking water in five-gallon earthenware crocks and a box of paper cups.

Doug dressed in his work clothes and, wearing his miner's hard hat with the light attached, leaned down to kiss Vergie good-bye and left for his first shift outside of the mines. He walked up the tracks briskly and covered the mile in less than 20 minutes. Anxious to get on the job, he had allowed 40 minutes before his shift was to start at 11 p.m. He had met his foreman, Carl Underwood, after the Superintendent had hired Doug. When his shift started, Carl greeted him, asking, "You ready for your first shift as a Car Dropper?" Carl raised his voice to be heard over the conveyor belt noise produced by the coal preparation plant.

Doug smiled and nodded his head. "I am ready to start," his voice boomed.

"Ok! We'll start by going over procedures, then you'll be working beside an experienced tipple employee. The batteries are charged over here for your light," Carl pointed to the charging station. Doug picked up and attached the battery to the cable for the light on his hard hat.

He did not know it then, but "Car Dropper", a job exclusive to coal mine tipples, would be Doug's job title for the next 41 years. The Car Dropper kept the steady flow of coal hoppers--really, railroad cars that contained coal—as they entered and exited the tipple. Empty hoppers sat on the track on side rails. To move the hopper to the loading point, the Car Dropper walked up the tracks, climbed onto the car, and turned the handbrake wheel to release the hopper and navigate it down the tracks. Once the hopper was filled, the

Car Dropper would move the car out from under the chute and move the next empty into place. It was critical to stop the hoppers in the right spot. Once the empties were delivered and parked below the tipple, there were no train engines available, so if the Car Dropper overshot the chute, there was no way to move it back up the track. Once the hoppers were loaded, the locomotive would pick them up below the grade of the tipple.

Carl showed Doug the check-in board where his timecard hung, waiting to be punched for the first time. Dewey Miller, Doug's assigned mentor arrived. He was about Doug's height but a more robust, big man. Now in his late 40s, he had been mining since he was 18. After introducing the men, Carl closed out his portion of the orientation, saying, "Time to get started, men. Good luck."

Dewey showed Doug the locker area for him to store his lunch box and other personal effects. The company maintained a bath house for the men to change and shower. The UMWA contract spelled out in detail that the company would provide the facility and furnish the men with soap. The selected bar soap was Ivory.

Doug spent the day as Dewey's second shadow. He found it difficult to hear above the continuous sound from the tipple and the trains. To see what he was to do in the job, he had to keep his thick glasses clean to see the detail of braking the coal hoppers and the parking spot under the chute. He cleaned them with his fresh, ironed bandanna and placed the newly required goggles over the glasses as the two men walked up the tracks. He folded the bandanna up and placed it in the inside pocket of his coveralls to be pulled out at least a dozen times in a shift. He would require a clean bandanna for each shift.

Doug would get used to the goggles as he had worn the thick glasses since he was twelve. Doug had cataract surgery in his teen years. When his vision did not develop like his older brothers, his folks took him to the doctor who could see the milky covering—cataracts—on Doug's eyes. It seemed very unusual for a young man to have cataracts, but the eye surgeon, Dr. Sinclair, told the family that it could occur due to some condition at birth. The doctor referred to it as a "congenital" condition.

This vision problem had probably handicapped Doug during his elementary school years. While the girls sat in the front desks at school, he sat with the boys in the back. He could never see the teacher's board work, so he got behind, and his frustration eventually led Doug to run off from the ninth-grade class at Matoaka High and he never returned to finish school.

Doug was thinking as he was watching Dewey "At any rate these goggles are better than having the welder's mask over my face at the shipyard. Sometimes I had to use those dark, lens goggles. That was tough."

At the meal break, the two men sat together and became acquainted. Doug shared he had recently moved from Rock to Tralee with his wife, and that he was proud dad of a boy. Dewey's baby girl, Judy, was about the same age. "She is not our first, but I think she should be the last. Her older sister Joan and brother Frankie...I thought...were going to be the only kids, but we got a surprise."

Doug laughed, "I think we should have another in the next year or so." The men didn't know it on that day but in

1964, Judy and Terry would graduate from high school together after spending 12 years as classmates.

Dewey told Doug that he lived in Covel, the company's coal camp about eight miles east on Route 10. "It was built for the mine up the hollow, but that played out just before the war. The Deerfield operation is part of American Coal, but since they didn't build a camp here, they are running a bus from Covel to the mines. I have a car but with gas rationing during the war, I just got used to riding the bus," Dewey explained.

"I have my name in for a house in Covel, but its full up. I hope something comes up. We can only stay in Tralee until November or December," Doug remarked.

"Yeah, it is full and with new men coming on to the mines, it may be a while. The colored section has a couple of empty houses and I think they are going to let whites go there until something opens up in the white section. When we first moved to Covel about half the camp was colored. They lived up the holler and the whites lived in the front of the camp. Now there are fewer colored miners, some have gone on to Ohio and Michigan to work in the auto plants. Some moved over closer to South Mullens where the colored high school is," Dewey explained.

"I don't know where I am on the waiting list, but I sure hope something comes through before we have to get out of the house at Tralee. I would live in the colored section if we could get settled." Doug responded with a worried look.

Meanwhile, Vergie set a routine quicker than she imagined. Doug's work schedule set the weekday routine. It was hard for Vergie to adapt to the sleeping schedule. Doug had to sleep much of the days Monday through Thursday, but he switched back to sleeping on his regular schedule on Friday and Saturday. He would take an evening nap on Sunday before starting his first shift of the week. Vergie and Terry tried to follow the schedule as well. It seemed to be easier for Terry.

Vergie didn't like to go to bed in the evenings without Doug. She was restless and probably a little afraid of a new, different place. Terry also stayed awake with his Mother. Vergie's Philco radio kept her company. She liked listening to swing music, but she especially enjoyed following the radio dramas. Terry pulled himself up by the rail of his crib and jumped and laughed when his mother laughed with Abbott and Costello. Vergie regularly listened to Dick Tracy and her favorite, The Shadow. She liked the suspense of The Shadow. Each program started with "Who knows what evil lurks in the hearts of man? The Shadow knows!" in a deep voice with chilling music.

One morning when Doug arrived from work, his wife met him with excitement. "Doug, Terry started talking last night. I wish you could have heard him," Vergie exclaimed.

"Did he say 'mama' or 'dada'?" Doug assumed it must be one or the other.

"No, he said, 'Gittum up Scout!' Just as clear," Vergie responded.

"Really? Gittum up Scout?" Doug said.

Just then, an echo of "Gittum up Scout" emanated from Terry's crib as he jumped up, holding the rail of his bed. Both parents laughed as Doug picked up his son. "I guess you are a real Lone Ranger fan," he exclaimed, because this was the catch phrase of Tonto, Lone Ranger's trusted companion on the radio western. Tonto repeated whenever the Lone

Ranger proclaimed, "Hi Ho, Silver!" to his faithful white stallion.

The move out letter arrived earlier than expected. It was the week of Halloween, and Vergie picked up the mail at the company store where the post office boxes were located. When she opened the notice, she felt a sense of panic. They had not yet heard from the Covel housing waitlist, and they had no lead on another location. When Doug woke up, Vergie shared the news.

"Could you talk to Mr. Shrewsbury tomorrow and see if he has any ideas of where we could go?" Doug suggested. She agreed.

The next day, after Doug had laid down to sleep, Vergie dressed Terry in his new sweater and sat him in the baby carriage that Doug's brother, Orville, had given them when they visited a couple of Sundays back. It was a fine carriage that Duvall's parents had given them when their son Bobby Lee was born. Bobby Lee was their only child, and he was close to seven. They didn't think that they would need the carriage again. Vergie usually took Terry's Red Flyer wagon, but the carriage would be warmer, and she did not need to bring back groceries on this trip.

Orville was the oldest of Doug's brothers, and he was a coal miner like Doug. He had been discharged from the Army after spending several months recovering from wounds that he received on D-Day at Normandy. Orville had little to say about his war experience, but when pressed, he would state: "I was one of the first to hit the beach and one of the first to be lifted off the beach."

Vergie pushed the carriage with her growing son down the road by the railroad tracks to the company store. The store

Forged by Coal

had most anything you needed for food, clothing, hardware and furniture. It also housed the business office for the mines including the payroll office where Mr. Shrewsbury had his desk.

Mr. Shrewsbury came to the payroll window. "Good morning, Mrs. Bailey. How you and the young one doing? I guess you got the letter."

"Yes, we did. We thought maybe you might know if there is any housing available in the county not too far from the Tralee tipple?" Vergie asked.

"I thought you might want to know about that. There is a vacant house up Route 10. It is one of seven that Pocahontas Fuel is selling. Could you buy it?"

"I don't think we have enough for a down payment."

"They might rent it out until they can get a buyer. I know the people in the office at Herndon. Let me ask them." Shrewsbury offered.

"Please do that for us. We would appreciate it." Vergie replied.

Shrewsbury told Vergie he would call and if she could wait, he should know in a few minutes if it would be available. When he returned to the window, he had good news. "The house is vacant and can be rented until next summer. The company is thinking about auctioning the property. These are the last seven houses that made up Monticello, the old coal town just a mile west of Herndon. It would be farther from Doug's work, but he could get a ride with one of the miners coming from that direction to Deerfield."

Vergie remembered Doug mentioning that Dewey Miller drove from Covel now. With more miners buying cars and riding together, the bus had been discontinued. She thought that Doug could arrange to ride with Dewey.

When Doug woke a little early from his sleep, the first thing he heard from Vergie was, "Good news Doug. We have a place to go to. Monticello. Just up the road."

"All right, things are working out. I guess I had better line up a truck for the move."

Glen and Abby helped Doug and Vergie load their household goods into another borrowed truck. This time, it took two loads for the four-mile trip up West Virginia Route 10. Abby teared up and Glen's face betrayed his disappointment as he picked Terry up for one last hug before passing him to Vergie.

"Don't be strangers. Come on back and see us." Abby said as she and Glen waved to Doug, Vergie, and Terry.

"I am looking to buy a car and we will be down." Now that they would be living in Monticello, they would be far from the company store or any store. They would really need a car now. They had also missed going to visit his folks and Mildred and Nat. Doug, Vergie and Terry waved as they pulled away and Glen and Abby waved back.

The Baileys lived at Tralee when they first moved to Wyoming County. The Tralee tipple is like the one that Doug worked at about a mile east of this coal preparation plant.

Photo Courtesy of WV Achieves

Chapter 9 – Monticello, Jefferson Never Slept Here

They did not live in the four-room house across from Gooney Otter Creek for long. The Flat Top Coal and Land Company owned the Monticello homes. In the 1920s, the company built seventy houses about a mile west of the Herndon mine for the miners who worked there. As the years went by, the mining operation required fewer and fewer miners. It had become more efficient when the company purchased continuous mining equipment, and the Herndon operation was becoming less profitable to mine.

There was only five of the original homes left on the hillside across the highway left. The others had been demolished with the lumber reused at other locations. Seven additional houses were across the Gooney Otter Creek from the highway where the Baileys would live. In the sixth house coming from Herndon. The Gooney Otter started at Covel where two smaller streams joined and flowed west along Route 10. This creek flowed by coal operations at Covel, Herndon, and Monticello. The Virginian Railway tracks had been laid parallel to the creek for its entire flow from Covel. The Gooney Otter ended where it emptied into the Barker's Creek between Monticello and Bud.

Their new home was nicer than the Tralee house, but it still had an outhouse. Vergie had hoped for an indoor bathroom. Both houses had running water, but they had to heat water on the coal stove for bathing, washing clothes and dishes.

The Baileys met their neighbors who welcomed them to their small new community. Vergie became good friends with Virginia "Jenny' Jones and Jean Repass. The women had

91

daughters close to Terry's age – Connie Jones and Marilyn Repass. The three became a non-stop play group while the mothers could have an afternoon talk with coffee.

The Baileys settled into the Monticello home just in time to celebrate Terry's second birthday. Vergie felt tired as she watched her son rip the paper from a box containing a blue metal toy steam shovel with working parts. He could not wait to share his new birthday toy with his new Monticello friends, Connie and Marilyn. Terry proudly showed them how his new steam shovel worked, loading sand from the creek bank in front of the house and pretending to move it around to build a road.

The day after Terry's birthday, Vergie felt a familiar morning sickness. When Doug got up, he found her packing his lunch box. "Doug, I think I am pregnant," she said with a sheepish smile.

Doug got up from the kitchen table and pulled his wife to him and kissed her. "That's terrific, sweetie. Let's have a girl this time." Doug knew that Vergie would like a daughter.

"With another little one coming, I hope we get good news soon about a permanent house in Covel. Terry is into everything, and I'll be getting bigger soon and it is harder for me to keep up with him." Vergie remarked.

Doug turned to Terry, "You are going have a sister or brother for Christmas," Doug told his son.

"Where!" Terry exclaimed as he looked around the room. The idea of Christmas and time were not set for the two-year-old, but he knew something was different. The idea of a brother or sister was maybe a little clearer since he had cousins on the Terry family side that were brothers and sisters. In fact, the cousins were multiplying Ruth and Louise

Tabor, Lowell, Lois, Lineal and Connie Davis, Donna, and Lane Gilley.

Lawrence James—known as Jimmy—the only son of Carrie and Larry had died the previous winter. He had developed leukemia and spent his last months in the Philadelphia Children's Hospital. He was almost 3 and half when he died. Terry and his parents had only seen Jimmy a couple of times during his short life. It was devasting and the deepest feeling of helplessness for the young couple to watch their child suffer. Jimmy was confined to bed and had extended stays in the hospital. To make the pain and suffering more bearable, Larry purchased a 16 mm movie projector and films of cartoons and the Three Stooges to entertain his son. He would take the projector to the hospital and project on the wall. Carrie said that the movies help to have precious memories of Jimmy's last days.

Marie and Robert were able to go to New Jersey for Jimmy's funeral service and to have a short stay with Carrie and Larry. Vergie had wanted to attend but the distance and having a young child made it difficult. She and her sisters all felt for their sister's loss.

Larry made it clear that he could not bring another child into the world and risk experiencing loss again. The Teels never had any other children. They did have Clarence, Carrie's brother with them. He would attend high school and remain in Lambertville, New Jersey throughout his life

As the summer of 1948 arrived, Doug bought a car. He parked the grey 1946 4-door Plymouth in front of the Bailey residence. The car burned oil but ran well. Now he could take Vergie and Terry over the mountain to visit on Sundays. He also planned to take Vergie to Bluefield to deliver the next child. He shared with his family and friends. "No more home delivery of babies." Doug said with his familiar grin. "It is going to be a lot easier on Vergie.

By that time, Vergie was feeling better. She had gained weight like her sisters had in their pregnancies. She hoped she would get her figure back after the delivery like Marie and Carrie. But, as her sisters always said, their Mother and Father were "big boned", so she might take after them like Mildred and Helen. When Vergie visited her doctor in Bluefield, he gave her a good report. She knew what to expect and that she was going to the hospital to deliver. Most babies were born at home. but the times were changing with pediatric wards being added to hospitals. Modern times were coming to the hills of West Virginia. This baby would be born at the Bluefield hospital

In Monticello, on a very hot August afternoon, Connie and Marilyn were outside playing with a doll. The girls handed the doll to Terry. He wasn't sure what to do with it. He had been given a Teddy Bear but had never played with a doll. He carried the doll, holding it like a newborn baby. When the girls asked for the doll back, Terry held on to the legs. The girls pulled the head trying to remove the doll from Terry's grasp. Suddenly the head of the doll came off in the hands of Connie. "Look what you did to my baby doll!" Connie shrieked. As Terry pulled away, he could see sawdust pouring out of the head and body cavity of the doll. "I didn't do nothing." he replied innocently.

Connie's mother, Virginia, was not happy about the abuse of the doll. Vergie offered to buy a replacement for the doll, but Virginia said it wasn't necessary. "The kids will learn how to treat their toys. It is alright," Virginia said. She stuffed some cotton into the doll and reattached the head. "You can't even tell the doll's been harmed after surgery," Virginia laughed.

At two years and 7 months, Terry would begin to have memories of going to his grandparents' home place in Rock. The rolling hills of the 88-acre tract of land were surrounded on three sides by the Bluestone River. Cora Lee Foster and Lake Erie Bailey, Sr. lived in this farmhouse on the hill since the day they married. Friends and relatives referred to them as Lake and Lee. "I grew up with being called Lee and that just seems to suit me." Doug's Mother had noted on several occasions if the subject came up.

Terry's father and all his Bailey uncles and aunts had been born at this house. His Uncle Melvin still lived at home. He was a truck driver for the Rock Cliff Beverage Company where his brother Junior managed the bottling operation. His Aunt Lois was working in Pulaski, Virginia and living with her Aunt Ocie. Since the war, Lois had worked at the munition's facility, the Radford Arsenal. At peak capacity, the plant had operated 24-hours per day, 7 day a week. Now it was down to one 8-hour shift, five days a week. Her job was being phased out.

Though Granddad Bailey, Lake Sr., was a carpenter for a mining company, he knew his way around the farm, growing crops and raising livestock. The family of nine subsisted on their chickens, pigs, cows, gardens, and apple trees. As the children married, the parents still shared their farm goods with the newlyweds and their extended families.

By tradition, the family killed and dressed a hog at Thanksgiving. All of the Bailey boys helped with the hog – hoisting the carcass up to begin the butchering process. The pig weighed in at close to 400 pounds – a lot of pork to share. They dressed the hams with brown sugar, salt, pepper, and other spices. After hanging in the smoke house to cure over the winter months, they would be ready to share at Easter.

Granddad Bailey directly supervised the production of the sausage. He had developed his recipe for just the right flavor. His sons took turns grinding the meat, feeding it into the top of the grinder and turning slowly to produce the strands of seasoned meat. The adult children would take the sausage, wrapped in brown butcher paper, with them at the end of the day.

With all of the work done, they settled down to eat their traditional Thanksgiving dinner: turkey, ham, green beans that had been canned the previous summer and now cooked with bacon for seasoning. All prepared mainly by Grandma Bailey with assistance from her daughters and daughters-in-law. They enjoyed baked sweet potatoes with brown sugar and cinnamon, mashed potatoes, cooked apples, and pumpkin pie. There was some discussion on installing an electric stove but at this time Grandma was insisting that she keep her coal burning stove. She told them all, "I know how to bake in this oven, and I don't trust the electric ovens."

Arriving back at Monticello late Thanksgiving night, Doug and Vergie found an envelope tacked to their front door. It was a notice to vacate by December 31, 1948. The Pocahontas Coal Company had hired additional miners who could operate the new equipment. To entice the new miners to relocate, Pocahontas had promised them housing, thus the eviction notices to the non-Pocahontas miners.

A familiar anxiety and dread set in with Vergie. "Where can we go and how can we move now so close to Christmas?" she exclaimed to her husband.

"We will work it out," Doug replied as calmly as ever.

At work the next day, Doug told Dewey about the eviction. Dewey reassured Doug that a place would come up. "Let me check with neighbors in Covel. And I am stopping off in Herndon to pick up some oil for the car. I will check with Johnny White. He has the Gulf station and knows everyone."

The next day, true to his word, Dewey offered Doug a tip from Johnny. "Doug, I have a place for you to check out. You probably ain't going to like it, but it could work until you get a house in Covel." Dewey announced.

"Where is it, Dewey?"

"There is an apartment above A. C. Cunningham's place."

"You're talking about that beer joint in the middle of Herndon on the highway? I don't think Vergie will like that." Doug replied. The apartment was above the tavern across the street from Johnny's gas station. In West Virginia, locals called taverns "beer joints". You could buy beer by the bottle or can and some limited liquor—usually legal spirits, but sometimes moonshine made in a mountain distillery.

"You ought to check on it. It may not be available for long." Dewey remarked.

After showering at the company's bathhouse, Doug drove an extra mile past their home at Monticello to Herndon and stopped at Cunningham's. A. C. stood sweeping a light morning snow from the front entrance.

Doug asked him about the apartment "Yes, it's available. The guy quit the mine and is going to Norfolk to work in the Ford plant. He said the coal wasn't for him. Should be out by Friday, but I think I have a renter."

"We have to be out of our place at Monticello by New Year's Eve. My wife is really upset over the short notice. And to make it even more of a problem, we have an active 2-and-a-half-year-old and she is expecting our second child." Doug told him. "I am looking for a spot until the company puts us in a place at Covel."

"Like I said, I think I have a renter. You can come up and take a look, but I think it's taken."

The two men climbed the steps to the apartment. At the top of the steps, they entered the living room directly from the stairwell. Doug said, "You have to be careful going down these steps since there is no door up here. I guess they were saving some space in the living room to have it set up this way. "The apartment seemed to be larger than Doug had first thought. Doug sighed noticeably and said, "Look A.C., we really need a place, and this could work. I know my wife would feel better for Christmas if she knew what we were going to do," Doug continued his plea.

A.C. took a breath and said, "You ever done much painting?"

"Yes, quite a lot. I painted with my dad who is a carpenter over in Mercer County. We painted some nice homes. Do you need a painter?"

After a slight pause, A.C. responded, "I think you and your Missus would make better renters than the guy that was thinking about the place. I can tell him I had to put you in because I knew your folks or something like that. Look, if you are willing to paint the place, I will furnish the paint, and the rent is $25. Do we have a deal?" A.C. proposed.

Without hesitating, Doug grinned, "You got a deal."

Vergie was not happy about the new rental when Doug told her of his conversation with A.C. "What about those steps with the baby...the noise...smoke...drunks!" Vergie pleaded. "And painting with a baby in the house can't be good for them. Or for Terry or me."

Doug reassured her that A.C. ran a decent place and that they would not move until after Christmas once he'd had the chance to paint the apartment. "It can't be too long before we get a house in Covel," Doug finally said.

The Bailey family began Christmas 1948 at Monticello. Between the holidays and moving preparation, Doug kept busy all month. After work each morning, he went to Herndon to clean the apartment and to paint. He snuck in sleep each afternoon before returning to work, so the painting took a little over a week. The family picked out a cedar tree above the railroad behind the house, which Doug cut down and set up in the living room for their Christmas tree.

Vergie bought a string of newly introduced bubble lights for the tree. The liquid in the tube bubbled when the lights heated up. At first, the spectacle of the lights fascinated Terry, and Vergie constantly reminded him that they were hot. Eventually, he could no longer help himself and the resulting burn cemented the lesson.

Terry understood that Christmas meant that somebody named Santa Claus would bring gifts. His interest in the stranger waxed and waned throughout the season. On Christmas Eve, the Monticello neighbors dropped by to wish a Merry Christmas to the young Bailey family. Marilyn and Connie wanted to know what Terry was getting from Santa Claus. Vergie told them Santa had a surprise for him. Since

Vergie was wearing her maternity clothes and showing her condition, the girls were also curious about the baby on its way. "We hope it's a girl," Connie told Vergie.

Vergie had baked cookies and a ham for their Christmas Eve supper. They would open gifts from "Santa Claus" in the morning and then head to Doug's parents' place and see all of his brothers and sisters.

On Christmas morning, Terry required no urging to see what Santa had brought. In front of the decorated tree stood a bright red tricycle. Terry had seen Connie and Cookie's tricycle but had never sat on the seat or tried to ride it. With a little support from his dad, Terry turned the front wheel with the pedals. He felt the trike move. He sat up proudly on the seat of the trike, but his eyebrows remained furrowed with hesitation. He soon found the trike's horn on the handlebar. He squeezed the rubber bulb of the horn in rapid succession. After watching with amusement for a few moments, his dad said, "That will be enough for now."

When it came time to leave for Rock, Terry wanted to take the trike with him. His Mother explained that they should not take the largest present with them but something smaller. With some reluctance, he selected a coloring book, crayons, and a toy car. The family loaded into the Plymouth around 10 am and headed east on West Virginia Route 10 toward the Bailey home place.

Terry steered the toy car from one side of the back seat to the next, mimicking his father as he drove to grandma's house. As Doug shifted the manual transmission into first gear to climb the 100 yards of the steep dirt driveway to the farmhouse, Terry shouted, "We are here!"

All of Doug's brothers and sisters were there, and that year, Denver B. (D.B.) Echols joined the group. He had just married Doug's oldest sister, Iva Lee Maxine, who the family called Maxine. D.B. was the brother to Faye Echols who last year had married Wallace. By that time, Wally had obtained a divorce from his war time bride, Alice, on the grounds of desertion through a special provision for military personnel. Spousal dissertation occurred with several returning service personnel, resulting in a divorce rate of 25 percent in 1946-- the highest rate in the United States until 1970.

As their children married and began having their own children, the Baileys remained a close family. Christmas was a special time. All of Lee and Lake's children and their grandchildren spent Christmas together. It became a tradition starting after the war and would continue through the next two decades until Lake and Lee died only six months apart, in October 1969 and April 1970. That Christmas was the fourth after the war's end and the day fell on Sunday. It would be the last one with only two grandchildren, Bobby Lee age 8 and Terry 2 years and 8 months. Of course, the family all wanted to know how Vergie was doing with her baby due next month. Over the years, the number of grandchildren grew until there were a total of 18 in1960.

Terry followed Bobby around the parlor for a few minutes before sitting on the floor covered with dark maroon wool carpet near the decorated tree. The formal parlor had replaced an extra downstairs bedroom was no longer needed to house Lee and Lake's children.   Only their youngest daughter, Lois Mae, had not yet married.

Lee served their traditional Christmas meal—ham raised on the home place, candied yams, mashed potatoes, green beans, and thin gravy. Plenty of sweet, iced tea and desserts, apple and pumpkin pies topped with whipped cream from milk of the Baileys' cow. And banana pudding because bananas were readily available this year.

The uncles, aunts and the grandparents lavished the two grandkids with gifts of clothing, toys, and candy. Terry felt overwhelmed at the number of boxes wrapped in pretty paper.

At the end of the day, the men had one final cigarette on the front porch before exchanging good-byes. Gradually, the car taillights disappeared beyond the top of the hilly driveway as each family headed back to either Mercer or Wyoming counties. Doug, Vergie, and Terry had the longest route but only by about 15 miles. Everyone lived less than 45 minutes from their birthplace.

It had been a wonderful Christmas. Terry had been excited almost every moment of the day. With his energy finally depleted, his sugar high from the desserts gave way to exhaustion. He fell asleep before Doug drove onto the Rock River Road.

Terry remained fast asleep as Doug carried him to his bed at Monticello for the last time. The next day, they would be moving about a mile up the highway to Herndon. Since Christmas had fallen on a Sunday, the mines stayed closed on Monday. The evening shifts week started on Sunday evening with the first shift ending Monday morning and the last shift of the five-day week ending on Friday morning. Doug thought this would be the best time to move the family. He would not lose any work and he could be back on the evening shift Monday night.

On Monday afternoon, Terry understood that he would not be sleeping in the Monticello house. His room was empty.

His parents had already packed all of his toys in boxes, which now awaited him at their new home. Even his new, red tricycle had been moved. That was the first thing he looked for when, for the first time, he climbed the steps over the Cunningham establishment.

The move went smoothly. Doug laughed, "We have the hang of moving now, since this is our fourth move in four years." After the second and final trip with a borrowed pick-up truck, Doug loaded their clothes on hangers into the Plymouth and helped his very pregnant wife get into the front seat with their son for the short drive to Herndon. Just as they were closing the car door, Connie and Cookie ran out to say good-bye to Terry. He slid out of the front seat, crawling over his mother to hug his friends. "Mom said she would bring me back here to play with you when she gets her driver's license!" Terry exclaimed. Terry was thinking that the girls always had a nice smell, like baby powder.

Forged by Coal

Chapter 10 –Trike Ride to Remember at Herndon

Herndon proved more convenient for the family, especially Vergie. She could walk to the grocery store, which was almost next door to the tavern. The store was nothing like a company store. The store did not have clothing, hardware nor any ordering procedures but did have the basic foods her family relied on. She just asked one of the two clerks for the items she wanted, and they obliged by picking the items from the shelves behind the counter.

One afternoon three days after Christmas, snow started falling. Doug had gotten up a little earlier than usual—about 3:30 pm—to continue unpacking from the move. Nearing her due date, Vergie was tired. The baby had begun to kick more often and at the most awkward times. Vergie had unpacked a lot of their boxes, but she relied on Doug for all the heavy lifting. Her condition also required that reach for top shelves and bend to reach low drawers. They had almost finished, but he could not help thinking they would have to do all again in only a few months' time. He still hoped they would move up the road to Covel, even if it happened on short notice. Neither of them was too keen on having two young children living above the beer joint. He thought it would round out their family nicely if the imminent new addition turned out to be a girl. One of each would suit them fine.

Vergie interrupted his thoughts, remarking, "Too bad it didn't snow earlier. We could have had a White Christmas. Maybe just as well. Crossing the mountain in snow might be a problem."

Doug replied, "Don't worry, I got a set of chains with the car. They are in the trunk. That reminds me, I think I will get gas and check the oil in the car before we eat," Doug said as he put on his coat and cap.

"Okay, dinner is almost ready. The roast will be about 20 minutes."

As he left the kitchen, Doug ruffled Terry's hair, thinking Terry must know not to get too close to the stairwell that was open to the hall that connected the kitchen and living room. Doug made his way down the step stairs to drive just across the road to the Lusk Gulf Station.

"Mommy, I want to ride my tricycle!" Terry proclaimed. Within days, he had become adept at riding the trike. He could steer with the wheel and propel the trike forward and backward as he had learned to ride in Monticello on the frozen dirt driveway in front of the houses.

"Ok but stay away from the top of the steps," Vergie responded distractedly.

While Vergie put away the dishes she had just washed and dried, Terry pedaled down the hall into the living room, then he turned the trike around and came back toward the kitchen. Arriving at the kitchen, he then turned the trike around once more and repeated the route. As he accelerated out of the kitchen, Terry gleefully shouted, "Wheeee!" His volume grew with each lap. In an instant, Vergie realized by the grinding sound of the wheels over the linoleum that his speed, too, had grown. She turned to tell her son to slow down and be careful, but before she had the chance, she heard a thump...thump...thump.

With horror, the young mother heard her son shouting, "Ohhhhhhhhhh!" She rushed to the hall. Much to her astonishment, she did not find Terry in the hall or the living room. She moved down the hall to the top of the steps as swiftly as her eight-month pregnant body allowed. At the bottom of the dark stairwell, she saw her son pinned down by the red tricycle. The sound of his screams between the loud sobs were all new for the son and for the mother. Terry and trike had gone down the flight of steps! Vergie reached for the light switch at the top of the steps and as the stairwell filled with light, she saw Terry looking at his right leg with his mouth open with the cries gushing out like an open faucet and eyes full of tears.

"Oh God, he must have broken his leg!" she thought and found herself instantly by his side. With a mother's instinct, Vergie picked her son up and held him close to her in a mother bear hug. Thank God, she thought. Though his leg was bleeding, he could move it. She remembered from her high school health class and from first aid training during the war that if he could move his leg and foot, it wasn't broken.

Vergie managed to lift her 35 pound, almost 3-year-old son and carry him up the stairs to the living room. The leg was bleeding from a gash above the right knee. Blood had smeared across Vergie's dress and apron. She laid him on the while she retrieved a towel from the bathroom to wrap around his wound. In the first aid training, she had learned to put pressure on a wound to stop the bleeding, so she used a dish towel to tie the other towel tighter around the leg.

With the bleeding controlled for the moment, Vergie considered what to do next. From her first aid course, she knew he might have a concussion or internal bleeding. "I need to get him to a doctor to check him for those things, and he may need stiches," the thought was punctuated by a kick. It occurred to her as she felt the kick, "The baby must know something is going on with their big brother."

Terry was still crying but not screaming. Vergie reassured her son that he was going to be all right. She felt his forehead for a fever but other than some smudges of dirt, dust from the stairs, he felt normal. "I need to go across the road and get your dad. I will only be a minute. Don't move."

She hurried as much as she could down the stairs toward the front entrance to Cunningham's. She found Doug on the other side of the door as she opened it. "Thank God you are back. Terry rode his tricycle down the stairs and has a big gash in his leg. We got to take him to the doctor right away!" Vergie exclaimed.

Running up the stairs several feet in front of his wife, Doug knelt next to Terry and shouted back. "Looks like a deep cut. He may need stiches. We can take him to the doctor at the Covel store. I know he is there today.

Vergie got her coat and Terry's, along with his cap with the attached earmuffs. Doug carried Terry down the stairs and around to the side of the building where he had parked the car. Vergie had thought to bring another towel to rest Terry's leg on in hopes that it would protect the seat cover from the same fate as her dress and apron.

Within five minutes, Doug pulled the car right up to the Covel company store's side. Doug ran into the doctor's office where he found the nurse and the doctor chatting. They had no other patients. "We need some help. My boy has cut his leg open. I will bring him in," Doug declared without waiting for a reply.

Dr. Frank Penn had been employed by American Coal to serve the miners of Covel, Garwood, Herndon, Bud and Alpoca. In 1948, he was starting to show some grey hair and had put on weight. He had been hired directly out of medical school in 1932 when he was 23. For the last 17 years, he had treated a multitude of ailments and injuries, and attended births and deaths. He was an integral part of the mining community.

"Yes, I can see from the blood that we have a bad cut here. What happened?" Dr. Penn inquired. Vergie explained the trike ride down the stairs while Doug carried their son to the examining table. Terry had only been to a doctor's office a couple of times. He was too distracted by his pain to feel anxious over seeing Dr. Penn for the first time. The Doctor removed the towels from the upper right leg to get a better look.

"Yep, you gashed it open. We can fix this in no time," Dr. Penn said. "But first," he requested as he removed the boy's right shoe and sock, "Wiggle your toes." Terry complied with great concentration and all of five toes moved up and down. "That a boy. Those toes are wiggling." Dr. Penn indicated with a slight grin.

After cleaning the wound, the Doctor swabbed a numbing solution on each side of the opening. He spread a boric acid cream over the wound and alcohol around the edges. Then he opened the sterilizer that had heated surgical instruments. He took out scissors and a needle with surgical thread. Terry lurched a little as Dr. Penn pushed the needle through one side of the wound and caught the other side of the skin to cover the open wound. "Ow, ow!" Terry howled.

The minute it took for Dr. Penn to sew the wound shut seemed like an hour to Vergie. He finished up by applying iodine with a swab and placing a bandage over the wound. "He should be fine. You will need to change the dressing each day for the next week or so. I will give you a roll of gauze and some tape. Keep it clean and dry, and it should heal quickly."

"You are about to become a mother again," Dr. Penn continued with a smile as he handed the scissors and needle to the nurse.

Vergie nodded and said, "About any day now. This scare almost sent me into labor."

"Is this your second one? The Doctor asked.

"Yes, we just moved from Mercer County and we're planning on going to the Bluefield Hospital for this one. Doug added, " It was too much the last time with home delivery in an upstairs apartment. We just thought it would be safer this way."

Dr. Penn agreed with Vergie. "I didn't think that I had seen you before. I have delivered a lot of babies in these coal camps. I am sort of proud my ability to deliver babies. I have to brag about using forceps when needed in delivery without marking the baby. You have a doctor in Bluefield?" Vergie told him she was seeing Dr. Butler there.

"I have met him. He is good. They have a full staff there. The nurses are probably the best around to help with newborns."

"Thank you so much Dr. Penn. How much do I owe you?" Doug asked

"You work for the company?"

"I work for American Coal at Deerfield. Do you charge us on my pay envelope?"

"The company pays me to provide medical care to each miner and the members of his family. You don't owe me anything. Just take good care of this young man. And I am sure we will see him for his shots," Dr Penn responded.

110

The nurse gave Terry a red lollipop. He looked at her and hesitated but then asked if he could have a yellow one because lemon was his favorite. She smiled and handed him two yellow lollipops. "One for now and one for late," she smiled.

Doug picked Terry up and carried him back to the car. As they drove back to Herndon, Vergie remarked. "I really liked Dr. Penn. He was good with Terry, very patient and had a nice way about him."

"It's good we got a doctor that close. One thing the company does that helps, for sure." Doug said.

As Terry savored the last slurp of his lemon lollipop, Doug asked him, "Are you doing okay, son?"

"Doing ok."

Satisfied with the response, Doug turned to Vergie, "How are you and the baby doing?"

Vergie replied with a sigh, "I am glad that it is over. We need to put something across the top of the steps. The baby kicked a little but seems calm now. I think me and my baby are going to be fine. We're both glad Terry is all right." After a pause, she grinned through exhaustion, "This is an adventure that I could do without, but we are going to have a tale to tell the family on Sunday."

Forged by Coal

Chapter 11 – Pamela Kay Bailey

On the evening of January 7th, Vergie was in a "half-asleep" way, as she liked to describe it. She wasn't asleep, and she wasn't awake. She was a full nine months pregnant, maybe a couple days more. In this half-asleep state, a multitude of thoughts floated through her mind. First and foremost, she just hoped the baby would be all right. Then, "It would be nice if it turns out to be a girl. I know we would have fun. Dressing girls and getting them toys is so much more fun than boys." At that moment she was startled by the baby's movement. The kicks were more forceful than usual. "Maybe you are getting ready to come out, but I don't remember this from Terry." She started to settle back into the sleepy state, thinking, "Maybe it is a girl!" as another movement occurred.

In a long few minutes, Vergie felt the baby settle. Vergie sighed, thinking, "Maybe a false start," then she drifted off into full sleep.

As January 8th dawned, Vergie opened her eyes slightly to see out the bottom of the window where the shade had not come to meet the seal. The snow had stopped in the early morning hours. "It looks like we got about 3 inches of snow last night," Vergie told Doug as he rolled out of bed.

"I am glad we have an indoor bathroom on a day like this," he responded as he stood up. "Wow the floor is cold!" In his bare feet, he made his way gingerly toward his house slippers, which Vergie had ordered from the Sears catalog and given him at Christmas with a note saying, "From your son, Terry. Merry Christmas, dad."

From the bathroom, Doug shouted, "The houses at Covel have indoor water pipes but outside toilets. This

bathroom is about the only thing I will miss from here."
"That's for sure." Vergie added.

It was Saturday and Doug had enjoyed Friday evening at home. As a night shift worker, his week started on Sunday night at midnight and ran through Thursday at midnight. To make the most of his weekends, Doug had become accustomed to napping on Friday morning and sleeping next to Vergie on Friday and Saturday nights. He had to take a nap Sunday evening before leaving for his shift at the tipple. It had taken a few weeks to adjust to this schedule, but it was now working fine. Terry, on the other hand, was accustomed to staying up with his mother until his dad had left for work around 11:15 each night. Terry didn't seem to need much sleep because he was up early too.

Vergie had put on her robe and started the electric stove burner. She heated up lard in a heavy iron skillet and fried Doug's two eggs, along with and one each for her and Terry. Then, she fried up some Spam. They typically had sausage or bacon, but Vergie had decided to try this new canned meat when she learned about it from her sisters-in-law. Doug's three brothers had eaten Spam in Europe and in the Pacific during the war.

As Vergie reached for the pepper to shake onto Doug's eggs, she felt the same forceful movements from the baby that she had felt the night before. She paused for a couple of seconds, trying to decipher the meaning. This feels different. I hope the baby is ok. "Doug, I guess you better put chains on the car and let's go over the mountain."

"The snow will be off the road by tomorrow when we go over to Rock and Mil's, so we won't need the chains" Doug responded.

With a higher pitched voice, Vergie said "We are going to the hospital in Bluefield today, I think I am starting labor!"

"Oh, why didn't you say so! Okay, I will get the chains on and warm up the car." Doug responded as he put on his jacket and cap.

Vergie had prepared her suitcase on New Year's Day, knowing the baby would be coming in January. Aside from the snow, she thought it would be a good day to have the baby. Vergie wasn't too worried about Doug driving in snow. All of the men in this part of the state had pride in their ability to drive in the snow and to handle the ice-covered roads. Vergie recalled just this last Christmas Day as the snow started falling when they crossed the mountain to return home. Doug had to stop at the foot of the mountain in Mercer County to strap the chains on. Then in second gear he successfully drove up and down the mountain.

Regardless of her confidence in Doug, Vergie could not shake her anxiety. I will be glad to get this over with. I hope everything is okay. I wish Doug would come on

"Terry, finish your breakfast. You're going to visit the Repass girls. Come on," Vergie said in a curt tone.

Terry looked up at his mother. "Okay, I just got toast to finish. Can I have apple butter?"

Doug's hands were stiff from the cold. Getting the chains on and fastening the hooks was almost impossible with gloves. He got the chains on and then started the car and checked the gas gauge. It was full. He had made a practice of filling up on Friday mornings as he came from work. Friday was pay day and he would settle up his gasoline tab with Bud at Milam's Amoco station just down the road. He liked Amoco gas, the white gasoline, that was better for the engine since it had the lead taken out. All other gasolines were red in color. It cost a little more than the gas across the street in Herndon— twenty-five cents a gallon versus twenty-two cents a gallon. When Doug paid his tab for gas, the station gave him S & H Green Stamps. Vergie collected the stamps, faithfully pasting them in the book after wetting them with a soaked sponge. She was saving them to redeem for new bed linens. The brand carried by S & H was much more attractive than the ones carried by the Company Store. S & H had a store in Bluefield, but they also did business by mail order.

Rushing out the door holding Terry by the hand, Vergie exclaimed, "Doug, my water broke. Let's get going. Don't forget, we have to take Terry to the Repasses first." The Repasses had agreed to keep Terry when Vergie went to deliver the baby. The Joneses, who also still lived at Monticello, had agreed to be the backup, in case the Repasses were away. None of the families had telephones, so they would just show up with Terry.

The car was just getting warm as Doug put Terry in the middle of the front seat by way of the driver's side while Vergie entered on the passenger side. Doug had brought the suitcase down for Vergie and a large brown shopping bag with clothes and a toothbrush for Terry. Vergie had stressed good dental habits for her son from his first tooth. She had read that taking care of your teeth promoted good health and that even baby teeth should be brushed. Her teeth and especially Doug's were yellowed from years of neglect, and they both had tooth aches. When they were growing up, looking after their teeth was not a priority.

Vergie was grateful that there was no traffic, making it a short drive to Monticello. The West Virginia State Road

Commission had already plowed the road, and though the snow was still falling, you could see the pavement. Even so, Vergie was starting to worry that she might deliver on the mountain. This was a very scary thought.

Doug drove slowly over the creek on the wood bridge and pulled up in front of the Repass house. Terry looking out the window, "Are we moving back here?"

"You are going to visit Marilyn and her sisters while your mother and I go get your sister or brother," Doug responded. Terry looked a little puzzled but then exclaimed. "Okay" and started toward the girls' toys in a large cardboard box in the corner of the room. Marilyn, one of the three Repass children, was Terry's age, "You want to see my new baby doll? She asked Terry. In less than a minute, Terry was looking at Marilyn's new doll and pulling out a coloring book from the box.

The Repasses were all at home. Earnest Repass was a miner, almost 30 years old. His wife, Geraldine, and their three children, Patty, Christine, and Marilyn lived in one of the four-room houses at Monticello. Geraldine was expecting her fourth child, due in May. They were hoping for a boy and had already picked out the name "Eddie", short for "Edward", which was Earnest's father's name.

"Don't worry about Terry. The girls love to play with him. He will be just fine. You folks watch that road crossing the mountain. Looking forward to seeing the new one here in three or four days," Geraldine said with a reassuring smile.

"Terry, we are going outside with the sled. Come on. We will build a snowman!" Marilyn shouted with her usual exuberance as she tucked her blond curls under her crocheted hat. "Dad's going to burn a tire too, so we will be warm."

Laughing, Doug said to Geraldine, "Thank you so much. I will check with you when I get back. I think we will have us a girl this time." Turning to the little girls, he suggested, "You gals will have another playmate and if you have a brother, he might have a girlfriend." He grinned.

Doug drove back on Route 10 and headed east to cross the mountain into Mercer County and on to Bluefield, the county's largest city. The snow had stopped, but there was some drifting across the road, especially in some of the many turns on Herndon/Arista Mountain. Vergie thought she felt the car slide a couple of times going down the hillside into Mercer County. She continued to worry about getting to the hospital and about how she was feeling. Passing the Mercer County marker sign, she realized, this baby would be another member of the family born in Mercer County. But it would be the first baby in either of the families to be born at a hospital. She tried several times to brush aside her unease.

After reaching the foot of the mountain on the Arista side, the road had been cleared of all snow. Doug always thought that Mercer County was better at clearing the roads. Vergie said that she didn't think they got as much snow, probably because of the lower elevation and its location, the most southeast part of the state.

The contractions had picked up by the time they pulled into the circular drive at the Bluefield Sanatorium, Bluefield's largest hospital. "I am glad we are here," Vergie said with relief.

An orderly met Doug and Vergie at the door. "I will park the car and come right back," Doug promised as the orderly pulled up a wheelchair and wheeled Vergie to the elevator.

When they arrived at the maternity wing on the third floor, they were greeted by a nurse whose nametag read "Gail Sizemore". She took Vergie's vital signs and noted that her blood pressure was up. "That's pretty usual" she reassured. "I am going to check with the doctor and let him know how you are doing." Vergie had none of this type of attention when Terry was born in their bedroom at Rock.

In a few minutes, Dr. Butler appeared with Nurse Sizemore. "Let's see how you are doing," the doctor remarked as he put the end of the stethoscope on Vergie's bulged stomach. His face seemed to tighten up as he listened. His eyes narrowed and his eyebrows furrowed.

"Everything okay, doctor?" Vergie asked with trepidation. The doctor nodded his head, "yes", but Vergie thought he looked worried as he stood up.

Doug sat in the waiting room with two other fathers-to-be. One of the men, RJ, looked to be a teenager. The other man, Tony, appeared to be much older than Doug. RJ told Doug and Tony that this was their first baby. "We have been married since July," RJ said sheepishly. Doug and Tony reassured RJ that it would be okay. Tony stayed quiet but appeared anxious, "This is our fourth kid. The last one was almost seven years ago. I'm getting too old to help raise babies." Tony declared.

A nurse came to the doorway of the waiting room and looked at Tony, "Mr. Conner, congratulations. You have a girl."

"That makes four girls," Tony said as he stood up to accompany the nurse to the recovery room to see his wife of 14 years and his newest daughter.

Doug and RJ sat silently, both thumbing through older issues of Saturday Evening Post and Look magazines. The nurse returned to tell RJ his wife had delivered a 7-pound 10 ounce boy.

Another 30 minutes passed, an orderly came to the doorway of the waiting room and quietly said, "Mr. Bailey?" When Doug looked up, "Please come with me". Doug stood up and followed the orderly down the hall.

"Everything okay?" Doug asked as they started down the hallway. "I think the doc has delivered your baby. He wanted to see you," the orderly replied.

Dr. Butler met Doug at the door to the delivery room. "Your wife had a girl. The labor went okay. Your wife did well. It took a lot of effort, and she is worn out." He paused before continuing, "I am afraid the little girl has a problem. Her heart isn't pumping like it should," The doctor explained.

"Is she going to be all right?" Doug asked.

The doctor shook his head slowly from left to right and responded. "There is nothing we can do. If the heart had a stronger rhythm and she could start to take in more air, she might get better. We will just have to wait but I don't believe she can make it this way." The doctor's words came slowly and reverently.

Doug felt himself tremble. He asked, "Does Vergie know about the baby's heart?"

"Not at this time. She heard the baby cry and saw her as we placed her in the bassinet. You should go in and be with your daughter and wife. The nurse will check in with you shortly," Dr. Butler concluded.

Doug slowly opened the door to the recovery room, and he felt like he was moving in slow motion as he approached

Vergie. "Honey, the doc said you did really good. We got a girl. Just what you wanted," Doug's voice cracked, but he forced a smile as tears flooded his eyes.

"She is so sweet, and I am so tired," Vergie replied to Doug as he leaned over to kiss her on the forehand. "I don't think she is as strong as she ought to be, though. I am worried about her. Something's not like it should be," Vergie voiced her mother's instinct.

Sighing, Doug replied, "Vergie, the doc thinks the baby has a heart problem. They don't think they can help her." His voice dropped off quickly.

Vergie's eyes teared up and her bottom lip trembled. "I just felt something wasn't right. Even last night I thought something was not right." Turning to the nurse, Vergie asked, "Can we see her?"

Nurse Sizemore picked up the baby and gently placed her in Vergie's arms. The baby girl was very still but her chest expanded with each struggling breath.

For a moment, the couple looked at their newborn daughter. The room stayed silent until Doug spoke. "Pamela Kay is a pretty name."

"Yes, her name is Pamela Kay Bailey," Vergie replied with quiet pride before silence again fell over the room.

"Very sweet, pretty name. I like it." Nurse Sizemore smiled as she bent over to look at the newborn. Her chest movement had slowed. Her skin had paled from healthy pink to a pale white, emphasizing the veins beneath it. Nurse Sizemore reached for the baby when her chest stopped moving altogether. At that instance, the nurse stood as if frozen in time for only two or three seconds but from the expression on her face and a sadness in her eyes it seemed like minutes. Nurse Sizemore sighed lowly, "Sweet baby has gone."

Pamela Kay Bailey had been with her parents in one room of a hospital all her short life. In that brief time, Vergie's hopes, and dreams for the daughter she would love and raise ended. Both parents cried softly as Nurse Sizemore rolled the bassinet out of the room and down the hall.

January 8, 1949, replaced the day Vergie's mother and brother died as the saddest day. It was so cold, so grey, so very sad.

Doug gave the baby's name to the hospital clerk who filled out the birth and death certificates to be signed by Dr. Butler. "I will take her to the Rock Cemetery for burial. There is space next to my brother Ralph's grave," Doug informed the clerk.

The nurse helped Vergie move to a semi-private room that contained two beds. To Vergie's relief there was no one in the other bed. She knew that she couldn't bear to be with a mother who had just given birth.

Doug entered the room and pulled the chair up to bed. The couple looked at each other without exchanging a word for what seemed like an hour. Vergie then asked," What are the arrangements for her...for Pamela?"

"I will take her to the Rock Cemetery. We have family there and I know there is space beside of my brother Ralph's grave," Doug responded.

"You should go over to your folks for the night. Tomorrow, you can take her over. Terry will be fine at the Repasses. I know they are not expecting to hear from us until tomorrow or Monday," Vergie added.

"I can stay here with you," Doug offered.

"No, you need to rest and arrange the details of the burial. I will just be sleeping anyway. And the doctor thinks I might be here for three days. They will take care of me. You can come on back in the morning."

"You are right. I will go on to Rock and order a coffin from the Bailey Funeral Home. Roland Bailey, the owner, is a cousin. I am sure they can take care of bringing over a coffin for her."

Vergie felt physically listless, but her mind swirled. Finally, she remarked, "Doug, I thought it would be safer and easier coming to the hospital to give birth. I can't understand it. I didn't tell you but yesterday and last night, I was starting to feel that something was not right. I didn't want to think it was going to be a problem and I didn't want you to worry."

Doug held his wife's hand tighter as he said, "I think the baby's problem was there all along, no matter where she was born. We would not want her to have to struggle, not be able to have a life. It doesn't seem right, but it may be for the best. We just don't know. There are lots of babies suffering and children stuck in iron lungs to breathe. That's got to be a hard way to live."

A nurse quietly entered the room with some medications. "Mrs. Bailey, I am nurse Dorothy Lusk. I have some medication for you, and I am going to take your temperature, pulse, and blood pressure." Doug released Vergie's hand and moved away from the bed as the nurse placed the thermometer in Vergie's mouth. Nurse Lusk took her pulse and checked her temperature. "You have some fever, and your blood pressure is up. I will let the doctor know. These are some pills that will help you rest," she pointed to one set of pills, then continued, "The larger one is to help you stop your milk flow." At the words, "stop your milk", Vergie teared up and swallowed, attempting to keep from crying.

"I will be back to check on you and will look in all through the night. The orderly will bring you a dinner tray in the next hour. You should try to eat." Nurse Lusk's soft tone was comforting as she backed away from Vergie's bed.

"Thank you." Vergie tried to smile at the nurse's kindness.

"You should go on and make the call to the funeral home and go to your folks. They will want to know, and they can help you with the cemetery," Vergie urged Doug.

Doug leaned over and kissed his wife. "Okay. I will be back early in the morning."

Doug used the phone at the nurse's station to talk with the funeral home. They assured Doug that they would take care of delivering a coffin for his baby daughter to the hospital by that evening. Nurse Lusk had overheard Doug's part of the conversation. When he hung up, Nurse Lusk reassured him that the hospital would take care of receiving the coffin. She said he could come to the rear of the hospital at the loading dock the following day and an orderly would help him.

Doug drove on to Rock. He stopped at the general store to pick up a pack of Camels. He had chained smoked since he left the hospital and was down to his last three or four cigarettes. He told the store clerk, Eugene Talbot, about their baby. He knew that would get the word out in the community where he and his parents were known. Eugene had worked at the store for years and knew Doug and his sisters and brothers. Doug had brought Vergie to the store when they lived at Mrs. Linkous's. "Tell your Missus we're very sorry for the loss of your baby. When she feels up to it, bring her by with that boy of yours. We have not seen them since you moved cross the mountain."

Back at the hospital, Vergie had started to doze off, but her mind remained focused on Pamela. She tried to imagine what Doug was telling his folks. She wished she could be with him and his parents. She realized that she had not even thought about her dad. She could not imagine his response. He had never known what to say or do when confronted with loss. Vergie remembered his reactions when her mother and brother had died. He was solemn but could not outwardly express his grief or even try to console his children. His reaction to people expressing condolences was mainly the nod of the head and a languid expression.

When her dinner tray arrived, Vergie sipped the iced tea but only pushed around the food on the tray. She wasn't hungry. She just wanted to sleep so that tomorrow would come sooner.

Doug continued to his parents' home. He opened the back door that lead into the kitchen and met his Mother who had seen the headlights of the car as he drove up the hill. Seeing sudden tears in his eyes, Doug's Mother knew something was wrong. "Is Vergie all right? What's happened?" Cora Lee asked.

With words muffled by tears, Doug laid out the sad details of the day for his mother and his father who had just come into the kitchen. They talked about burying Pamela at the Rock Cemetery the following afternoon. When there was nothing left to be say, Doug told his folks good night and went upstairs to the room that he had slept in for twenty years. He tossed and turned, on what was the hardest night in his memory.

Before daylight on Sunday morning, Doug found himself in the kitchen adding coal to the cook stove. He knew his mother would be up shortly to fix breakfast, but all Doug needed this morning was cup of hot coffee and to get back to his wife. He did not how he would find the strength to bring their little baby girl to the cemetery. He said only a few words to his mother as she handed him a cup of coffee. Before he left for the hospital, Cora Lee told him to come to the church if he got back before the Sunday service ended.

Vergie awoke before daylight as well. The sleeping pill had worn off, and she wasn't sure if she wanted another one. It had made her groggy and confused. She knew she was no longer carrying a baby. She felt empty. When Doug entered her room, it renewed her tears, and he cried with her. He embraced her as she leaned back on the two pillows propping her up. "Doug, take our baby, Pamela to Rock," Vergie whispered in her husband's ear.

It was a lonely, silent drive for Doug as he drove from Bluefield and turned onto the Rock Road. Pamela Kay was in the small coffin on the back seat.

The word rippled out quickly from the general store and through his parents' church on Sunday morning. As it had been decided early that morning, Doug arrived at the Rock Methodist Church as it was letting out. Doug parked on the hill outside the church where his Mother played the organ and his father was a Sunday school teacher for the men's class.

As Lake Bailey made his way out of the church, he spotted Doug and cut a path over the church lawn toward his son. With organ music in the background, Lake Bailey put his arm around his son and said "Doug. It's hard to figure how these things happen. I am so sorry." He stared at the back seat of the car as Doug gave him a strong hug. When the last of the parishioners straggled out of the sanctuary, the organ music stopped, and Doug's Mother came out of the church looking straight ahead for her son. Quietly, she kissed him on the cheek and took his cold hands in hers.

Doug told his dad that he needed a pick and shovel to bury Pamela. He wanted to lay her to rest beside Ralph if they agreed. Lake Bailey shook his head and said, "You know we have the space there for the family. I didn't think I would have a grandchild there before we were using the space."

The brothers, Orville, Junior, Wallace, and Melvin had gathered around. "We will take care of the grave, Doug. You go home with dad and mom. Come over to the cemetery around 3:30 and we should have it all set." Orville suggested to Doug, and his brothers nodded in assent. Doug looked at his family and in a choked whisper said, "Thanks."

Vergie stayed in the hospital on doctor's orders. She tried to imagine her daughter being buried today without her. Doug felt very much alone even though his family had climbed with him up the steep hill to the burial site where they lowered the small wooden coffin into the narrow, 6-foot-deep opening in the earth. Lake had requested that the Methodist preacher be there with the family.

The preacher read the passage from Revelations 21:4. "And God shall wipe away all tears from their eyes' and there shall be no more death, neither sorrow, nor crying, neither shall there be any more pain: for the former things are passed away." And he followed this reading up with Matthew 18:10. "Take heed that ye despise not one of these little ones; for I say unto you, That in heaven their angels do always behold the face of my Father which is in heaven." To end the short service, for what is there to say about a child who lived only hours, the family joined the minister in reciting the Lord's Prayer.

Doug, with his head still bowed, thanked everyone and especially the preacher.

Walking down the hill, Cora Lee hung back with Doug, who lagged the others. "Doug, come over and get some supper,"

"I am going back to the hospital and be with Vergie".

"You must eat, and you can make a plate for Vergie too. You know how bad that hospital food can be," his mother grimaced.

"Okay, but then I really do need to get on back," Doug said as he took his mother's arm to start down the steep path. The recent snow had made the path slick, but his brothers had thoughtfully put down some dirt and coal cinders on the steepest parts.

Years later, Doug could not remember what his mother had prepared for the Sunday dinner or even if he had eaten anything. He did remember that his mother prepared a basket of food for Vergie that he had almost forgotten as he entered the hospital. He returned to the car to pick up the basket. As he waited for the elevator, he realized that he needed to see his wife and he felt that she needed him. Why was the elevator taking so long?

Part III – Covel Coal Camp

Chapter 12 - Moving to Covel

It had been two months since they lost Pamela. Vergie wondered why people used that word: "lost". Pamela had died the same day she was born, and Doug had taken her little body to the Rock Cemetery for burial. They had visited the grave site three times, once in six inches of snow. Pamela wasn't lost. She wasn't with her mother, father and brother or the rest of the Baileys or Terrys, but she wasn't lost.

Doug climbed the steps to the apartment above the beer joint and shot Vergie a huge smile. In the weeks after Pamela's death, he had worn a grim and dignified look, which was very much out of character. "We got us a house in Covel, Vergie." The good news had restored his trademark grin.

"Oh great, it is about time, when?" Vergie replied.

"Any time after this Friday," Doug beamed. "Let's go see the house on Saturday to see if it needs anything and plan to move the next weekend." He knew how very much she wanted to get out of the apartment. The tricycle misadventure had proved that it was not the best location for an active boy. The boisterous bar noise on the evenings and weekends made it difficult to sleep. Vergie was already looking forward to getting away from this place and putting the memories behind her.

Doug's expression became serious again as he continued, "It's the only house available in the camp. The folks are moving to help at their parents' farm in Basin." He paused, "The only thing is…it's in the colored section of the camp."

"What do you mean colored section?" Vergie looked puzzled.

"You know, part of the camp is for colored miners and the other part is where whites live. The house had colored in it, but we can clean it up and I can paint, and we can get in good shape to move in quick." He looked at his wife's face and reassured her. "It is going to be ok. If we don't take it, there are others on the list that will. Mr. Hill, the company payroll clerk, says we can move to the white section as soon as there is an opening."

As she considered what he had told her, Vergie conceded, "Ok let's go see it. We can change our mind if we don't like what we see. But I really want to get out of here." Vergie stated in a tone that was considerably less than enthusiastic.

* * *

Vergie anxiously waited for Saturday to arrive. She wanted to see the house and the section of the camp reserved for coloreds. When the day came, Doug stood at the top of the stairs and reached his hand out to his son, "Come on Terry, we are going to see the house where we are going to move." Terry tentatively approached the stairs. Since the big trike accident, Terry had been very careful when he approached the top of the steps. He knew he did not want to tumble down again. Hand-in-hand, they made their way down the stairs.

Terry sat between his mom and dad on the front seat as Doug drove about a mile to the entrance of the Covel coal camp. The couple had only driven through the camp a few times. Doug had been there to pick up his pay and sign up for benefits. Terry remembered going to see the doctor when he had his accident and cut his leg. "Are we going to the doctor?" Terry asked.

"No, we are going to look at a house," Vergie replied.

Doug turned left off State Route 10 and guided the car onto the one lane, wooden bridge that crossed the Gooney Otter Creek branch that flowed from Garwood. This branch traveled only 400 feet to merge with the upper branch that flowed from the holler where the Covel mine had been located.

Most of the miners' houses sat on the creek bank down in the holler between the steep mountains. By contrast, three two-story houses lined the hill next to the paved highway, Route 10. An additional three two-story houses were also located with the miner's homes. Management employees—superintendent, foremen, store manager and payroll staff—lived in these larger homes.

After passing a dozen identical houses, the car slowly crossed a second wooden bridge before turning slightly right to travel under the tall Virginian Railroad Trestle. From Terry's low angle view through the windshield, the bridge appeared to touch the clouds.

Doug pulled the car into the gas pumps at the company store, where he spotted his cousin, Glen Thornton, working as the gas attendant. Glen asked, "Hey, Doug, do you want it filled up?"

"Yes, I need to fill up since we are crossing the mountain tomorrow. Going to my mom's at Rock and then to Littlesburg to Vergie's sister's place," Doug said.

"Good idea, ain't no gas on Sunday. Say hello to your ma and pa for me. I haven't been over to Rock since I don't know when. My old Ford needs some kind of work every week it seems."

Doug watched as his cousin maneuvered the pump. Glen had lost a leg in a lawn mowing accident as a youngster. His tall, thin frame amplified the limp from his artificial leg. "That'll be $3.07 Doug," Glen held out his hand.

"Just put it on my chit, I will let the folks know you asked about them." Doug replied. "Say, we're going to see an empty house up the holler. Do you know anything about it?"

"Only one empty now. It is in the colored housing," Glen replied.

"That's the one. Company is going to let us have it. We are living over Junior's beer joint right now. Vergie's tired of the noise and the smell and I am too," Doug shrugged his shoulders as he moved toward the driver's door of the car.

"It's the first house on the left after you cross the cement bridge up the holler," Glen indicated in the direction of the bridge.

Doug got back in the car and drove on past the store on the right and the elementary school on the left. "Terry, there is where you will go to school." His mother pointed to the three-room white clapboard building with a green shingle roof. Just above the company store on the same side of the road sat the Missionary Baptist Church, a cinder block building with a steeple – the white folks' church. The church for the Blacks was situated at the end of the holler. In most ways, the frame building looked more like a traditional church than the cinder block Baptist church. Its steeple loomed larger and housed the church bell that rang out on Sunday mornings.

The family crossed the one lane concrete bridge and spotted a house immediately on the left. This had to be it. There were no shades or curtains in the windows, which set it apart from all the other identical houses that lined each side of the road.

Doug down shifted to first gear, coming to a slow stop as he pulled into the yard. He turned off the engine and pulled the emergency brake with his left hand before saying to Vergie, "This is it. Let's see what's here." Terry climbed out after his mother with both feet landing on the grass and weeds that made up the yard. The house was unlocked, and Doug found the key on the windowsill in the living room, just as Mr. Hill promised, adding, "If you want the place, take the key. If not, leave the key there."

After exploring the house for a few moments, Vergie said in quick succession. "The house is spotless. The linoleum doesn't have a streak on it. The walls look like they have been freshly painted and the windows are clean, clear inside and out." The house had been cleaned top to bottom.

"It does look good and smells like bleach and soap," Doug responded.

"It's a bigger place and Terry can have his own room," Vergie noted.

"Let's take it," Doug picked up the key and looked to Vergie for her accord.

With no work needed on the place, Doug borrowed a pickup truck and moved all their belongings to the house in Covel the following Saturday. He had help from some of his buddies from the tipple. When Doug stopped at the company store to fill up the truck before returning it, Glen asked, "How you going like living next to the coloreds?"

"They don't bother me and I sure ain't going to bother them."

"I hope it won't be long before you get a house down here with the whites," Glen drawled out.

"At the end of the day, all of us are black that work in coal mining." Doug responded.

Doug did believe in the equality of each miner. They were each member of the United Mine Workers of America, and the Union saw that all its members—Black and white alike—were treated as per the all-important contract, which governed the relationship between mining companies and their miners. Doug followed the example of John L. Lewis, the Union President, who was famous for standing up for the miner regardless of race or national origin.

While they unloaded the truck, Vergie let Terry play in the fenced yard. Terry relished having a yard in which to run and jump. He played cowboys and Indians like in the movies that he saw with his folks in Mullens or Princeton and on the Lone Ranger radio program.

Terry had not seen many Black children in his short life. All his Monticello playmates had been white. He had seen Black families on Saturday visits to Mullens. For their part, the Washington children eyed their new little neighbor with curiosity, since it was the first time, they had lived next to a white family. All the Washington kids were older than Terry. Kathy Washington took a special interest in him, thinking of him as oversized living doll. She had several dolls--all white--that she had kept in perfect condition. Vergie felt amused when Kathy walked Terry around the houses, pretending she was his teacher or even his mother. The Washington boys ran with other boys in the camp. They liked to play baseball in the parking lot between the school and church lot. They often would play against boys from the white

134

section of the camp. There was tough competition among the teams.

Vergie was on the porch directing the men folk where to take the furniture when she caught sight of her neighbor, Gladys Washington. Gladys lived next door with her husband Clarence and their three kids, Clarence Jr., Morris, and Kathy lived next door. Gladys was a little stand-offish at first, but Vergie wanted to get to know her closest neighbor, so she engaged Gladys with questions about her family.

She learned that Clarence had grown up in Alpoca, one of Judge Lee Washington's six sons and five daughters. Judge had started out as a pick and shovel miner right after World War I. Rumor had it that he had "hoboed" a train from someplace in Alabama after he had a disagreement with a white man and had to get away. Judge was well known for his family of 11 children and a wife that was as strong as most men. Now that Judge was reaching retirement age, he liked to visit with his children and especially his grandchildren. Vergie learned from Gladys that the family that had occupied the house had been there almost ten years ever since they had married. The husband's folks had a farm up at Basin and needed help since his dad had become ill.

One of Judge's daughters also lived in Covel. She lived in the last house up the hill from the Bailey home. Florence Washington Jones ran a little convenience market out of her home. Florence started her small store for the folks in her section of the camp, but it didn't take long before she had customers from the white section of Covel. The company stores usually closed by 6 during the week and stayed closed on Sundays. Florence bridged that gap by selling basics – bread, milk, and a few canned goods

Vergie became a customer the day Kathy told her about Florence's market. She needed a can of cream for Doug's thermos of coffee. Florence sold the familiar red and white can of Carnation evaporated milk for ten cents more than the company store.

The Bailey family lived in the "colored" section for about three months before Mr. Hill notified Doug that there was a house available in the white section. It bordered the Gooney Otter Creek which sometimes flooded the yard but never reached the house. By that time, two other white families had moved into the "colored "section. More Black miners had left for jobs in the big cities, especially new automotive plants in Ohio and Michigan that had turned from military equipment production to automobiles. Automobile ownership was increasing nationwide with the post war prosperity and the urge to travel. Doug had heard that Black people were treated better in the cities, even that they could date whites in Ohio.

With the decrease in the number of Black families, the county board of education had decided to close the Covel school for Blacks in the next year. The school had served children from Garwood and a couple of families on Herndon Mountain. Now, the children would be bused with the older children who attended Conley Junior and Senior High in Mullens. The elementary students would be dropped off at the Bud-Alpoca Colored School.

The company had also decided to discontinue separating the blacks from whites in housing. The whites could stay in the colored section since there were fewer black miners needing housing. Since they had put in for the housing and the new home was next to their friends, the

Repass and Underwood families, Doug and Vergie decided to make the move again, hoping to stay put for a much longer time.

When they saw the new home, Vergie sighed in disbelief, "This place is a mess. It is not as clean or neat as when we moved into the one up the holler."

"They were mad since he was fired. They didn't care how they left the place," Doug remarked flippantly.

Rumor was that the miner had been fired for showing up drunk on a Monday for work. The company expected you to move within days if you lost your job at the mines. They needed to make room for your replacement. In this case, the company gave the man and his young family ten days' notice to vacate. The loss of your mining job if you lived in company housing meant you literally lost it all, job, pay, and your home.

The closet doors needed repairing. A company carpenter like Doug's father would take care of replacing two of the doors that had been busted--probably deliberately. Mr. Hill told Doug he would be given credit to get paint from the Company store for the kitchen and living room. The bedrooms were in fine shape. The yard was smaller than the one up the holler. They now situated between two houses where there was only a house on one up the holler. The places weren't as nice, but at least they lived closer to friends. The Repass family had recently moved from Monticello to Covel and were the next, door neighbors.

Doug and Vergie's social life blossomed in the new location. They played cards – canasta, gin rummy and 500 rummy with the Underwoods, Lusks and Repass families. They also enjoyed a new board game, Monopoly. Doug especially liked Monopoly and felt a charge of luck whenever the roll of the dice offered him the chance to purchase Park Place and Boardwalk.

Since New Year's Day fell on a Sunday in 1950, the miners' union contract said they would get Monday, January 2 as a paid holiday. On New Year's Eve Day, the Baileys of Covel visited Rock to wish Lake Bailey a happy 57th birthday. Lake liked to tell folks he would be a year younger if his mother had delivered him just thirty minutes later. She had given birth at 11:30 pm on December 31, 1892.

It was completely dark by the time the family arrived home at seven in the evening. The three had plans to ring in the New Year at the Lusk home playing a new game called Monopoly. They also played cards, listened to the radio, ate popcorn, and drank cokes and beer. There was a silence from the adults as the NBC radio network, featured live from New York, a popular favorite, "What are you doing New Year's Eve" performed by the Orioles, a rhythm and blues group from Baltimore. "Those guys can really sing." Vergie broke the silence at the end of the song. "Orioles, they must have named themselves after the baseball team." Boots interjected. "No, I read it was after the Maryland state bird and to follow up like the group, The Ravens." Margaret Repass added. "They can sure sing. You know those black folks got a natural talent." Boots continued.

Finishing a bottle of beer, Doug proclaimed, "You can't beat the Pabst. I never cared for the Schlitz. Too bitter."

Lindell Lusk said, "Good thing I got us Pabst, then."

Boots and Margaret Repass joined the party as well. They let their girls stay home next door to play with their own toys and snack on cake and ice cream. The Lusks' daughter, Nancy, sprawled out on the floor with Terry coloring in coloring books. Nancy had a princess coloring book and Terry had one showcasing Roy Rogers, King of the Cowboys.

"You know, they are sending television pictures from a station in Huntington now. I read about it in the Bluefield Daily Telegraph. Do you think we will ever have television here?" Vergie asked. They had been regular subscribers to the newspaper since they got married, and Vergie kept up with the news.

"We barely get radio stations now," Boots chuckled. "I think we are going to have to have television signals closer to us than Huntington."

Doug chimed in, "I heard they put the World Series on the television. Now that would be something to see. I would buy one of those sets if I could see the series."

"Maybe we will watch it here someday," Boots conceded.

As the radio host counted down to midnight, the Lusks, Repasses and Baileys paused their game to wish each other a "Happy New Year!". The children joined in revelry with their own shrills. In the New Year tradition, Doug kissed his wife, then with a look of eagerness, he said, "Here come the 1950's. Let's see what the New Year and the '50's will bring us. It's hard to believe, in the '40's we had the war, got married and had a kid. I think the '50's will be good and hopefully peaceful."

* * *

News Year's Eve 1949 marked the start of the 1950's and did bring changes for the family and the small company town of Covel that Doug, Vergie, and the others gathered that night could not imagine. They could not have anticipated the changes that would occur in their families, the automation of the coal industry, or the cultural shift that would occur for this generation, No one in the Lusk house that night would suspect that before this new decade would end, Covel would no longer be the property of a coal company.

Chapter 13 - Here Come the 50's

Terry kept growing. He was growing out of his clothes and shoes. Vergie walked with him to the American Coal Company Store to try on some Buster Brown shoes. The three-story wood frame building also housed the payroll office, the doctor's office, and the Covel Post Office. The inhabitants used a freight elevator to move goods between the floors while the customers had to climb steps between the floors. In the 1930's, one of the floors had served as a movie theater but that closed after Mullens added a second theater and ran current films. Now, that space served to store and display more merchandise, which swelled with Christmas goods even before Thanksgiving.

At the company store, miners could buy on credit with deductions from their pay. On pay day, they received pay envelopes containing cash or script. Few miners had accounts at banks and checks were difficult to cash. Some miners received empty envelopes when they had run up expenses at the company store that equaled or exceeded their earned wages.

Vergie knew that prices there were higher than stores in Mullens, Princeton, Bluefield, and Beckley, but the convenience outweighed the price. The company store carried quality merchandise. Aside from the Buster Brown children's shoes, they sold Arrow shirts, Levi jeans and, of course, Dickie's brand work clothes for the miners.

The company store served as the social hub of the community. Miners, their wives, and children would catch up on the latest news about the company, mining operations, union activities, upcoming school events, the latest gossip or even the weather.

* * *

It rained more than usual that spring, causing the creek bank to overflow a couple of times. When the creek overflowed, it flooded the alley behind the Bailey house, but the flow hadn't gotten past the fence. Vergie worried that they could have a flood someday. Doug reassured her, "Water has never got up in these houses. The house is built four feet off the ground." The houses across the dirt road were only raised about two feet from the ground.

Each house had a metal fenced yard with a concrete walk to the front and back steps going up to the front and back porches. Most of the yards had about thirty feet to the fence from the house. A sparse covering of grass and weeds provided the ground cover tor the yards. The Baileys had an oak tree in the back corner of their lot. Doug had hung a swing from a limb that would support a single child. Terry and his playmates enjoyed the swing.   Most houses did not have a tree.

The alley had been built to provide access for trucks bringing coal to the coal bin structure known as the "coal house." The union contract stipulated that miners could purchase coal for heat and cooking at a discounted price. Everyone cooked on a coal stove, and once a week, they heated water from the kitchen sink to fill the ubiquitous steel bathing tub. This zinc coated round tubs were large enough for a full-size man to squat in, and to economize time and hot water, two children at a time would often share the tub. Between uses, the tub hung on the back porch. The soap of choice for most families was Ivory. Everyone knew that Ivory was 99% pure. Vergie questioned, "99% pure what – soap?"

The houses had the minimum of 65 amps mainly for lights. The light in each room hung down from the ceiling by the electrical wire that powered the single bulb.

The miners' homes had outdoor toilets, two seaters. Vergie had wondered why there were two seats, because she had never heard of folks going together to the outhouse. Their outhouse abutted the neighbor's outhouse. Terry was used to going by himself. One of his earliest experiences of returning from the toilet, he asked his mother, "Do you think one of the Repasses is sick? I heard this loud straining sound coming from their toilet this morning. Like someone was really hurting." Vergie smiled and reassured her son. "Sometimes people just take more effort to go, or they need to eat some prunes."

In the dead of winter, the residents used chamber pots in their bedrooms. The containers—usually white enamel or porcelain—served as a miniature toilet. When someone was sick or needed to get up during the night.

Terry asked his mother, "Why is this called a chamber pot? It's a pee pot or poop pot."

Vergie thought for a few seconds before replying. "Terry, you may have a better idea, but I think people just don't want to use those words: "pee" and "poop". Bedrooms used to be called "bed chambers", I think that's where the name for the pot came from."

The seasons are well defined in the Appalachian Region of West Virginia. The dead of winter gives way to the spring with its renewal of the leaves from the deciduous trees to the warmer summer temperatures that dry the dirt roads that create a thick dust cloud when a coal truck travels over them even at a speed of 15 mph.

The mines shut down operations the first two weeks of July for vacation. They used that recess to perform maintenance on equipment and air circulating systems. During the vacation time, the family visited Doug's parents with the purpose of helping in the home place gardens. They picked green beans, corn, and dug potatoes, all by the bushel baskets. They also gathered strawberry husk tomatoes, which were better known as ground cherries. Doug favored the plentiful and easy-growing fruit, which made great preserves for biscuits and toast. Taking a break from the summer harvest one afternoon, Doug, Vergie and Terry went fishing and had a picnic on the nearby Bluestone River. The hot topic that summer was the plan to build a dam near Hinton on the Bluestone River. The result would be a huge lake, perfect for boating and water skiing. The Baileys didn't even know anybody that owned a motorboat. And except in the movies, none of them had had seen water skiing. They did know some folks with a canoe or rowboat to fish out in the river.

* * *

On a crisp late summer day, Vergie spotted Thomas Caves, the school's principal, at work in his yard. He and his wife lived just three houses up on the same side of the road as the Baileys. He wore his customary work clothes: matching work pants and shirt. Tom Caves took pride in his yard. Without a doubt, he kept the greenest, most immaculate lawn in Covel.

The sight of him and the chill in the air turned Vergie's thoughts to Terry starting school in the next year. The Covel elementary school had started a primary program to ease children into school before starting first grade. Mr. Caves had suggested this to Vergie as "an opportunity for Terry to start school maybe a year before he turns six."

Thomas Caves also taught fifth and sixth grades. H had been a miner when he became smitten with a young schoolteacher named Gertrude Murphy. After some time, courting, she convinced him to start college at Concord College at Athens, West Virginia to become a teacher himself. They eventually married and came to the Covel school as a team after World War II. Mrs. Caves, who was the first and second grade teacher, would have the primary class as well, which meant she would be Terry's first teacher.

The Caves were the only family living in company housing who were not directly employed by the coal company. They did not have children, making their home one of the few houses in Covel without them.

Mr. Caves always wore a suit and tie at school. He had conducted the school census for the county in the Barkers Ridge magisterial district, which included Covel and all the coal camps east of Mullens. He knew that Terry would be coming to the school. He had remarked to Vergie, "I think you have a smart boy. We will look forward to having him at the school."

Vergie smiled and replied, "He does ask a lot of questions."

On Halloween night, Vergie dressed Terry in a cowboy costume, his favorite since he had heard the radio programs of the Lone Ranger and Hopalong Cassidy. The Saturday

145

matinee movies in Mullens had brought the radio characters alive on the big screen. The Repass girls showed Terry the ropes of trick-or-treating. Every miner's house had the porch light on to invite the kids. Most families gave out "penny" candy. Some families gave regular size candy bars or even apples, but everyone knew that Charlie and Amy Hill gave the very best treats. This year, they gave each child a waxed harmonica that they could play and eat it later. They asked each trick-or-treater to sign a notebook as a receipt for the treat – strictly one to a person. Christine Repass, the oldest of the sisters, wrote her name and each of her sisters' names, and finally, Terry's name.

While the children collected candy and enjoyed their treats, some teenagers managed the tricks. The boys hung a stuffed scarecrow from the railroad bridge. When the younger kids walked under the bridge, the teenagers jumped out with flashlights and shouting, "Look, somebody hung themselves!", as they pointed up at the hanging scarecrow. Many of the younger kids were scared and became noticeably upset when they looked up at the dangling bodies from the railroad trestle., Terry did not seem to mind.

Later in the night, the teenagers overturned some outhouses. They were careful to set the structures down lightly to avoid permanently damaging the walls or the door. Still, it created a challenge for the victims to restore them the next morning. As folks went about their regular morning routine, they were not very happy to see their old Sears catalog pages flapping in the yard, and they certainly weren't happy at the idea of the double seater setting exposed to the neighbors and the elements. Most folks found the nearest upright outhouse, and neighbors kindly shared until each "outdoor john" could be put back upright.

* * *

Thanksgiving came with the annual hog killing and big dinner at the Bailey home place at Rock. Everyone left looking forward to reassembling at Christmas.

One morning a week after Thanksgiving, Vergie was busy fixing Doug's breakfast and packing his lunch. She had just put the ground coffee into the top of the pot when it hit her. She recognized the familiar stomach sickness that she had felt in 1945 and 1948 and the expectation of a new life suddenly filled her. She knew she was pregnant.

The first few months of the pregnancy were rougher than either of her first two pregnancies. Out of concern, Vergie made a couple of trips to see Dr. Penn, but he reassured her that all was coming along fine. "You are going to have a July baby, as best I can figure. Be sure you don't overdo it—especially lifting. Let your old man help with hanging out the wash." "Doug is good to help." Vergie reassured the doctor. "I know you are worried but there is no reason to think that this baby will have the problems that your daughter had. Just look at how your son is doing. He is growing and is active." Dr. Penn reassured Vergie as she was preparing to leave the office.

With Pamela's death ever in their minds, Vergie and Doug felt anxious about this pregnancy. The days and weeks seemed to creep by. Vergie tried to appear upbeat and show the excitement most expectant mothers showed, but her angst broke through the thin façade.

All the while Terry grew more and more independent. He would ride his tricycle out at the edge of the road. Vergie allowed him to ride it as she walked to the post office at the company store. She checked the mail daily, looking to hear from Carrie. Carrie and Larry had learned that their son, Jimmy, had leukemia. The Baileys only saw the Teels once a year, when everyone gathered to celebrated Easter at Mil's home. Terry was a year younger than Jimmy, but at the last Easter, he had been just as tall, thanks to the Bailey genes. Along with their cousin, Lane, the boys played together. They hid behind large boulders near the creek at the Tabors' home, pretending they were a trio of cowboys. That was before Jimmy was diagnosed.

Now, Carrie kept them informed about Jimmy's health by writing weekly and sometimes twice a week. Each letter from Carrie held hope that Jimmy could recover. He had been in and out of the hospital in Philadelphia, about an hour from their home in Lambertville, New Jersey. The doctors there were trying new drug strategies and remained hopeful that there could be a breakthrough.

Larry bought a 16mm movie projector with sound to show films to Jimmy while he was confined to his hospital room or, when he wasn't actively undergoing treatment, to his bed at home. Jimmy and his parents laughed together at the Three Stooges or the Looney Tunes cartoons, especially Bugs Bunny. The laughter brought some relief to Jimmy and helped his parents—even for a short time—to forget that their son had a terrible disease.

Whenever she received a letter, Vergie made sure to write back the next day. She sat at the kitchen table with her fountain pen, bottle of ink, and note paper and wrote in the tidy script they had been required to learn in the Glenwood and Princeton public schools. Vergie wrote to Carrie with news of her pregnancy.

Terry eyed his mother as she formed the letters. He thought it looked like coloring, but there were no lines on the paper and she only used black ink. How dull! When he asked what she was doing, Vergie explained what writing was and told him, "When you go to school, you will learn how to write. I am sending this to your Aunt Carrie who lives far away," Vergie showed Terry the envelope and pointed, "See, this is Carrie's name and where she lives so the postman will know where to take the letter." Somebody from Covel takes the letter to Aunt Carrie?"

"No, they take all the mail from Covel and other towns nearby and put it on train to a big post office. Then they sort out the mail by destination...that is, where the mail is going."

Terry nodded his understanding.

"We put a stamp on the envelope to show that we paid to send the letter. It cost three cents." She held up a stamp for him to see, "This stamp has President Thomas Jefferson on it." She surprised Terry by licking the stamp and sticking it to the envelope.

"Does the stamp taste good?" Terry asked, hopeful that it might taste like the penny candy his neighbors had handed out on Halloween.

"No, we just have to get it wet so that it will stick to the envelope."

Next, she pulled out a brightly colored card, explaining that it was a get-well card for Jimmy. Terry watched quietly while she wrote in the card and put it inside another envelope. Before she could add the stamp, Terry asked, "Can I lick the stamp?"

She handed it to him. "It don't taste like anything," he noted as if he hadn't believed her explanation. He stuck the stamp to the envelope.

With the letters sealed and stamped, the duo made their way to the post office, where Terry reached high to put the letter in the mailbox slot. "Now the lady that works in the post office will put it in a big bag to take on up the hill to the train."

Just after the first day of spring, on one of their expeditions to the company store, Vergie and Terry saw Mr. Caves, the school's principal.

"Boy, is he growing!" Mr. Caves seemed astounded as he looked down at Terry on his tricycle.

"Yes, he will be five next month," Vergie smiled. "It's hard for me to believe."

Mr. Caves paused "Why don't we let him try school? We have room in the primary section. I think he is ready, and he looks tall enough to be a first grader."

Vergie said she would talk to her Doug about the proposal.

Mr. Caves looked at Terry, "Would you like to come to school?" He pointed to the white three-room structure across the road.

Terry stood straddling his tricycle and considered the question. Yes, I want to go to school."

Vergie and Doug decided it would be fine for Terry to try school. He could walk up the road with the Repass girls. Terry started school in a three-room building at Covel in April 1951, just before his fifth birthday.

Chapter 14 - School Starts

Vergie could not believe that Terry was old enough to go to school. It seemed like only a year could have passed since they took him to his grandparents for the first time. Preparing for the school year helped get Vergie's mind off her pregnancy. Since this was the first time Vergie had no pregnant sisters during her own pregnancy, she knew she would have all the "mother-to-be" attention. She would be happy with either a boy or a girl this time. She just wanted the baby to be healthy, and it was helpful to have a distraction from the worry.

Doug didn't say much, but Vergie knew her husband and could tell that he had concerns. He could not help but remember how hard it had been to lose Pamela less than two years before. And the entire family still reeled from Jimmy's recent death.

One day at work during lunch, Doug told Dewey that they were expecting again. Sensing apprehension from Doug, Dewey responded, "That's great Doug. Now, don't worry, it will be fine. Kids need brothers and sisters. Look at us. I can't even think how it would be if I had been the only child."

Doug sighed and said, "Dewey I just don't think I would want Vergie to go through this and lose another baby. Somehow, I think if it's another boy, it will be ok. I don't know if that had anything to do with losing the little girl."

Dewey nodded his understanding, "We don't know why these things happen. I just think we have to believe it's for the best and let go."

"I guess worrying about it ain't help anything anyway." Doug said as he closed his lunch box and stood up to return to work. "By the way, Terry is going to start school next week. Isn't your girl, Judy, with Mrs. Caves?" Doug asked.

"She is. That'll be nice, them being in the class together." Dewey smiled as the men started back up the tracks toward the tipple.

Terry started school April 2, 1951, just eight days shy of his fifth birthday. His mother had ordered a copy of his birth certificate from the Clerk's office in Princeton, the county seat of Mercer County. She carried the certificate as they walked to school on the mild spring day. Vergie showed the birth certificate to Mrs. Caves, who wrote the full name, Terry Douglas Bailey, in the schoolbook register on a page with the heading "Primary (Pre-First Grade)". The tidy page had four other names written in blue ink before Terry's. Mrs. Caves filled her fountain pen and wiped away the excess drops of ink with a small cloth. She then added to the register Terry's birth date, his parents' names, and their address.

"We are all set. Usually, we want the children to be five, but he will do just fine," she smiled warmly at Terry. Vergie kissed her son on the forehand and said, "See you at lunch. Christine will come in to get you and bring you home to eat."

"Christine is an excellent student—one of our top students. I am glad that she will be looking after him here at the start, Mrs. Caves nodded reassuringly

Terry looked wide-eyed at the desk that Mrs. Caves had assigned to him—his very own desk. He slid into the seat, which attached ingeniously to the writing surface. He placed his things—pencils, crayons, wide ruled tablets and his first schoolbooks—into an open storage space about a cubic foot under the seat of the desk.

Blackboards lined walls at the front and right sides of the classroom. Above the chalkboards, Mrs. Caves had pinned green cards with the large yellow letters of the alphabet in both print and cursive. Terry recognized the letters of the block printed version of the alphabet. His mother had given him a coloring book with each letter on a different page, and he could even recite the letters. But he puzzled over the cursive figures.

Terry sat behind a boy that he had seen in the camp a couple of times. Glen Miller lived on the same side of the road and two houses up from Terry. Glen had turned five and started school in December. The boys became fast friends, and Glen showed Terry the ropes, including how to use the water fountain. He also showed Terry how to find the indoor bathroom, which was not an entirely new concept for Terry, as he had used them at his grandparents' home and Aunt Mildred's home, and of course the family had one in the apartment at Herndon.

Mrs. Caves called the primary students up to the front of the large classroom and asked the five youngsters to sit on the area rug in front of her chair. He was amazed at how loud the gentle teacher's voice became when she addressed the full classroom.

Terry stared at Mrs. Caves as she read aloud from a picture book. She held the book so that it faced the primary students and glanced over the top of the book to read the sentences printed on each page. All the children sat enraptured, as Mrs. Caves read and made eye contact with each one, in turn.

As she read, Terry realized that Mrs. Caves might be a grandmother. She had grey hair like his "Grandma Bailey".

That was about the only physical similarity between the two women. Mrs. Caves was much plumper. And shorter. She smelled sweet something like a bunch of flowers after a light rain in the spring. She wore makeup on her fair skin, which accentuated the red in her lips. Terry rarely saw women wear makeup. His Mother powdered her face when they went visiting in Mullens, but she did not wear it every day.

As Terry returned to his seat in the first row, he noticed the first and second graders sitting in their desks working in workbooks, writing on blue-lined paper sheets or reading books. All day, he watched the older children as they went about their work.

He longed to play at the table with sand on it – "the sand table". There, he saw toys and other things that students could arrange on the table. He always enjoyed playing in the sand outside his house in Monticello. He was thinking how much fun it would be to play in the sand on this table inside the classroom.

At lunch time, Christine rushed into the classroom to collect her sister Marilyn, a first grader, and her new charge, Terry. The threesome made short time in walking home for lunch. Without the daily responsibilities for Terry's care, and nervous over his first day at school, Vergie had lunch ready for him well before he arrived home for lunch. She had prepared a Peter Pan peanut butter and grape jelly sandwich on Miss Sunbeam white sandwich bread. She filled a cup with Sun-Maid raisins and poured a glass of Foremost milk to wash it down.

Terry told her about listening to Mrs. Caves read and about the sand table. She could tell how much he wanted to go to the sand table by the way he said, "I think that will be fun!"

"Don't forget you have to wait until Mrs. Caves tells you that you can go to the sand table," Vergie cautioned.

Within the hour, Christine and Marilyn arrived back on the front porch and knocked on the door for Terry to join them on their return to school. They did the same for the next six weeks, until school was out for the summer of '51.

On Terry's second day of school, he followed the regular schedule. He walked with Christine and Marilyn to school. When they arrived, there were three lines of children waiting to go into the building. Each school morning, the students lined up in single file by classroom and grade, forming a T along the concrete sidewalk. The three-room school had three teachers—one for each room. The right top of the T was formed by Mrs. Caves' primary, first and second grade classes. In the center stood Mrs. Whitt's third and fourth grade classes and finally Mr. Caves' fifth and six graders made up the left top of the T.

Mr. Caves walked to the point where the lines converged and, in an authoritative voice, led the students in the Pledge of Allegiance. Terry had never seen this ritual before, so he looked around at his classmates and mirrored them by putting his hand on his heart and looking up at the flagpole that stood outside the schoolhouse. The Works Progress Administration (WPA) had installed the school's flagpole and concrete sidewalks in the 1930's as part of President Franklin Roosevelt's economic relief effort, which came to be known as the New Deal. A sign at the base of the flagpole credited the WPA. Most of the parents of Terry's classmates, and his own, had a reverence for President

Roosevelt. He had been the president for most of their youth, seeing them through the Great Depression and a world war.

After the pledge, all the students filed silently up a set of six stairs and into their respective classrooms. Mrs. Caves' classes turned to walk into the room at the left, closest to the road. The center room housed Mrs. Gladys Whitt's students, and in the room across the hall from Mrs. Caves, Mr. Caves taught the fifth and sixth grades.

Once in his seat, Glen turned around to Terry and said, "You will know the words to the flag pledge soon. We say it outside every day. Except when it rains. And then we say it to the flag above the blackboard." Terry did pick up parts each day and before the month was out, he could say it all. He didn't know what some of the words meant, but he knew how to say it.

The primary students had clay that they could mold into shapes and figures. Mrs. Caves provided a sheet of heavy brown paper torn from a large roll to put on the student desk before playing with the clay. One day, Terry took a ball of the clay and pressed it down on his desktop without the brown paper. He mashed the clay down and then rolled it. Mrs. Caves noticed that there was no paper under the clay and told Terry in a stern voice, "You are supposed to have the paper on your desk when you are using clay. You should always have the paper down." Mrs. Caves then handed Terry a wet sponge to clean his desk and then a cloth to wipe it dry. This would not be the only time in school for Terry to be corrected

Mrs. Caves gave each of the students a sheet that was printed in light blue or purple for the primary students to color. She would make these pages one at a time in a tray by pressing a blank sheet of paper onto a gelatin surface that had the image in the gelatin. (This process is called hectograph which was the forerunner to the spirit duplicator. Neither of these processes are used today.). When the page was lifted from the gelatin, the image appeared on the paper. The paper had a smell to it when it was first made but was gone in a few minutes. All the students enjoyed coloring

The primary and first grade students used larger round pencils than the other students. Mrs. Caves said, "Your hands are smaller, and they need a larger pencil or crayon that is bigger." Terry thought about what she said and did not understand that if your hands were smaller why would you need a larger pencil?

Each morning and afternoon, the students crowded onto the playground for a fifteen-minute recess. The playground had been outfitted with a variety of equipment. Some children played tetherball at one of the two tetherball poles. The younger children enjoyed swing sets and a merry-go-round, while the older boys played basketball.

But what caught Terry's eye was a game the other kids called "shooting" marbles. On the day he learned about marbles, the first words out of his mouth when he saw his mother were, "Can I get some marbles when we go to Murphy's this Saturday?"

Without hesitation, Vergie replied. "Sure, you can get some marbles."

That Saturday, Doug took Terry to the G.C. Murphy Five and Dime Store, Murphy's for short. It was the largest retailer in Mullens with entrances on two streets, Guyandotte Avenue and Howard Avenue, Mullens' main street. Crossing the store threshold, Terry practically ran to the back of the store where the toy department was located.

Terry looked over the selection of marbles, and finally picked a mixed bag of solids, stripes and cat eyes, forty in total. Doug handed his son a crisp new dollar bill, telling him that he could pay for the marbles at the register. "Terry, remember to get the change for the dollar. There is no tax on this since it is less than a dollar," Doug told his son. Grasping the dollar in his left hand and the marble bag in this right, he walked quickly to the register. He passed the dollar to the clerk, and she returned twenty-one cents. Triumphant, Terry turned around and held out the change to his dad.

"You can put the change in your piggy bank, son."

At home, that afternoon, Doug drew a circle near the coal house and knelt to show Terry how to shoot the marble. "Terry, the trick is to hold the knuckles hard against the ground in a fist with the thumb pulled back behind the thumb, then flick out as hard as you can if you need distance. With practice you will catch on and learn how hard to flip the thumb nail against the shooter marble to bust open the pot." Doug explained. "After the marbles are scattered, you aim your shooter marble at one of the marbles in the ring with the idea of hitting it to knock it out of the ring. You keep doing this until your marble goes outside of the ring or you don't knock a marble out when you shoot. When that happens, you lose your turn and the other player shoots his shooter marble." Doug continued.

In a few minutes, Terry was hitting the marbles with his shooter marble from a distance of three feet. Doug prompted him to try it from a few feet farther back. This proved to be more difficult, but he gradually started hitting the marbles with enough force to break up the bunch of marbles in the center of the drawn circle.

Once he felt a little confident, Terry invited Marilyn Repass to come over and play marbles. She had not played before either, but she picked it up quickly. In less than an hour, she was doing better than Terry.

On Monday, Terry took his sack of marbles to school. At recess he asked Wade McBride if he wanted to shoot marbles, to which Wade replied. "Okay, are we playing for keeps?"

"I don't know. What does keeps mean?"

Wade grinned as he responded, "If I knock or shoot your marble out of the circle, I get to keep it. If you knock my marbles out of the circle, you get to keep it."

Terry thought for a couple of seconds. "I don't know. I just got these Saturday, and I don't want to lose them."

Overhearing the conversation and sensing Terry was out of his depth, Paxton Hill blurted out, "Wade, you know keeps is not allowed at school. Mrs. Caves told us we can only play marbles for fun." Paxton was also a member of the primary class, and it was widely known that she was one of the best marble players at the school. She was athletic, good at running, bike riding, softball and about any activity she set out to do. Some of the boys were jealous and called her a "tomboy" but not to her face.

"Okay, Paxton, we will play for fun. Are you going to play with us?" asked Wade. "Yes, I want to play."

Each of the three put five marbles in the ring. "Girls go first," Paxton stated before aiming her shooter marble into the ring of marbles. She successfully knocked out ten marbles before finally missing. Then it was Terry's turn. He hit a marble with his shooter, and it came within a half inch of leaving the ring. Wade shot next and was able to get two marbles out before missing. On Paxton's next turn, she cleaned out the last three marbles. There was no doubt who was the best marbles player.

As Paxton and Terry walked in together, she promised, "We will play some more, and I will show you how to hit the marbles better. You will catch on."

"Thanks, I would like that," Terry responded.

Paxton followed through on her promise. With her pointers, Terry got better but Paxton always won. Terry and Paxton formed a friendship that lasted until Paxton's family moved when she was in the seventh grade.

Chapter 15 - New Member of the Bailey Family

It was a warm, cloudy day with rain expected on Sunday, July 22, 1951. With the sky still dark, Doug lifted Terry, who was still in a deep sleep, out of his bed. Doug carried him three houses down to the Repass family home, where Doug and Vergie had left him two and half years before. This time the location was just down the road in Covel. The reason was the same, the couple's next child was about to be born.

Doug drove over the mountain, thankful that the road conditions were better than they had been on their last trip to the Bluefield Hospital delivery room in January 1949. He and Vergie were nervous, worried and anxious like most expectant parents. Neither spoke about Pamela but both knew she occupied the other's mind. The trip seemed long. Doug only interrupted the silence to ask how Vergie was doing, to which she briefly responded, "Okay."

They each glanced at the turn-off road for Rock as the car traveled past it on Route 10. Memories of the last six years flashed through each of their minds, before their attention returned to the present moment.

Doug exhaled in relief when he pulled into the hospital's driveway. "It won't be long now," he said as he opened the car door for his wife. As they walked through the double doors, an orderly met Vergie and Doug with a wheelchair.

"Have a seat and we will go to the delivery room on the third floor," the orderly spoke in a low tone. Through the corner of his heavy, wire-rimmed glasses, Doug watched his wife board the elevator, then he turned to the admission desk to give his and Vergie's information to the nurse.

"You have UMWA insurance. Can I see your card?" Doug took his insurance card from his wallet and handed it to the nurse. She gave it back with a brief glance and a semi-smile and said, "You are all set. Have a good delivery." Doug knew that the coverage would cover the total cost for the delivery and a shared hospital room. The union (United Mine Workers of America) had done a good job in getting health coverage for the miner and his family.

It was a good delivery. About six hours after arriving at the hospital, Vergie gave birth to a boy with jet black hair. She greeted her son, "Welcome to the world, Richard Keith Bailey." The couple had agreed on the name, because "Richard" had been in the Bailey family for years, and Vergie was partial to "Keith".

Doug's first glimpse of his new son through was through a glass window in the maternity ward. After Terry's birth at the Linkous house, Doug was holding him within the hour but it would be three days before he could hold Richard, who they came to call "Rickey".

Doug drove back to Covel to check on Terry and to tell his ride, Dewey Miller, that he would not be going to work the rest of the week. Then he headed to the Repasses home to check on Terry.

"You are going to stay here for the next few days until your mother and brother come home from the hospital," Doug told Terry, who didn't seem to upset at the news. He enjoyed playing with the Repass girls. They had lots of toys and interesting things in their room.

New Member of the Bailey Family

After breakfast on Monday morning, Dr. Penn came into Vergie's room with a nurse. The nurse pulled the curtain that partitioned the room for privacy. "How are you feeling today? Is your husband coming in?" The doctor asked the questions brusquely.

"I am feeling better and enjoyed breakfast. I've already nursed my son. Doug will be here before lunch," Vergie responded. Dr. Penn smiled slightly as he looked at the chart the nurse had handed him. "Your boy looks pretty healthy. He will get stronger as he nurses more. I would say you have a fine young one to take home. I will be by to check on you and you can always send a message through the store to get in touch with me if you need anything," Dr. Penn said in a reassuring tone. When the nurse pulled open the curtain, Vergie saw Juanita in the bed next to hers.

Vergie shared her hospital room with a woman from Piedmont named Juanita Gilbert who had given birth to a daughter the same day Rickey was born. Juanita Gilbert was a chatty roommate. Vergie had learned that this was her third child, but only the second one to be born in the hospital. Juanita knew Vergie's sisters, Marie, and Helen, who also lived at Piedmont. She went on and on about how nice their families were. "The Davis boy—Lowell—is a talker and he is so cute. But I guess you know that. He will probably be a salesman or a politician," Juanita remarked.

"Yes, all of my nieces and nephews are great kids. Rickey and Terry are lucky to have cousins on both sides of the family that get along so well," Vergie reflected politely.

Upon his return, Doug stopped by the hospital's gift shop and purchased a vase of flowers to take to his wife. He also had Sunday's Bluefield Daily Telegraph newspaper tucked under his arm. He and Vergie both enjoyed the newspaper, especially on Sundays.

As Doug entered the room on the maternity ward and saw his wife, and with his big grin, said, "How's my wife and new son doing?"

Vergie shot back a broad smile and responded, "We are doing fine." Doug helped his wife up to go see Rickey through the glass at the nursery. He was easy to spot with a full head of black hair. "You know, he doesn't seem to kick his blanket as much as the other babies," Vergie noted.

"Probably just content under his blanket,"

Two days later, Doug came to the hospital one last time to bring his wife and their son home. Vergie held Rickey as they traveled by the coal operations and camps in Mercer County and crossed the mountain into Wyoming County. It was a very hot and bright July day. Suddenly it occurred to Doug, "You know, I just thought of it – since you and Rickey both have July birthdays, we can have one party for the both of you."

"No way, we both should have our own birthday celebrations," Vergie shot back with a determined look.

Doug pulled the car into the dirt driveway of the Covel home. It was a makeshift parking spot, as homes in the coal camps had not been built with automobile ownership in mind. As Doug and Vergie got out of the 1940 Ford coupe, the Repass girls came running up to greet them, trailed closely by their parents and Terry. Everyone wanted to see the new baby. Vergie laughed and told the girls, "His name is Richard, but we will call him Rickey. I need to get him into the house and into his crib. He needs to rest and sleep for a while. You can come see him later."

Terry stayed behind the three girls, wanting to come forward. But he stayed back until Doug reached down and gave him a pat on the head, saying, "Come on boy, and meet Rickey. You are going to help take care of your little brother."

His mother said, "Yes, Terry, come and meet your brother." Terry tugged at his mother's cotton dress as they started up the steps to the front porch. Doug gathered their things from the car. He juggled Vergie's suitcase and two vases of flowers—the small one that he had brought to his wife and one from her sister Carrie. Vergie had been stunned, having never received a flower arrangement from a florist delivery. Carrie had called Bluefield from New Jersey order the delivery.

Inside the four-room house, Vergie placed Rickey in the crib beside the bed in the room she shared with Doug. Then she turned to hug Terry and kiss him on the forehead. "Terry, what do you think of your brother Rickey? Isn't he cute? And look at the black hair. You can help us take good care of him. Rickey will need to be looked after until he can take more care of himself."

Terry looked at his brother who looked like the Repass girls' dolls with the eyes that closed when you laid them down to sleep. Terry looked up at his mother and exclaimed, "I can help take care of him, mom." Vergie smiled and said, "I know you will, Terry."

As promised, Dr. Penn knocked at the family's door on Thursday afternoon. This first of August was as hot as Vergie could remember, so she had opened the front door and pulled shut the screen door to keep the flies out. She opened the door and invited Dr. Penn to enter. "How are you and the baby doing?" Dr. Penn asked.

"As for the baby, he is nursing, sleeping and pooping," Vergie replied with a laugh. "He isn't active, but a baby less than two weeks old doesn't do much. As for me, I am not sleeping well. It's too hot and I'm still pretty sore."

Dr. Penn picked up Rickey and turned him over. He pulled on each of his legs and palpated them. Then he checked Rickey's reflexes by tapping on his tiny knees with a small rubber tipped mallet. "Looks like he is taking to nursing." Dr. Penn noted as he saw the needle on the scale move. He asked Vergie to sit so that he could take her vital signs. "Looks like your blood pressure is running high. It's common after childbirth and usually settles down within a couple of weeks. We will check it again next week."

For Vergie, the boiling summer of '51 seemed to crawl by. Her days were filled with taking care of Rickey. Babies have needs of filling them up and emptying their diapers as Doug would say. Doug bought a window fan for the bedroom and though Vergie said it was blowing hot air into the house, the cool did come when September arrived, especially of the evening. Once Labor Day passed, Terry went back to school and the next weeks seemed to clip by fast. Vergie started planning for Christmas. This year would be bigger with two sons. She surveyed the Sears and Aldens catalogs for the newest toys and for something for her and Doug. She liked the Aldens catalog for the women's fashion, and it only took a week to get an order from their store in Chicago.

November brought another Thanksgiving at Doug's parents' home. The clan was decidedly larger, with Rickey being the newest of the cousins. Doug's Mother remarked, "Our family is growing fast. In five years, we have tripled the grandchildren." In addition to Rickey and Terry, they now had

166

Bobby Lee, Arthur, Jan, and Vickey. All the Bailey brothers and sisters except Lois had children. Lois had married Charles Farley in September. "Just think what it's going to be like in the next five years." Grandmother Bailey remarked.

Vergie thought, "Well, we have made our contribution to the line of cousins."

Charles was home for Thanksgiving on leave from the army. He had been drafted as the Korean conflict expanded. Over the meal, he and his brothers-in-law who had been in World War II discussed how the army had changed in the years following the war. Lois felt uneasy as she sat listening to the men. She was not looking forward to Charles being thousands of miles away in a war.

The war talk caused Vergie to remember that her oldest brother Kenneth had served in the army and was in Germany when her mother and youngest brother Donald died. She had received a letter from sister, Carrie telling her that their brother Clarence who had joined the Marines was going to Korea. Vergie was thinking and had prayed for the safe return of Clarence and now Charles. She and Doug had suffered loss of brothers, Donald and Ralph but none of their brothers had died due to war. She prayed that that would still be the case.

Faye, Doug's sister-in-law, was expecting her and Wallace's first child. She was about four months from her own delivery. Faye remarked to Vergie, Wally and I are thinking of naming our baby Richard if it's a boy. Wally's middle name is Richard for his great-great grandfather, I think. Wally says that this area was settled by Richard Bailey before the Revolutionary War. With your boy named Richard, I hope that don't cause any confusion," Faye stated with a smile.

167

Vergie laughed, "I think we will be able to tell them apart. We've taken to calling Richard "Rickey", anyway. Do you think you will do that?"

"I think we will try to keep it as Richard or maybe use his middle name too: Richard Lane." They agreed that would work fine, and in March of 1952, Faye did give birth to Richard Lane Bailey.

* * *

As the months rolled on, Rickey did not seem to be growing as fast as Terry had done as a baby. On Rickey's first birthday, he was not as tall as Terry had been. Doug joked, "Looks like he is going to take after your side of the family, Vergie."

"Yes, he's short, and he has our coal black hair too." They also started to notice Rickey struggling with crawling and standing up. In fact, his development started to decline and by his second Christmas he could not stand as easily even holding on to the railing of his bed.

When Vergie pointed this out, Doug said, "I think we better get Doc Penn to check on him. Terry's spring school term started on Monday, January 5. Doctor Penn would be in his office that afternoon. Vergie and Rickey were first in line waiting for him when he arrived with his nurse.

"What's up with our young one, here?" Dr. Penn questioned.

Vergie explained what she and Doug had observed. Rickey was not standing as steady as he had done. He seems to be dropping down quickly. He also was not walking as steady or for as long a duration as he had just a week or so ago. "I think he is losing some of his development for some

168

reason." Vergie's shoulders crept up to her ears as she talked in a concerned tone.

Dr. Penn examined Rickey who was 18 months old by that time. "His leg muscles don't seem to have the strength that we would expect to see in an active baby at this age. I think we should get you an appointment at Bluefield to check him out some more. I will get them to run a blood test to see what that might show." Vergie nodded in agreement, and they set an appointment for the following week at the clinic connected with the Bluefield hospital where Rickey had been born.

When Vergie told Doug about the follow up appointment, he asked, "Are you sure you can handle driving Rickey to Bluefield for the appointment?" Doug asked.

"I think so. With the appointment at 11, I will have time to get Terry off to school and be back before he gets home," Vergie explained.

Doug was no longer readily available to drive during the day since he worked the day shift now. With the expanded operation at the Deerfield tipple, he and Dewey had gained seniority and opted to move to the daylight schedule. So, encouraged by her sisters Marie and Carrie obtaining their drivers' licenses, Vergie had gotten her own driver's license just before Rickey was born.

On the day of Rickey's doctor visit, Vergie put Terry's lunch in his hand and watched him join the Repass and Dudley girls as they walked up the dirt road toward the school. She changed Rickey's clothes and tucked him into the back seat of the car with his teddy bear and his favorite blanket, which she noticed it was beginning to look threadbare from washing.

Rickey was not used to having the back seat all to himself. Terry and he usually shared it. Nevertheless, he stayed only on his usual side behind the front passenger seat where his mother usually rode. This time it was a little strange for him because she was driving. He pulled on his blanket and covered his teddy bear up to the neck. After settling in, he started looking out the window. He was very interested in the slow-moving train pulling the long line of coal cars through the Springton crossing. He liked the sound that the engine made and the turn of the wheels that carried the heavy load of coal.

When they arrived, Vergie buttoned Rickey's coat and fastened the neck strap on his ear-muff cap, then picked him up to take him into the out-patient area of the hospital. It was colder in Bluefield than it had been at home. There always seemed to be a breeze in the city built on a hillside. In fact, Bluefield was nicknamed by the Chamber of Commerce as "Nature's Air-Conditioned City." In the summer months, free lemonade was distributed if the temperature went over 90.

Vergie had completed a stack of paperwork and was now sitting in an exam room with Rickey on her lap. She responded to a long list of questions from a nurse before the nurse explained that they would need a blood sample to look for possible problems with cell development or viruses. The nurse smiled at Rickey as she said, "This will sting you a little." She rubbed alcohol and a numbing solution on his arm. Rickey frowned with a twisted face but did not cry as the needle was inserted in the vein and the nurse drew blood into the syringe.

"Hello, I am Dr. Blair," the doctor announced as he entered the examination room. "And this must be Richard

Bailey, a brave patient." He lifted Rickey up onto the examination table and talked in a soothing tone while he pulled on Rickey's legs and arms. He looked over the chart which contained vital information taken by the nurse. "I understand that your son is not standing and moving like you think he should at this time. His leg muscles don't seem to be as firm as we would expect for his age." Vergie asked what he thought the problem could be. "I can't tell from my examination what may be causing this, but we should know more after we receive the blood test results." Dr. Blair assured her that he would be in touch when he received the laboratory report.

Vergie left the office feeling frustrated that she didn't have any more information than when she came in, and this increased her anxiety. However, she decided that she and Rickey should have a treat before starting back home. They walked to the lunch counter at Kresge's and ordered milkshakes. Vergie loved strawberry and Rickey ordered chocolate. When they emptied their glasses, they were ready to cross the mountain back to Covel.

The following week, Dr. Penn sent a message by Glen Thornton at the company store, asking Vergie to come see him with Rickey. "Doc will be in his office until 5, Vergie, if you want to catch him today," Glen stated.

"Thanks Glen. I will bring Rickey right over."

Dr. Penn had a stressed look about him as he greeted Vergie and Rickey, "I heard from Dr. Blair, he gave me a call at home before I left this morning. Mrs. Bailey, I'm sorry to say it, but Dr. Blair concludes that Richard has infantile paralysis. Based on symptoms and the results of the blood test, it looks like he has contracted the disease." Dr. Penn delivered the news with a calm, matter-of-fact voice, but his furrowed brow betrayed him.

Vergie was silent for a few seconds that seemed like minutes. Then she blurted. "I don't understand. What is infantile paralysis?"

Dr. Penn came closer to Vergie and crouched a bit to look her directly in the eye. He explained quietly, "Most people call it polio, Mrs. Bailey."

Tears formed in Vergie's eyes, and her body seemed to collapse as she muttered the word "polio". The images from magazines and a newsreel that she and Doug had seen at the movies rushed through her mind. Children laying inside of contraptions called iron lungs that mechanically forced their breathing. Children walking in heavy metal braces or confined to wheelchairs. The images were as clear as the examination table in the office.

"We are going to watch him and test his reflexes. At his age, it can be a mild case that he can outgrow. We won't know that for a while." Dr. Penn explained.

Vergie felt a familiar veil of fog starting to form as she heard the doctor's words. She knew she needed to shake off the numbness and ask what could be done for Rickey, but she struggled to form the questions before Dr. Penn added, "Your son will need rest, heat applied to his legs on a regular basis, and to avoid getting sick from other diseases. Polio is contagious, so you will need to keep his bed, bed linens and everything he comes in contact with clean and away from others." Then Dr. Penn added, "I know you have a son at home and he is about six, correct? Polio is very contagious, especially with the young."

Her mind and heart raced. It couldn't be true. She had seen with her own eyes that he was all right. The idea that Terry could also get polio was too much to consider for this 25-year-old, third time mother.

"We had to report your son's polio to the Health Department in Charleston, and I told them you have another child. A doctor from their office called to tell me that they are in the process of obtaining a vaccine that was developed to prevent polio. It has been approved, but they haven't been able to manufacture a large enough supply to administer to all children yet. He said they are giving priority to children in homes where a sister or brother has the disease. As soon as they can obtain the supply, they will arrange for delivery to doctors with these patients. Are you okay with your little Terry getting the vaccine? Not many people have had this shot, but the results have been good from what I know. There is, however, always a risk," Dr. Penn stated in his typical continuous flow.

"I will talk to my husband, but I think we should let him get the shot. I think we have got to do this," Vergie replied.

"I will let them know to put an order in for us. You are the only patient that I have that has an active case of polio in the family. We want to keep it that way if we can," Dr. Penn indicated.

When Doug came in from work, he could tell from his wife's face that she had some bad news for him. After she explained the findings from Rickey's test, Doug said, "You know we will do whatever the treatment calls for. Like you said, Doc thinks he can outgrow it."

Vergie sighed, "Doug, Rickey can give polio to others if we don't keep them far enough away and keep his things really clean. We have to keep Terry from getting it."

Vergie and Doug explained to Terry all the ways that he could help Rickey, but they explained that he must follow steps to stay well after he touched Rickey or any of his toys. "You must always wash your hands before and after you are with Rickey or touch any of his things like his blankets, toys or crib. We will always leave Ivory soap and a pan of water by the sink. And never put your fingers in your mouth." Vergie reminded Terry of the last rule every day, which he thought was strange since he only put his fingers in his mouth to lick melted chocolate or cake batter.

A week later, Vergie awoke from an afternoon nap to a knock on the screen door. It also woke Rickey who gave out a whimper.

Glen Thornton stood at the door. "Hi Vergie, how you doing? Doc Penn called the store and asked them to send someone down to tell you that you should bring your boy, Terry, up to his office tomorrow for a shot. I think around noon."

"Okay, thanks Glen. I will work it out to be there with Terry."

That evening at supper, Vergie and Doug talked about the vaccination that Terry was going to receive. They had some doubts. It was a new medicine and most people who took it stayed under the watchful eyes of medical workers. Terry would be one of the first patients to have it administered by his regular doctor. After some brief debate, Doug said decisively, "We got to do it."

"I know," Vergie agreed, "we certainly don't want Terry to come down with this."

Vergie arranged for Lucille Dudley to come to the house to watch Rickey while she went to the school to get Terry to take him the doctor's office. Lucille was another new neighbor who had made over Rickey, which is to say that she fawned on him. After all, she had three girls and badly wanted a boy. Vergie went to Mrs. Caves classroom and told her she was there to take Terry to the doctor. "Yes, we have heard that Terry is going to get this vaccination. We all are all praying for him. How is your young one doing?" "He seems to be about the same and hopefully, he will get better as he grows. We are following the doctor's directions on treatment." Vergie replied.

The doctor's office was nestled in the terrace level, which had been built halfway underground at the end of the store facing the railroad trestle. As they approached the office, several people stood outside, as the waiting area was full. Vergie bent down to Terry and confided, "It looks like we are going to have a long wait"

Nurse Maude greeted Vergie and Terry. "The doctor is ready for you. You just need to sign this form giving us permission to give this vaccine to your son."

"Ready for us? What about all of these patients?" Vergie asked skeptically

"Oh, they aren't patients. They just heard about this vaccine and come to see who is getting it." The nurse replied. Vergie thought Glen Thornton must have told a few folks about this. She saw those men on the evening shift, some of Terry's classmates and some interested mothers had assembled to see how this vaccination worked.

Vergie signed the consent form just as Dr. Penn walked out into the waiting room.

"I think people want to know that the vaccine is okay. And if it is, they want to have it for their children. People know how bad polio can be, and they have heard that the vaccine will be available to all children in a few months. They are curious but they want what is best for their children. Terry would be one of the earliest children to be   administered the vaccine outside of a research facility and maybe the first patient ever in West Virginia. So, if it's okay with you I would like to allow a few of these folks to watch the vaccination. It would help get the word out that this is a safe thing to do for the children. And word of mouth goes a long way here." Vergie nodded her agreement.

Dr. Penn told his nurse to pick out about ten or twelve folks to come in. "Get some miners and some wives. But no children." He added. The nurse returned with six men and six women from the community. The room was silent as Dr. Penn picked up the hypodermic syringe. Terry's eyes widened when he saw the big needle with the large container attached. In fact, it was a standard adult hypodermic syringe, but Terry thought it looked made for a giant. Dr. Penn directed Terry to pull down his blue jeans. Terry looked around the room sheepishly and cast a questioning glance toward his mother. She assured him it was okay. So, Terry turned around and pulled his jeans to his knees in front of a dozen onlookers. Then he climbed on to the examination table as Dr. Penn directed.

Dr. Penn cleaned the injection site on Terry's left buttock with a cotton swab soaked with alcohol, then administered the polio vaccine. He assured the spectators that the shot would typically be administered in the arm, "But the health department has recommended a larger dose for Terry since there is already a case of polio in the family. I thought this fellow might have a very sore arm, so he should be fine with this." As the doctor depressed the syringe's plunger, Terry grimaced as hard as he could with every muscle in his face, and his neck bulged, but he did not cry. It stung, but it wasn't as bad as his trike accident.

Terry rolled off the examination table and as he stood, he pulled up his white Fruit of the Loom briefs, followed by his Wrangler Blue Jeans.

As the months passed, Rickey grew stronger and more active. Everyday Vergie gave Rickey the warm baths and massaged his legs. Several times a day she also moved his legs in a kicking motion that the nurse had shown her. Vergie was steadfast in her commitment to her son.

By his first birthday, Dr. Penn reported to his parents, "It looks like he has a mild case and is outgrowing it. I think he is going to be okay." Rickey did "grow out of polio" as Dr. Penn had suggested. He learned to walk and became "more sure-footed," as Vergie would describe it. There were no outward signs of his developmental struggle, but his parents knew that he had worked harder at his development than his older brother or the several youngsters growing up in Covel. Vergie and Doug felt relief and gratitude, and they, along with their extended families gave thanks to God and Jesus.

As he grew up, Rickey remembered little of his bout with polio. He learned about the ordeal from his mother who related the details of the illness to him when he was older.

While Rickey was recovering, Terry helped with his baby brother. Eventually, Rickey grew and became interested in playing with toys and other youngsters. Despite their 5-year age difference, the two became playmates. They loved to make-believe they were cowboys like the Lone Ranger or Gene Autry. In matching costumes that included a six shooter with holster and belt, they played for hours. They had regular gunfights with cap pistols. The toys used rolls of red powder paper that made a "pop" sound as the hammer of the play gun hit the small impression on the roll of paper. With each pull of the trigger, the roll of paper advanced to the next bit of powder until it ran out. Then, the boys waited until they could replace the cap rolls at the toy department at G.C. Murphy on their next trip to Mullens.

Chapter 16 – School and a Visit to the Grandparents

When Terry went back to school in the fall of 1951, he'd become something of a celebrity for having received the polio shot. Noting the widespread curiosity, Mrs. Caves told her classes all she could about the shot. She said that all of them would be getting one within the following year, which made Terry laugh to himself, "That's a lot of kids with their pants pulled down for a shot." Of course, he had forgotten that was not the way the vaccine would be administered at school.

Terry quickly adjusted to the daily routine of school. When school was in session—from mid-August to the end of May—Terry walked to school with the Repass and the Dudley girls. The three-room school had two restrooms. The girls' room was on the side of the building next to the road and the boys' room was on the side of the building that abutted the hillside. The students could only use them before and after lunch or during recess, which was held twice a day for fifteen minutes in the middle of the morning and again in the middle of the afternoon.

Lunch lasted 45 minutes, so if you lived in Covel, you could run home to eat. Since the kids from Garwood, Clarks Gap and other parts of Herndon Mountain came by bus, they had to stay on school grounds for lunch. For the first months of school, Terry walked back home with the Repass girls to have lunch with his mother and Rickey. But when the weather started becoming pleasant in the spring, Terry asked his mother to pack him a lunch so that he could eat on the playground at school and play with the other kids. From then on, she made him a peanut butter and jelly sandwich or cheese and lunch meat sandwich with an apple or banana every day.

She also packed an oatmeal cake or a raisin cake. She occasionally included a very special treat like a snowball cake or coconut marshmallow iced chocolate cake.

Terry especially liked spending recesses and lunch outside. He joined with his classmates and some older students in playing tag and tetherball. The playground had two poles for tetherball, one for the younger students and the other for the upper grades. Terry wasn't as good at tetherball as most of his classmates. He missed hitting the ball more often than the others, but he still liked being with the kids. He also could not catch balls as well as most of his classmates.

Vergie gave Terry company script to buy milk or ice cream at school. Usually, ice cream won out. It was part of a new program started by the county Board of Education with some funding provided by the Federal government's Agriculture Department. Larger schools had implemented hot lunch programs, but Covel Elementary only had milk and ice cream brought weekly by the Foremost Truck. The school had recently added one of Terry's favorites to their offerings: strawberry ice cream cups. Terry and the other kids handed over their script as though it was money. In fact, they thought of it as money, not realizing that the script was not accepted all over the country like real U.S. currency. The equivalent of five or ten cents bought a dairy treat.

* * *

Between the recesses and lunch, the teachers conducted lessons in all the basic subjects. Each grade had a set of textbooks to match the subjects. Books were provided in Wyoming County while some of Terry's cousins lived in other West Virginia County's that had a textbook fee to rent or you could buy your books.

School and a Visit to the Grandparents

Spelling was a daily subject with a written spelling test on Thursdays and a spelling bee with class standing in front of the chalkboard taking turns at the list of words. The teacher would use words from previous weeks or bonus words until there was only one person left standing. Terry came close a few times but never made the last best speller in the class.

When school let out for the summer, Vergie asked Terry if he would like to visit his grandparents in Rock. "Yes, let's go see Grandma and Grandpa!"

"Your dad and I thought you would like to ride the train to stay a few days with your grandparents."

"Yeah, a train ride would be fun! When are we going?" Terry remembered the times they had ridden the train to Rock, Matoaka and Princeton to visit relatives. Most of the time it was just with his mother but sometimes his dad went.

"This Monday, but you would be riding by yourself this time. Your Uncle Junior will be at the Rock Train Station to pick you up, and you will stay with him until your grandpa gets off work and can come by to pick you up and take you to your grandparents' house to stay until we come over on Sunday."

Terry hesitated for a moment and thought about riding the train, then he said, "That would be fun. I like going to Rock to see Grandma and Grandpa."

Vergie and Doug had talked about Terry making the train trip alone and staying with Doug's parents. Doug had assured Vergie, "My mom said she would like to have Terry with her. She has other grandkids, but they are babies. Since Terry's the second grandchild and old enough to mind her and help in the garden, she wants him to come over. Bobby Lee has done that in the past, but this year he has scout camp, basketball camp and they are traveling for vacation. I think it would be fine for Terry to go on his own."

On Monday morning, Vergie packed her son's clothes— mainly jeans, tee shirts, socks, and underclothes—in a large paper shopping bag. She also packed a sandwich in a small brown lunch bag. When it was time to leave for the train station, she left Rickey with Lucille Dudley and the Dudley girls while she walked Terry to the railroad tracks to catch the train. She walked with him up the long flight of concrete steps.

The Company had built the railway stop years ago for the miners and their families to go to the company store located near the tracks of the Virginian Railway on the hillside above the Covel camp. The original owner of the mines had built a small brick store, but it had since been replaced by a larger, three-story store located in the center of the camp. From the platform at the top of the steps, you could look back at the camp and see the tops of the frame houses with smoke rising slowly from the chimneys toward the blue sky. Even in the summer, each Covel resident kept a fire going in the kitchen cookstove to prepare the meals.

They arrived at the tracks with plenty of time to spare. Vergie knew that she had to be there to flag the train. It did not automatically stop every time it came through town. It did slow down some to drop off the incoming mailbag and catch the outgoing mailbag attached to a crane on the side of the tracks. As the train slowed, the conductor looked out for passengers flagging the train. He would then signal the train's engineer by waving a flag that the engineer could see in a mirror. This made it possible for small towns like Covel to have passenger service without stopping the train every day like it did in larger towns like Mullens, Matoaka or Princeton.

Vergie pinned a note written in ink to Terry's white tee shirt: "Terry to get off at Rock." As she did it, she told her son, "Terry, the conductor will say, "Rock" and that is when you get off. If the train stops anywhere before he says Rock, you stay on the train. Do you understand? Tell me what I just said."

Terry repeated his mother's instructions. Vergie smiled and said, "Good. Here is a quarter for you to buy a Coca-Cola and an oatmeal cake. Don't lose the quarter. The conductor will come through and ask if you want anything." Terry thought about these instructions and was already looking forward to the pop and cake.

Vergie stood by the track with Terry as the eastbound steam locomotive approached the remnants of the original Covel company store, slowed, and came to a complete stop.

The conductor stepped off the middle passenger car in his black uniform and hat. He placed a step stool firmly on the ground, then motioned for Vergie and Terry to come forward.

Vergie explained to the conductor, "Terry needs a ticket to Rock. Could you see that he gets off there? His uncle will meet the train."

The conductor replied in a matter-of-fact manner, "Child's minimum fare is ninety cents. That would cover him to Rock." Vergie handed the conductor a dollar bill. He pushed the lever on the coin dispenser attached to his belt and caught the dime that dropped from it. He gave the shiny new Roosevelt dime to Vergie.

"Terry has money for a pop and oatmeal cake. Will he be all right and will you see that he gets off at Rock?" Vergie asked again fretfully.

"Don't worry. Children travel on the Virginian every day. We will see he gets off in Rock. It is good to have the note pinned on him. I will see that he gets his cake and pop too," the conductor replied with a reassuring smile.

Vergie hugged Terry and gave him a kiss on the forehead as he climbed up the step stool and then on the steps to board the train. At the top step, Vergie handed him his suitcase shopping bag, then the conductor picked up the step stool and followed Terry into the car. Terry took the first seat by the window on the Covel side of the train. He could see his mother looking up at the windows. He waved and she waved back instantly. The train jerked forward, and Terry was on his way for his first solo travel adventure.

Terry looked out the window as the train picked up speed crossing the Covel trestle. Terry felt a sensation of newfound freedom as the train moved away from his home community. Looking down, he could see the houses in the center of the camp and the houses near the highway entrance. He could not see his house from this end of the trestle, but as it traveled to the other end, he could look back and see his house by the creek, fourth from the end of the road. The train continued to gain speed as it approached the mountain grade. Terry saw the houses and the company store in Garwood. Some of his friends lived here and rode the bus to the Covel school.

The second railroad trestle crossed over the highway and Terry saw an empty, slow-moving lumber truck passing under the trestle and through Garwood. Just then, the train started through a mountain tunnel. The tunnel's lights revealed the concrete tunnel sides as the locomotive traveled through. Throughout the trip, Terry took it all in. He noticed the noise of the engine, the chugging sound of the steam as it spurted out from the release value of the engine, the smell of the coal smoke and the continuous movement of the car. He had not noticed any of these things in the past when he was distracted by his mother or dad or by his coloring book. He was mesmerized with his face to the window, staring into the green hollows when the train entered Mercer County. Terry had a new sense of wonder for this adventure.

The train slowed down at Springton and came to a complete stop. Two women got on the train. They smiled and greeted Terry as they passed his seat. Terry overheard one of them say, "What a cute boy, riding the train by himself." Terry noticed that they had a perfume odor like his mother's as they passed down the train aisle.

In a few minutes, the conductor bellowed, "Next stop Matoaka, Next stop Matoaka." When the train came to a stop in Matoaka, the same two women who had gotten on at Springton got off the train again. Terry looked out the window and saw two crates being unloaded. The conductor stopped by his seat.

"You should get your pop and cake now. It will not be too much longer before you are at Rock," the conductor explained.

"Yes, I would like a Coca-Cola and an oatmeal cake," Terry said as he reached for his quarter. Ordering and paying made Terry feel very grown-up.

The conductor handed Terry his cake and then pulled off the Coke's cap with an opener, placing a paper straw in the bottle as he handed it to Terry.

Terry sipped the icy cold drink from the bottle and quickly ate his oatmeal cake. As he finished the cake, he remembered that his mother had packed him a sandwich. It worked out well since he still had just enough pop left to finish off with the sandwich.

"Rock, Rock, next stop!" the conductor announced as he walked through the passenger car at a quick pace. He looked straight at Terry to be sure the boy was paying attention. Terry swung both legs to the side of the seat and then quickly stood in the aisle while the train was still moving. He grabbed the back of the seat as he lurched slightly with the train movement. The train came to a complete stop, then Terry held on to his shopping bag as the conductor helped him off the train. "Welcome to Rock. This must be your uncle coming over," The conductor glanced in Junior's direction. Terry felt a personal pride in having accomplished something new. He felt like he was a much older kid now that he could ride the train, order his own treats and in a way be treated as if this was a very special time, which it was. The memory of this trip would remain with him throughout his adult life.

The Rock Train Station probably in the 1920s but was unchanged when Terry disembarked from the locomotive to visit his grandparents.
From the Bobby Davis Collection

Junior with his usual big Bailey grin, waved at Terry. Junior thanked the conductor and took the shopping bag from Terry.

"Hi Terry, you ready to visit with your grandparents?" Junior asked. Despite his name, Junior was the second son of Lake Bailey, Sr. Years later, Terry would wonder why his grandparents waited for their second boy to nickname him Junior. He never thought to ask them or his dad. With the shopping bag luggage in hand, Junior led Terry to the local bottling plant where he worked. The Rock Cliff Beverage plant bottled soda pop in a variety of flavors. Terry liked the orange and strawberry drinks best, but one of the most popular drinks was Rock Cliff ginger ale. The pale gold beverage had more fizzy carbonation than the fruit flavored ones.

"You will wait here until your Granddad comes, Terry." Junior pulled out a tall stool with a seat back. Terry climbed on to the stool for a view of the soda being bottled. Junior reached onto the moving conveyor line, picked up an uncapped bottle and handed it to Terry. From the smell, Terry could tell that the factory was producing the grape drink today. "The drink is cold because we cool the water before it's mixed with the flavoring," Junior explained. Terry gave a big smile as he told his uncle, "Thanks!" Junior returned to work, walking down the line and observing the conveyor belt line of a continuous stream of grape soda bottles.

Lake E. Bailey, Sr.— "Grandpa" to Terry and his cousins—arrived just as Junior was clocking out from his shift at the soda bottling plant. "Hi Terry, good to see you," he grinned. The grin was almost identical to Doug's expression.

Forged by Coal

Junior rubbed the back of Terry's head and spoke. "We will see you Sunday when your folks come over." As he picked up his lunch box and headed out the door for the half mile walk to his home.

Terry rode in the front seat as Grandpa drove down the Rock Road and then turned on to the road that followed the Bluestone River toward the Baileys' homeplace of over thirty years. Terry was feeling very special to be in the front seat of the new Chevrolet, a bright two-tone green. "Terry, I just got this car last month. Getting used to it. It's automatic. Takes less to handle this one. Rides good, don't it?" Grandpa Bailey exclaimed. Terry did not know what "automatic" meant but he knew that it was something Grandpa valued and spoke in such a proud tone.

Grandma Bailey stood at the kitchen door and watched as Terry and Grandpa walked down the hill from the parking area to the house. Terry carried his paper luggage and Grandpa had his own dinner bucket and thermos.

"Terry, glad you are here! How was the train ride?" Grandma asked as she hugged her grandson. Terry related some of the things he saw on the train ride, but he emphasized his purchase of the oatmeal cake and bottle of Coca-Cola.

That night, Terry was excited to sleep upstairs all by himself in the big bed with the overstuffed mattress covered in one of Grandma's handmade quilts. Before coming upstairs to sleep, Grandma Bailey had asked Terry to say his prayers. Terry knew the "Now I lay me, down to sleep …" well and recited it.

The weather was great, without a drop of rain as the week continued. Each day, Grandma or Grandpa introduced Terry to a new farm chore. He hoed rows of corn, gathered

188

eggs each day and fed the pigs. One day, while Grandma milked the cow, she confided, "We are going to sell the cow—probably this fall. It doesn't make much sense to take care of her for milk two people need. It's a lot cheaper to buy milk and butter." When she had finished, Terry picked up the heavy pail of milk with both hands wound tightly around the wire handle of the steel bucket.

Terry learned how to pick ground cherries from between the rows of the corn plants one morning. By the time Grandma told Terry it was time to go in for lunch, he had filled several buckets with the small yellow, husked fruit that resembled tiny tomatoes. After lunch, Terry watched his grandma make jam from the ground cherries by boiling them in sugar on the coal stove. The sweet aroma filled the downstairs and delighted Terry, cementing for decades a special memory of this time in Grandma's kitchen.

On Sunday, his aunts and uncles and their families came to visit as usual. Vergie, Doug, and Rickey were among the first to arrive for a Sunday of family, food, and local news. Terry enthusiastically recounted his week, paying special attention to the gardening and of course, the train ride. He ultimately deemed it, "a very terrific time."

Chapter 17 -The Eyes Have It

In the third grade, Terry and his cohort of classmates moved up to Mrs. Gladys Whitt's classroom. Early in the school year Mrs. Whitt noticed that Terry wasn't reading as well as she expected based on what Mrs. Caves had indicated on his report card from the previous year. She had informed Mrs. Whitt that she was getting a top, smart student in Terry. He had earned 100 percent on each of his weekly spelling tests in second grade. Yet he failed the first two tests in the third grade. Mrs. Whitt consulted with Mrs. Caves about this change.

The two teachers tried to isolate the problem. Mrs. Whitt opened the spelling book to this week's lesson and asked Terry to spell "snake".

"C N A K E," Terry sounded out.

Mrs. Caves took the book from Mrs. Whitt and put her finger on the spelling word. "Don't you remember us saying the letter S looks like a snake?" At this point, the two teachers saw that Terry was squinting at the page.

Mrs. Whitt declared, "He can't see the word clearly. He needs to see an eye doctor."

Mrs. Whitt wrote a note to Vergie, sealed it in an envelope and gave it to Terry, saying, "Don't lose this. Be sure you give it to your mother." Terry followed the instructions when he got home, and Vergie opened the envelope and read the note. She was not surprised to read that Mrs. Whitt and Mrs. Caves believed that Terry had poor eyesight and probably needed glasses. Doug's eyesight had been poor since he was a very young man and he had cataract surgery.

When Vergie told Doug about the note from the school, he responded, "Let's get him an appointment with Doc Sinclair in Bluefield. I don't think there are any eye doctors in Mullens or at least no good ones." Dr. Sinclair had been the ophthalmic surgeon for Doug's cataract surgery in 1939. By this point, however, it turned out that Dr. Sinclair was no longer taking new patients--especially children--but his partner, the younger Dr. Fugate, could accommodate Terry, so Vergie set up an appointment with him.

Vergie asked her friend, Louise Clark, to go with her to Terry's appointment. Doug had to work, but she knew she didn't want to go alone. It had been a stressful seven years with six moves, three pregnancies, a baby's death, polio and now an eye doctor appointment for a possibly very serious eye condition. Louise knew how to drive, and all her children were in school, so Doug arranged to ride with Dewy Miller and left the car for Louise to drive Vergie and Terry to Bluefield to see Dr. Fugate. Vergie felt relieved to have someone with her.

Terry rode in the back seat while the women talked in the front seat most of the way to Bluefield. Louise drove a little slower than Doug, so it took a few minutes longer than usual to arrive in town and park. Doug always parked at a meter on the street or at his cousin's business: Bud Meyer's Automotive, so Terry was surprised when Louise turned into the parking building. He loved the novelty of a car driving inside of a building. It felt like an amusement park ride as Louise turned around the curves at each end of the building before accelerating up a ramp to the next level. She parked in an open spot on the third level.

The threesome walked a block and a half to Dr. Fugate and Dr. Sinclair's office. Vergie held Terry's left hand as they navigated the sidewalk and she reminded him, "You remember what I told you. A gentleman always walks on the side closest to traffic when he is with a lady." Terry made a real effort to remember the guidance because it seemed important to his mother.

Several patients sat in the doctor's waiting area, some with a patch on one eye and some wearing sunglasses. Vergie told the receptionist that Terry Bailey had arrived for an appointment with Dr. Fugate, then answered some questions for the receptionist and showed her Miners Benefit Card.

After almost an hour in the waiting room, the receptionist called Terry's name. Dr. Fugate greeted Terry and his Mother wearing a white, starched coat with a fountain pen and a small flashlight clipped to the pocket, "Nice to meet you, young man. You know, your dad comes here to see my partner, Dr. Sinclair. Let me ask your mother what is going on with your eyes, ok?"

"Yes, Doctor, Terry's teacher sent us a note saying that he can't see his books or the chalkboard clearly. We thought he had been doing fine, but I do remember him bumping into some things. This happens when he is playing outside. Recently he ran right into the clothesline pole at his grandparents!"

Terry remembered running into the pole—a two by four—that was supporting the center of the clothesline in his grandparents' back yard. It had almost knocked him down.

Then Dr. Fugate turned to Terry, saying, "Let's take a look at your eyes." His nurse turned off the room's light and the doctor took out his pocket flashlight to look at Terry's eyes. First, he pointed the light at Terry's right eye and directed Terry with hand gestures, "Look this way, up, down and this way." Then he repeated the same directions for the left eye. Lastly, he asked Terry if he knew all of the letters of the ABCs.

"Yes, I know my ABCs. I am in third grade!" Terry shot back, wounded.

"Good, then tell us the name of the letters we point to on the chart.".

The nurse turned on the room lights and Dr. Fugate pointed to the chart on the wall with his flashlight. Terry progressed through the chart, starting at the top with the "E". When he reached the fifth line, he read, "P...E..." then he paused before continuing, "...not sure, looks like it could be O or Q."

"Let's see if we can help you out here." Dr. Fugate placed a device over Terry's face with two openings for him to look through to view the eye chart. Some years and many eye examinations later, Terry learned that the device with so many choices is called a phoropter. The doctor asked Terry to focus on the fifth line while he changed the lenses in his machine and asked over and over again, "Is this better or is this better?" Each time he asked the question, Terry heard a sharp click from the phoropter. Terry thought the doctor must have asked one hundred times before he finally removed the phoropter and asked Terry to sit back. Terry felt jittery from trying so hard to see his very best.

"Mrs. Bailey, your son's vision is about 20/40, and it is going to become poorer because it looks like he has cataracts developing. We can help him with glasses for now, but his prescription will have to be changed over time, and eventually glasses will not help. He will need surgery at some point to correct the problem." Dr. Fugate stated starkly.

"I always thought only old people got cataracts. Do you know why this is happening?" Vergie asked.

"Most cataracts do develop with age, but sometimes, for reasons we don't fully understand, young people like Terry or even a baby can have cataracts," Dr. Fugate explained. "Did anyone in your family or your husband's family have cataracts at a young age?"

"Yes. Doug, my husband, has thick glasses from cataract surgery as a teenager. None of our brothers or sisters have cataracts as far as I know. Our parents don't either," Vergie replied.

"Yes of course. I should look at your husband's chart. It probably is something that Terry had at birth. Now it is growing over the lens of his eye. I will check Dr. Sinclair's records for your husband. From what you're telling me about his condition, I would say Terry got his cataracts from Douglas. We would call them genetic cataracts if they came because of your husband's genes. That means it is something your son inherited from his father. On the other hand, they could be the result of an infection during pregnancy, which would make them congenital. I am not sure we can tell either way, but Terry does have cataracts on both eyes."

"Either way, it doesn't seem like we could have prevented him from having them," Vergie responded with a slow sigh.

"But we can help you now with some glasses. I am writing a prescription, and we can order the glasses for you here or you can go to the optical company up the street."

Vergie replied, "We will get them with you."

Dr. Fugate made the prescription notes on a form and handed it to Vergie, saying, "Give this to Beverly behind the l4cation.

reception desk. She will help you pick out frames and she'll take care of making the order. And this boy will be even more handsome with glasses," Dr. Fugate smiled at Terry.

Vergie and Louise helped Terry to select frames. Dark brown frames were selected. There was only one other student, Glen Miller in Terry's class with glasses and his were more a dark red color. When he had made his choice, Beverly completed the form and told Vergie the glasses would be ready in two weeks. "We will send you a post card to let you know that they are here. You should come in with Terry so that we can be sure they fit right, and we can go over how to take care of his glasses," Beverly instructed Vergie and Terry.

When the post card arrived two weeks later, Louise agreed to make the trip to pick up the glasses. Terry could see the difference immediately, especially reading his books. Only a year later he needed a pair of glasses with bifocal lenses. His vision was deteriorating so that he required different focal lengths for close and distance vision. He would be the only child at Covel Elementary with bifocal glasses.

When Doug came home from work and saw his son in his new glasses, he smiled and told Terry, "Mighty handsome. I think you should try out these spectacles at the airport in Bluefield this Saturday. They are having a grand opening with flights. What do you say?" as he looked at Vergie. "Airplanes! That would be fun. Let's go." Terry almost shouted.

On Saturday instead of the weekly trip to Mullens, the Bailey family headed to the Mercer County Airport between Bluefield and Princeton. The airport, the parking lot and all open spaces were crowded with folks that wanted to get a look at the airplanes and hear the dignitaries praise the opening of the airport. Terry was restless especially hearing the politicians speak. Doug shook his head, "I think Congressman Jim Key could talk all day. Let's check out these planes. Looks like we could take a short flight for $15. Want to go?" Terry jumped up. "Yes!"

Vergie shook her head, "I don't think I want to do this. Remember I got sick the last time we went to the carnival and road the rollercoaster. I don't think Rick would like it either. Too noisy and scary." Doug looked down. "Okay, it would be $60. Let's skip it." Terry sighed. "I think it would be fun. I have never flown." His dad nodded, "None of us have either, Terry." Vergie took a deep breath. "Doug, you should take Terry and go on the flight."

"Are you sure? How about Rickey? "

"I think it might hurt his ears. You know he has had some earaches. You and Terry would enjoy it. I think Rick and I will be fine right here on the ground."

Doug took Terry by the hand, and they got in the line to get a ticket for the exhibition flight. After about 45 minutes in line that seemed like a half-day to Terry, father and son boarded one of the three planes that were making these opening day flights. Doug motioned for his son to sit by the window. The stewardess dressed in her official grey uniform with matching cap, announced over the public address system. "Welcome aboard, this special Piedmont flight on this wonderful opening day of the Mercer County Airport. We especially like to welcome our first-time flyers and urge you to fly with us to one of the airports that connect you to the country and even the far reaches of the world. We have flights to Atlanta, Charlotte, Pittsburg, and Baltimore. Please watch as I demonstrate how to buckle your seat belt." After the demonstration, she continued. "Since this is a very short flight, smoking is not permitted. Smoking is permitted on our regular fights after takeoff and before landing. "

Terry pressed his face to the window and was amazed to see the propeller on the wing, disappear as the engine revved up and the noise in the plane's cabin made it almost impossible to hear someone next to you. Looking down as the plane rose into the air, Terry could see the cars traveling on U.S. 460, the main road between Bluefield and Princeton. The houses and businesses along the route look so small from the air. Terry was amazed as he experienced his first flight. In 1954 at age 8, he and his dad at age 30 had their first airplane ride.

Chapter 18 – Discipline. Could this be Love?

One late fall day at the Covel Elementary, Terry and his classmate, Glen Miller were directed one at a time to bend over and hold their ankles while Mr. Caves gave each one three smacks with the paddle that were loud enough to be heard from the front of the room into the main hallway. Most of the students knew that someone was being disciplined with the wood paddle administered by the school's principal, Thomas P. Caves.

What infraction had brought Terry and Glen to receive this punishment? A cardinal school rule had been broken by the two boys. A Burnside pot belly coal stove heated each of the rooms in the schoolhouse. When the stoves were lit for the first time each fall, the teachers made sure to teach the students one important lesson: stay away from the stove! These stoves would cause severe burns at the slightest touch. In third grade, Terry and his friend, Glen Miller—not the band leader—learned that lesson.

Mrs. Whitt, the third and fourth grade teacher, had cautioned the boys about "horse playing" near the stove. She reminded them of this when she saw them too close to the stove a few days later. After the third time, she said pointedly to Terry and Glen, "Boys come with me." They followed her up the hall and into Mr. Caves' room. Both boys were quiet and had the most sobering look on their faces as they crossed the threshold of the 5th and 6th grade room. Neither of the boys had ever been in the room where the principal, Mr. Caves taught.

"Mr. Caves, I told Glen and Terry not to be playing around the stove. But they were there again this morning," Mrs. Whitt explained the interruption.

"Boys you could really get burned badly if you fell or were pushed against the stove. You cannot be playing around it. I hope you'll remember that from now on," Mr. Caves chided as he opened his desk drawer and pulled out a wooden paddle with six holes drilled in it. At least half of the school knew someone was getting a paddling.

With the corporal punishment complete, Mr. Caves gave each of the boys a note to take home for a parent's signature.

> Your child, <u>Terry,</u> received <u>3 </u>licks with a paddle today because of <u>playing too close to the</u> <u>stove after warning</u>.
>
>   Sign here _____ and return this note to the school tomorrow."

That evening Vergie showed the school note to Doug. He read it and looked at Terry through his thick glasses which magnified his eyes into a deep stare, saying, "I got a share of paddling in school. I don't want you to start this. Do you understand? If you get another one, I am going to give you twice as many licks with the belt." Terry thought about this for a split second. He had only been hit with his dad's belt a couple of times--once when he colored in Marilyn Repass' new coloring book, and she started crying. His dad didn't say much then except to tell Terry not to mess with another people's stuff as he took his belt off. It hurt a lot more than Mr. Caves' wooden paddle.

Discipline. Could this be Love?

"I understand, dad", Terry sputtered in a higher pitch voice. This turned out to be the first and only school paddling that Terry ever received. He would receive the belt only once more from his father.

Paddling was not a daily occurrence at the Covel Elementary, but Mr. Caves did administer them fairly whenever boys and girls committed a particularly serious offense. Almost always, the students at Covel took their punishments from Mr. Caves in steadfast silence and obedience. An exception to this occurred in Terry's last year at Covel Elementary.

The exception was Floyd Shrewsbury who was from Clarks Gap. He and his three siblings were not fond of school, but Floyd did enjoy the playground. At recess one day, he and Jerry Cruey had a disagreement over a turn at tetherball, and soon the two were in a fist fight. Floyd was taller but thinner than Jerry. Overall, they were well matched. Mrs. Caves was on recess duty, which obligated her to intervene. When she tried, one or both boys accidentally pushed her. Whoever the culprit, this stopped the fight.

Mrs. Caves took the boys to Mr. Caves and reviewed what had happened. "Floyd and Jerry were fighting on the playground. When I came over to them, they kept at it until I stepped between them. Look at my dress, red clay from their scuffle." She exclaimed. Mr. Caves said, "Floyd and Jerry you know we don't fight in school. It's not the thing to do and you know we have rules against fighting." He then reached for the wooden paddle.

Floyd took a deep breath, ran his tongue over and under the inside of his lips. "You ain't going to paddle me!"

Floyd shouted and darted out the room and back into the school yard.

Mr. Caves took a deep breath, turned around and said to two of the strongest and fastest sixth graders, "Wade and Billy, go get Floyd and bring him back here."

Wade and Billy rushed out of their seats, delighted to get out of class and to chase a classmate. This was a mission that they were ready to accomplish. When Floyd turned to see them leaping down the steps into the school yard, he started running. His run was short lived as the other two quickly overtook him. Each boy grabbed ahold of Floyd by the armpit and the two marched him back into the school and in front of Mr. and Mrs. Caves. Mr. Caves paddled Jerry without a word, then turned to Floyd who was pulling as hard as he could to escape Wade and Billy.

"You need to take your punishment just like Jerry," Mr. Caves stated and paused for a response. Floyd flushed red in the face and stopped pulling at the other two boys and leaned down to take the requisite five licks.

Floyd's school attendance was poor, but he never had any more trouble at Covel. When he reached his 16th birthday, he dropped out of school. About a third of the class at the high school, mostly boys dropped out before graduation.

Another unusual event that Terry would remember on how Mr. Caves dealt with impending tragedy involved, the mother of one of the Mr. Caves' students. Mrs. Opal McKinney, taller than most women and very stout, just like her son, Mark came to the school to see Mr. Caves. It was well known in the camp that Mrs. McKinney had some problems with her emotional behavior. People did not refer to this as mental health in the 1950's they just said "she ain't right in the head." She was under Dr. Penn's care and taking prescription medications.

She came into the classroom and sat down in the chair beside of Mr. Caves desk. She calmly opened her purse and pulled out a ten-inch kitchen knife, then muttered, "You ain't treating my son right. He is a good boy."

Mr. Caves stood up and backed slowly away as he could see the sweat start to appear on her face and slowly trickle down each of her cheeks. "Yes, he is and it's going to be all right. Now let's be calm and everything will be all right. Please put the knife on the desk." Then, without taking his eyes off Mrs. McKinney, Mr. Caves once again called on Billy and Wade for their assistance. "Billy and Wade, go over to the store and ask Mr. Cline and a couple of men to come over and help us." The pair complied with Mr. Caves' request by rushing out the back door to the main hallway and ran to the company store.

As Mr. Caves continued to back away from the mother, he tried to reassure her that everything would be all right. "We understand and I am getting some help for us. That's why I sent those boys over to get us help. Can we just sit until our help gets here?" Mr. Caves implored. Mrs. McKinney stood up with the knife firmly in her right hand and her arm extended toward Mr. Caves. "You and the teachers have not given my boy a chance. You keep picking on him. It ain't right how he's been treated." She exclaimed in a slightly slurred speech.

Billy and Wade accompanied by the store manager, Mr. Cline and a couple of other men arrived through the back door, Mrs. McKinney was startled to see the men that she recognized. She turned in their direction, still holding the knife that she now waved left to right as she moved between the aisle of student desks. Students still seated at Mr. Caves urging, started to make deep gulping sounds as they looked on with a startled expression.

A heavyset man, Richard "Wimpy" Pedneau came up another aisle of desks and approached Mrs. McKinney from the side. He brought his arm down against the women's right arm to knock the knife to the floor. Then the other two men and Mr. Caves pinned her arms to her side. The woman began to scream and yell profanity as they pulled, almost dragging her out of the school and toward the store. "Let's take her down to the Doc's waiting room," Mr. Cline shouted to the group.

Mr. Caves told the students to stay seated and asked Wade to notify Mrs. Caves that he was dealing with an emergency and had to go to the store. Most of the students appeared stunned but Terry and Glen followed Mr. Caves instructions and rushed to Mrs. Caves room.

Mr. Caves joined the other three men in the doctor's office. Mr. Caves gave Dr. Penn a quick summary of what had occurred. Mrs. McKinney was given a shot while the men held her. In a few minutes, Dr. Penn assured the men that he and the nurse had Mrs. McKinney under control as she became lethargic from the shot.

For some time thereafter, Mrs. McKinney was hospitalized at the state's mental facility in Weston. She was eventually released and continued under medical care. Mr. Caves never spoke to the students about the incident, but he did reassure the parents that the woman was getting the help she needed.

The incident with Mrs. McKinney was very unusual and was a very rare occurrence. For the most part parents saw the school as a positive, almost the center of the social function of the coal camp. Most miners had school age children. Mothers supported their school with an active Parent-Teachers Association with the meetings have very good attendance.

The Parent-Teachers Association held a Halloween Carnival each year as a fund-raising event for the school. The carnival featured costume contests, apple bobbing, cake walks among. The cake walk was a favorite. Music was played from a record player until someone whose back was turned to the circle of people marching around, lifted the needle off the record. A hidden spot marked the winner when the music stopped. The coal miners' wives, who were known for their good cooking, brough lots of baked goods to the carnival.

For several years, the Company provided a hot dog roast after Halloween if there was no damage done to property. Many coal camps, including Covel had a history of mostly teenagers doing some property damage including turning over outhouses. The hot dog roast did work mainly through peer pressure and parent control. The roast was held in the school yard following the Saturday after Halloween.

~~~ ~~~~~~~~ a wall lamp.

Covel-Garwood Children To Receive Reward for Good Halloween Behavior

By Register Staff Writer

COVEL - GARWOOD—Youngsters, both white and Negro, of the Covel-Garwood communities are to be rewarded for their good behavior Halloween night.

In keeping with a standing offer that it would treat the young folks if they did no desroy any property, the American Coal Company has announced it will finance the cost of a wiener roast.

Four - hundred - fifth wieners, buns, and garnish have been ordered for the affair.

Beckley Raleigh Register newspaper clipping.

In the fifth and sixth grades, the last activity of the day was West Virginia Club or Library Club done on alternate Fridays. The West Virginia Club taught students about the history, geography, and government of the state. Library Club was silent reading and then oral book reports. All students were required to read a number of books and make several oral and written reports. The "library" was enclosed shelves in the back of the classroom. The library held many children's classics – Treasure Island, Gulliver's Travels, Little Women—

and more current series like the Hardy Boys, Bobbsey Twins and Nancy Drew.

Terry enjoyed the Hardy Boys series and was sort of a showoff when it came to oral book reports. He would try to imitate a book character's voice and not give away the ending just to see if he could get a reaction from his classmates.

The student always started West Virginia Club meetings by singing the state song: "The West Virginia Hills." Mr. Caves prompted the students to "Sing out, be proud, be loud."

Oh the West Virginia Hills! How majestic and how grand.
With their summits bathed in glory like our Prince Immanuel's Land!
Is it any wonder, then, that my heart with rapture thrills
As I stand once more with loved ones on those West Virginia Hills

* * *

Birthday parties were very special events in Covel. These usually were attended by kids of close to the same age. Parties had about a dozen or more children attending. Playing the games, opening of presents and cake. Kool Aid was the most common beverage. Orange and strawberry flavors were the most popular.

"Terry, here is an invitation to my birthday party," Paxton said it tersely and handed Terry an envelope as he was riding his bike by her house. Sarah Paxton Hill, who everyone called Paxton, was the only daughter of the Company bookkeeper and his wife. They lived in one of the two-story homes in the center of town. They were the ones who gave out the best trick or treat that you had to sign a sheet to get.

Terry took the invitation and muttered, "Thanks." He stuffed it in his back pocket and rode on. When he got home, he opened the invitation,

You are cordially invited to attend a party
in honor of Sarah Paxton Hill's Tenth Birthday
August 5, 1957
RSVP 86-W-11

Terry showed his mother the invitation. "What does RSVP 86-W-11 mean?"

"They want you to let them know if you are coming to the party by calling them at their phone number," Vergie replied.

"But we don't have a phone."

"Just tell Paxton, you are coming. You do want to go? It should be nice."

"Sure, I guess so." Terry stated.

"Terry, on second thought, you can go over to the Dudleys and ask them if you could call Paxton to tell her you are coming to the party. I have an idea she would like that." Vergie indicated.

"I don't know if I should do that," Terry replied.

"Come on, I will go over with you," Vergie responded as she stood up.

Terry sighed but started thinking how to make the call and what to say as they walked across the road to the Dudleys. Lucille came to the door and invited Vergie and Terry in. Vergie explained Terry's need to use the phone.

Discipline. Could this be Love?

Terry picked up the phone and took a deep breath. He had only talked on a phone a couple of times when his Aunt Carrie had called at his Aunt Mildred's and the phone had been passed to him to just say hello.

The number 86-W-11 meant that the Hills had a party line phone. When it rang, it was one long, one short ring thus the 11. The Bailey family would get a phone in the next year, also on a party line and the number would be 86-J-13, one long and three short rings. Numbers were called by picking up the receiver and telling the operator the number you wanted after she said, "Number, please." If it was not a local number, you would ask for the long-distance operator to give her the number.

Mrs. Hill answered the phone. Terry paused and then said, "Is Paxton there?" Mrs. Hill recognized that it must be one of Paxton's classmates. "I will get her, just a minute." Was the response. "Hi, who is this?" came a clear voice that was Paxton. She had a more direct, clearer voice than most of the other girls. "I will come to your birthday party." Was Terry's response. "Is this Terry?", Paxton shot back. "Yes, it is me." Terry managed back. "Good, see you then thanks for calling." And then the phone clicked as Paxton hung up.

Vergie picked out a present, a turtleneck sweater from the company store, for Paxton. She wrapped it with care, placing a gold bow on the package. She had Terry write the card in his own handwriting. "Be sure to tell Paxton if it doesn't fit or she wants another color, she can exchange it at the store. Have you got that?" Terry nodded his head. Vergie wanted her son to make a good impression. She was a little nervous that Terry might not be up to going into one of the homes of the coal company's management. Mr. Hill was not a miner. Terry nor his mother had ever been in the Hill's home. She knew Mrs. Hill wasn't like most of the miners' wives. She had been brought up in a city and was new to coal camp life. According to town gossip, she had fine china and silver. The Hills did not socialize with the miners, and they took trips to New York, Washington and Florida.

The day of the party, Terry—with his shoes shined and hair combed—traversed the 200 yards to the Hills' home carrying the present. Paxton opened the door wearing a light green dress. The sight of Paxton in a dress surprised him. She always wore jeans to school and around town. In fact, Terry had never seen her in a dress. Most of the kids in town, thought of her as a tomboy. She could bike and run as fast as any of the boys. She climbed trees and played baseball. She never played with dolls. And of course, she had taught Terry how to play marbles.

Terry entered the hallway of the Hills house. He expected to see ten or more other kids, but he saw no one except Mrs. Hill. Just then, he heard footsteps on the front porch. Connie Jones stood at the door. Paxton greeted Connie and said, "Let's start the party."

"Are we going to have other kids here?" Terry asked.

"No, you and Connie are the two that Paxton wanted to invite," Mrs. Hill responded.

"I just thought that the three of us would have fun. I don't think anybody else would want to come," Paxton remarked in a pragmatic way. The party was much calmer than others Terry had attended. He was used to more kids running around and making noise. "This." Terry thought, "is different." Mrs. Hill had served the food on real plates with silverware, and they drank the punch out of real punch glasses instead of the usual paper plates and cups.

Mrs. Hill took Terry aside and said, "Connie has been here before because they play together, so she knows where everything is. If you need the bathroom, it is upstairs. I'm glad you could come. Paxton says she likes riding her bike with you and that you are smart.

For the first time, Terry reasoned Paxton must want him to be her boyfriend. Terry had not thought of the idea of a girlfriend. He really did not know what to think but he knew he was feeling different. This made him a little nervous. Terry had known Connie since their parents played cards together in Monticello and they played in the yard between their houses. He thought of her as a friend just like one of the boys. But something different for Paxton. Perhaps he was developing a crush on her, whatever that might be. At any rate, the crush would be short-lived. Before he had time to figure out this crush idea, Paxton was gone. Mr. Hill was promoted to the regional office for American Coal in Bluefield and Paxton moved within a few weeks of the birthday party. Terry would not see Paxton again, but he never forgot her and especially the birthday party.

The game of Post Office became popular as the Covel kids moved into their teenage years. Terry first played the game at the age of twelve at Elsie Dudley's 13th birthday party. The rules were simple: if your name was drawn out of the hat, you became the postmaster. You knocked on the door, which could be the floor, wall, or a nearby door and if you were male, you picked a girl to kiss to deliver the letter, that is "sealed with a kiss". The girl then became the postmaster and the process continued until everyone had been kissed and the cold germs had been sufficiently spread.

The other popular kissing game was spinning the bottle. If you were male and the bottle pointed to a girl, you kissed her. She would then spin the bottle. If it pointed to a guy, you lost your turn.

These games at birthday parties where the threshold for the teen years as the opposite sex became of interest. This was probably no different in the coal camp communities as would be in other communities, large or small as boys and girls entered puberty.

Chapter 19 – Religion, Scouting

"Terry, it is so hot in here," Rickey whispered as the two sat on the church pew at the Rock Church of God on an August night in 1957. Both boys had beads of sweat dripping down their necks as they listened to their Aunt Duvall preach a forceful, loud sermon. They had come with their parents to hear their aunt, Uncle Orville's wife, preach in a Christian revival.

Despite being raised in the Christian Church, the Baileys did not usually attend these revival services. Doug had accepted Jesus and had been baptized as a teenager shortly after his older brother Ralph had died in an automobile accident. Vergie had completed confirmation class as a teenager and joined the Littlesburg Methodist Church. She remembered her communion and baptism with the pastor sprinkling water over her head along with the other nine members of her class.

After being married by the Methodist minister at the parsonage, the couple had attended the Rock church regularly, since it was only about a mile from their home. Vergie served as the church secretary, where she was appreciated for her "beautiful penmanship." They maintained their membership until they moved across the mountain to Wyoming County. Once they were residents of Covel, they visited the Missionary Baptist Church and the nearest Methodist church located in Herndon, about a mile away. They had chosen not to join either one, deeming the Baptist church too "hellfire and brimstone" and the Methodist church "too stuffy".

The coal companies had supported the building of churches in the coal camps. Early coal operators felt that providing an outlet for spiritual wellbeing helped maintain community and keep miners and their families near the mines. In Covel—as with other camps, was segregated —there were two church buildings, one for white worshippers and the other for colored worshippers. Terry noted that the colored church really looked more like a church with a steeple while the white church was made of cinder block in a plainer style. Terry asked the pastor of the white Baptist Church, Richard Davis, why the differences?

"It was before my time, Terry. The colored church was built when the camp started in the 1920s while this one wasn't done until 1940. I suspect it had something to do with the carpenters and the supply available at the time. Maybe the union would not let the company take money out to help pay like the company did in the 20's."

All the churches in the coal camps typically conducted annual or semi-annual revivals like the one where the Baileys now sat. They were intended to renew religious fervor and bring in new members. Terry watched mesmerized as Aunt Duvall plead with the attendees to make that altar call and accept Jesus. The sweat on her face glistened as she walked by their pew, and he was reminded that he could not wait to ride home with the windows rolled down to let the mountain air to cool them off. Terry thought, "She sure is different than when we see her at Sunday dinners in Rock. She's usually soft spoken and not like this."

Suddenly Shirley Jones darted out of the pew where she had been seated with her parents and rushed down to the church's alter. She knelt and stated almost in a shout – "Yes

Jesus, I accept you. Thank you." Duvall moved toward Shirley to place her hands on Shirley's shoulders and to give her words of encouragement as Shirley stated before the worshipers that she accepted Jesus as her personal savior. Duvall looked out over the attendees and could see that a young couple was coming to the alter. She felt a sense of accomplishment in reaching these folks this evening along with relief that her call to preach was "bearing fruit."

Duvall said she had gotten "the calling"—by which, she meant she felt personally called by God to conduct these services. She had been in prayer and meditation while Orville was serving in Europe and then recovering from a wound he received in Normandy on D-Day. Duvall and their son, Bobby Lee had waited anxiously for news of Orville's recovery in England. He did successfully recover and was now working as a coal miner.

Duvall convinced the church's pastor, James Sizemore, that God had called her to be the preacher and conduct these services. He acquiesced, reasoning, "Who am I to argue with God?"

Finally, the service ended and the crowd—which may or may not have been delivered from evil—*was* gratefully delivered from the heat of the sanctuary. On the way home that evening in the car, Terry listened to his folks talk about the service.

"Duvall sure gave a strong call tonight. Vergie nodded her head in an approving manner. "She really tried, and I give her that. She felt like she needed to do it and she did. But she's no Oral Roberts," Doug referred to a young charismatic preacher from Tulsa, Oklahoma who had conducted tent revivals in southern West Virginia and was starting a program

Forged by Coal

to televise these meetings. The Oral Roberts revivals included a healing service at the end. People with all forms of illness would be brought forward for "the laying on of hands", in expectation of being healed by God through the prayers of the preacher.

Doug continued. "You know Shirley Jones was a Oliver. She and I were in school together. She married Robert Jones who was killed in the Pacific. I think they were married just a few days before he shipped out. "Vergie shook her head, "Sad the number of brides that the war took their husbands.

* * *

One annual church event the Baileys always attended was the big homecoming event at the Rock Methodist Church. Past members who had moved and extended family members and friends would make the homecoming Sunday an annual priority. Terry and Rickey enjoyed visiting "Grandpa's church", especially when there was a meal afterwards. And what a meal it was, lots of fried chicken and all the trimmings and homemade desserts of all descriptions – pies, cakes, banana pudding, one of Rickey and Terry's favorites. The beverage of the day was contained in wash tubs filled with ice was bottles of the soda pop produced within sight of the church at the Rock Cliff Beverage Company.

By 1955, as her two boys became older, Vergie decided to take them to Sunday School at the Baptist Church. Like most of the mothers in the coal camp, she thought it was important for the children to have the experience and it was a Christian duty that you should provide your children with religious training. In the summer both the white and Black churches conducted a week-long Vacation Bible School, during which the children attended Bible classes, made craft

216

projects, and played games. The week culminated with a well-attended program where the children performed and showed their parents what they had learned. It was at one of these programs that Terry elicited an unexpected laugh from members of the audience. The participants sat onstage answering Bible trivia and when Pastor Davis asked Terry, "When did Peter deny Christ?"

Paster Davis expected Terry to answer, "When the cock crowed."

Terry, proudly proclaimed, "When the crow cocked."

He furrowed his brow in confusion when the audience broke out into laughter, and he remained confused whenever miners brought the story up at the company store.

TEN   BECKLEY POST-

VACATION BIBLE SCHOOL FOR CHILDREN of the Covel and Herndon communities was directed by the Rev. and Mrs. Louis S Lindlmore (right). Among children attending were (left to right) Billy Branham, Peggy Pennington, Terry Bailey, Billy Raney, and Debbie Clark.

Beckley Newspaper Clipping

Another church that played a part in the community was located about a mile away, The Herndon Methodist Church. This church sponsored the Boy Scout Troop and the Cub Scout Pack that the boys from Covel joined. The church welcomed boys from other churches or ones who didn't attend a church to join the troop or the pack. Scouting was founded with a religious component. Scouting for boys and to a lesser degree for girls at the time, was second only to school activities as an outlet for social activities with other kids.

When Terry was 11, he joined the Boy Scouts of America and attended meetings in the basement of the Herndon Methodist Church. Every February, the Herndon church honored Troop 140 with a Scout Sunday. The scouts—Cub Scouts in their blue uniforms and Boy Scouts in their khaki uniforms—attended church to be recognized.

When Rickey became a Cub Scout at the age of 8, Vergie became a Den Mother for his pack. The Den—also sponsored by the Herndon Methodist Church—had enough members to meet in Covel at the school so that they did not need to travel to Herndon.

Scouting afforded the boys growing up in coal towns an opportunity to see life outside of the coalfields. Camp Roland, a summer camp in Bland County, Virginia showed the boys a rural, natural setting free of coal trucks, coal tipples, railroad tracks and the relentless coal dust that settled on their coal camp homes. The summer camp experience also introduced the coal camp scouts to boys from other areas of West Virginia and Virginia, rural and urban. Camp Roland offered swimming, canoeing, skills development in wilderness survival, crafts in leather and wood working, as well as games between troops and individual scouts.

Boy Scout leaders during this time were Curt Hellmandollar, Harold Jones, G. C. Cecil, and Mack Quensenberry. These leaders guided the youngsters in activities outside of the routine of the coal camps. The boys earned merit badges by studying subjects that interested them and following through on projects and examinations to show that they had met the objectives for the badge.

Chapter 20 – Gardening, TV, & the Company Store

The 1950s would bring changes to the life of the coal miners' families in Covel and the rest of the Appalachian coalfields. How the miners spent their free time, how the family purchased goods and even who would own the miner's housing would change drastically from the previous decades of the coal camp life. These changes and the impact can be detailed through the Bailey family.

The Baileys would have a garden to grow their vegetables. This would be abandoned by the 1960s as access to well stocked supermarkets like the A & P and Kroger in Mullens made it more convenient to obtain a variety of food. They ordered more each year from the ever-expanding mail order catalogs and did less shopping at the company owned store. No single technology would have more of an impact than the expansion of television to the hollers of Southern West Virginia. These developments as seen from young Terry's perspective would expand his outlook and change his goals that would not continue the life in Appalachian coal country.

When Doug, Vergie and Terry moved to Covel, they joined a self-sufficient, self-contained community, not that different from the distant villages in Europe during the feudal system or the early settlements of the colonies in the New World. Covel, the coal company owned, and operated community contained the housing, water supply, dry goods, food supply, school, medical service, church, post office and social outlet. The camp like hundreds of others in the coal fields of Appalachian was insulated from the outside world by the owner – the coal company. During the decade ahead, much of this was going to become history.

* * *

"I think I will put out a garden on the hillside this spring," Doug announced one March morning in 1954. He had been thinking about planting a garden for vegetables. From his upbringing on the farm, he knew how to plant, tend and harvest. The garden would provide fresh produce, but it would also be a source for canning. Vegetable gardening was a common practice in the area, and most of the wives knew how to can, with the company store carrying mason jars and seasonings for the task. Vergie had received vegetables from her mother-in-law and her sister Mildred's gardens. There was pride in growing your own.

Many of the other miners had also grown up on farms. The yards around the camp houses were too small for large vegetable gardens, but it was not unusual to see tomato and pepper plants growing near the edge of the porch. The hillside above Route 10 had been cleared and some of the other Covel residents had tended gardens on it with success.

The hillside turned out not to be as fertile as bottom land, but it did produce a good crop of corn and root vegetables like potatoes, carrots, and radishes, encouraging Doug to continue the gardening for a few years. Terry and Rick were helpful in the harvesting process. With guidance, Terry was able to dig potatoes and both boys could pick corn and pull carrots from the ground.

Terry, Rick, and the other coal camp youngsters had already been introduced to berry picking. Strawberries and prolific bushes of blackberries grew wild on the hillsides above and below the railroad tracks. Terry didn't like the picking mainly because he thought he could see a snake near every large rock, but he loved the strawberry shortcake and blackberry cobbler that his mother made. The fruit desserts were extra good with the Foremost brand ice cream from the company store. And for strawberry shortcake, Vergie insisted on making heavy whipped cream using Pet or Carnation evaporated milk.

In future years, the harvests from these hillside gardens came in handy when there was a work slowdown and a strike at the mines. That way, miners and their families had a food source independent of the company store.

* * *

Mail order was more popular. Sears Roebuck, Montgomery Wards, and Aldens had been around since the start of the 20th century. Vergie liked the clothes from Aldens. They carried the plus sizes that she needed after gaining the weight from three pregnancies. Terry and Rick looked forward to the big Sears Roebuck catalog that came just before Halloween each year. The company marketed the catalog as their "Wish Book", and the boys marked all the items they hoped Santa would bring.

One of the Terry's most anticipated Christmas Wish Book items was the Daisy Air Rifle. Most of the boys in the camp, wanted a BB gun at some point or another. Terry received his rifle on Christmas morning 1957. Dad gave him very strict safety warnings and insisted that he was not to shoot birds. This was Terry's first and it would be his only BB gun, but he had shot his cousin, Lane Gilley's gun and a few times, some of the boys in Covel had let him shoot their guns. Terry along with the Jones boys, the Fine boys and Connie Otey target practiced at the rock wall that provided a border for the creek.   Contrary to what you see movies today, they almost never used pop or beer bottles for target practice, since they were worth three cents apiece when returned to the store.

One Saturday afternoon, Terry arrived home after being out with some of the other boys from the camp. He announced to his folks, "The Dudleys have a television! Elsie said I could come over and see it. So, I did, but I didn't see much but black and white squiggles and noise like the radio needed tuning."

"Howard told me they had bought a set from the store in Mullens, but he said they needed a better antenna to get the signal from Huntington. The store is supposed to bring him a bigger antenna when they receive them." Doug recalled.

"Sears has televisions in their new catalog." Terry quipped. "Are we going to get one?"

"You can't hardly get a signal here, down in this holler," Doug replied. "Let's see how the Dudleys' television works with the new antenna. Maybe we can get one if they have a lay away or monthly payment plan for them."

Vergie chimed in. "It's got to have a better picture than what I hear from Howard. They are not too happy with theirs."

"Huntington and Oak Hill television stations are both mountains away. The Bluefield station is scheduled to be on before next year. That should help," Doug surmised.

A couple of weeks later, as Doug left the company store, he saw a posted sign:

Meeting to Get TV
In Covel – Scout House
7 pm, Tuesday, May 13
All Interested are Welcome

He and Vergie attended the meeting, which was led by Carl Underwood, one of Doug's buddies and an electrician with the mines. He proposed a mechanism by which the community could improve television signals from both closest stations. If they installed an antenna on top of the mountain that could pick up the signal from more than one station, then the signal could be wired to extend from the mountaintop down into the camp and then to each house.

Howard Dudley, who had the most experience with his own TV antennae, piped up, "From what I was told, you lose all the signal before it gets off the mountain. So, how's that going to work?"

Carl responded, "Howard, you are right, but the signal can be boosted as it comes through the wires. In fact, to get the best result, you have to do that several times as the distance from the antenna to the destination increases." Carl explained that there would be boxes that would contain the boosters at certain intervals along the wires as they came down the hill and through the camp to each house—something like electricity. To come to this conclusion, he had read up on the topic and talked with the owner of the television repair store in Mullens. The owner was anxious to expand television reception for obvious reasons: more tv set sales and service.

"Where you going to get electricity to power these boosters?" asked George Akers, one of the few retired miners living in the camp.

"I talked to the mine superintendent, Mr. Moorefield, and he said they would get us electric power from the warehouse at the bottom of the hill. He promised they would pay for the power and provide us with the electrical wire, of which the mines have plenty. We will need this antennae wire, two bare copper wires with insulator separating the two."

When there were no more questions, Carl finished his pitch, saying, "If you are interested in taking on the project, I am asking for help in running the wire, installing the antenna and building the boxes for the boosters to be in. The company is not going to buy the boosters or the antenna, so each family would have to pay to hook onto the antenna.

"How much?" George Akers asked.

"It depends on how many people want to do this. The more families, the cheaper the cost per family."

Before the meeting was over, the group agreed that as a first step, they should get the TV signal down to the company store. That way folks would see what they were getting and could subsequently sign up for their houses. This was the start of what would be known as community antennae television (CATV). Under Carl's leadership, a volunteer crew of miners installed the system, running the cables down the side of Herndon Mountain to the company store.

The countdown came at 4 pm on a Saturday. Mr. Cline had a Zenith® TV set ready for the demonstration. The store was abuzz. Almost nobody at the store had ever seen a working TV in the coal camp. When the wire was finally connected by Carl to the booster at the store's electrical room entrance, the stations at Huntington and Oak Hill came through.

The Covel CATV system started with two channels: WSAZ from Huntington and WOAY from Oak Hill. Within the first year, WHIS from Bluefield started broadcasting, and it was added to the system. Since the Bluefield station was the closest, it of course had the strongest signal. Some late TV purchasers bought antennae and could get a signal from Bluefield, but to get all the available channels, TV owners had to sign on to the Community Antennae system.

The system required more maintenance than Carl had planned. The boosters which technically where amplifier circuits using vacuum tubes required tube replacement at some place. The kids playing on the hillside often heard the hot vacuum tubes sizzle when they encountered rain or snow. When a tube failed, people complained that their TV had "gone out". Carl had a couple of other men who worked different mining shifts agree to replace tubes and check out the system as required.

Within weeks, almost everyone in town had purchased a TV set. The company store sold their stock of Zenith®, Bendix®, and RCA® televisions as fast as they could get them shipped in. The Baileys bought a 17-inch Bendix®, though Doug expressed some disappointment after seeing an ad in the Bluefield Daily Telegraph just a week or so after getting the television set. "If we would have just waited, RCA® is coming out with a 21" big screen next month."

Television had an almost overnight impact on the coal camp, bringing the world outside of the West Virginia coalfields straight into the homes of the miners. What were once rather insular towns now had access to national and world events through TV programs like the fifteen-minute Camel News Caravan with John Cameron Swayze. President Eisenhower was seen by more people than any other president in history because of his appearance on television. A new era of cultural experience started to shape the Appalachian experience.

The influence of New York and Los Angles was reaching into the hollers of Appalachia. Television began to consume more time. Wives tuned in daily to soap operas like The Guiding Light, a serial drama. The miners watched boxing, wrestling, baseball, football and Roy Rogers, the King of the Cowboys. Teenagers tuned into a new program out of Philadelphia called American Bandstand, hosted by a guy named Dick Clark. Younger kids watched Mickey Mouse Club. There was also a local program just for preschoolers called Ding Dong School with Miss Francis. The Snoop and Scope show from Bluefield was hosted by a couple of guys that became local would-be, cowboy stars as they presented western movies from the 1930s and 1940s. All and all it didn't take too long before everyone knew the TV schedule for each evening.

Television presented a common cultural experience for the coal camp population. People often started their conversations with "Did you see on TV last night...?" And if they were watching TV, they saw one of only three programs in the timeslot.

Television wasn't the only major system to impact the coal camp culture. The almost monopoly of the company store came to an abrupt halt in Covel. In November 1954, there was a rapid hard knock on the Baileys' door. Doug opened the door to find Ernest Repass who blurted, "The store is on fire!" Terry and Rick scrambled onto the front porch. They watched as smoke bellowed up from below the railroad trestle.

The Covel company store was an impressive three-story structure that had been built in the 1920s as the camp was developed. It housed a store carrying food and general merchandise, a post office, the payroll clerk's office, and the doctor's office. A movie theater had originally occupied the top floor of the store, but it had been removed shortly after World War II to make room for storing larger merchandise. As car ownership expanded after World War II, the company installed ESSO brand gasoline pumps.

The structure was wood framed with floors oiled to preserve and provide waterproofing for the hardwood. The building's heating system was a large coal furnace that heated a boiler that provided steam to the radiators throughout the building. The whole system was still original and on that very cold night, the furnace overheated when a valve failed to open. The resulting explosion caused a fire that burned through the night as the miners and their families watched in disbelief as they were helpless in trying to contain the fire. More explosions followed, some smaller and some major. Doug explained to his family, "Those are cans and bottles. Their contents are boiling from the heat and making them blow. There's a lot of ammunition there too." They heard shotgun and rifle shells going off in rapid succession as the fire raged. People were in disbelief and the fire frightened most of the children in the community. There were memories attached to the store.

By the next afternoon, all that was left of the company store was a huge pile of charred rubble with an occasional recognizable item that had somehow escaped the massive fire. The fire department, which was in Mullens about ten miles from the camp, was not able to save the building. The explosions and the shell discharges had presented a safety concern for both the fire fighters and onlookers. Fortunately, no one was injured.

The company store was the heart of a coal camp. It was always the largest building. While the school and church were important, they did not serve as the economic or social hub for the community. Coal companies had to provide the stores when the camps were first built, because there was no public transportation to cities and automobile ownership was almost non-existent at the time. It was an expansion on the general store of the nineteenth century. Some items were available for self-service, but clerks had to assist customers with retrieving most items. Locals tended to be hunters, so the company store maintained a good supply of shells. Miners could and usually did run a credit account with the store. The company deducted the total of a miner's tab from the miner's pay, and it was not unusual for a miner to owe more than he made – especially around the Christmas season.   Thus, the inspiration for Tennessee Ernie Ford's song. 16 Tons - Saint Peter don't call me cause I can't go, I owe my soul to the company store.

When the coal company rebuilt the store, they used a new concept of a metal shell building. The new building was not as large or as impressive as the original company store that had burned. Since it was only one story, inventory was limited to food and some hardware. Mr. Cline, the store manager, decided not to carry clothing or appliances any longer, citing the fact that more miners were getting their dry goods and appliances in Mullens, Beckley and Bluefield. The night the store burned was in some ways, the beginning of the end of the coal company camp economic system. The change in Covel was accelerated by fire.

Chapter 21 - Family, Community & Entertainment

The Baileys of Covel were not unlike most folks living in a coal camp. Doug had come from a farm where his parents and siblings knew how to tend the land and do all the necessary chores to keep the farm productive. The farm didn't provide their income for living. It was their living. Their food—both vegetables and meat—came from acres atop a knoll surrounded on three sides by the Bluestone River. They ate fresh fish, thanks to the river. Apple trees dotted the yard around the two-story wood frame farmhouse.

Times changed for the generation that was born in the 1920s. Farming and for some other Appalachian families, living off the land became less of a choice. Changing culture and values shifted with the rest of the country to "working for the man." Some folks called it public work which did not mean government or public assistance but that you worked outside of the home, and someone paid you to perform a task or produce a product.

Before the expansion of the coal industry in southern West Virginia, the sparsely settled hills had only self-sufficient families living from the land. This changed as mineral rights were purchased by corporations from Pittsburg, New York, and Boston. Doug was the second generation from his family to enter the coal industry. His father was a United Mine Worker union member who worked as a carpenter to repair company houses in coal camps. Doug's oldest brother, Orville had returned to the mines after he was discharged from the army.

Vergie's family was also dependent on the land. Her father was an independent barter, cattle broker, and family farmer. Two of Vergie's sisters married coal miners that lived in the coal camp at Piedmont. The sisters, Marie, and Helen were at home at Piedmont when the word came that their mother and brother Donald had died.

Large families were the norm. You needed working hands to keep growing crops and tending the livestock. When folks started moving into public work and did not have time nor need the farm, the number of children per family started to decrease. Probably this was by design since the expanded needs and cost of raising a child was growing.

Family connections were essential. The expectation that you visited the home place was a given. Doug and Vergie would take the boys to Rock for the Baileys and Littlesburg for the Terry connection, almost every Sunday and always Thanksgiving, Christmas, and Easter.

The cousins relished playing together whenever they visited. They enjoyed adventures around the farm, especially exploring the garage, the barn and its hayloft, and the smoke house where the family cured meat and smoked it with oak and apple woods. As one of the oldest grandchildren in the Bailey family, Terry became a playtime ringleader, but there were times where his judgment, knowledge and lack of experience caught up with him.

One Sunday, when Terry was ten, he set his mind to demonstrating a scientific principle to his younger cousins at his Grandparent Baileys' home. He had recently learned how to create an electromagnet by wrapping battery wire around a large metal bolt and attaching the wires to a battery. His cousins were interested in Terry's project. Ever a scientist and a showman, he told them, "I have an idea. If we get more electricity, the magnet would be stronger. I think I know how to do that." With this statement, Terry removed the wires from the battery and led his six cousins to the dining room where he held one wire in each hand and inserted each wire into the electrical socket on the side wall.

Bang!

The sound rang out from the dining room with a puff of black smoke and an awful smell and one grandson, Terry pushed down halfway across the floor. Terry felt a tingling in his body as he heard the stampede of adults approach from the living room, the front porch and kitchen to see what had happened. While Terry sat stunned, some younger cousins stood crying and a couple of the older cousins knew enough to declare, "It wasn't me!"

The fuse had blown, and Terry saw that the wall had a good-sized circle of black soot, and the electrical receptacle was melted. The "shock" of the experience had left Terry a little out of breath, and now he was worried about repercussions. Vergie leaned over her son and asked if he was alright. Doug's first reaction was a little less understanding. He was angry about the damage and possible harm to Terry and the other kids. He was preparing to give Terry a punishment with the belt, but the rest of the adults persuaded him that Terry had been punished enough. So, he calmed the situation with a big chuckle, saying, "Well, I guess that's one way to learn about electricity. I bet he won't do that again."

Granddad reassured everyone, "I have some paint and can touch this up. I think I have another receptacle in the garage too and plenty of fuses in the basement by the fuse box."

As a teacher near the end of the next decade, Terry would demonstrate the electromagnet using a dry cell battery.

But the legend of that first electrical experiment would live on for years at family gatherings.

* * *

The Bailey grandparents' bedroom was explicitly off-limits to the grandchildren. Terry had never been in the bedroom, and as far as he knew, none of the other grandchildren had either. But one of those Sundays when Terry was ten, he opened the door to his grandparents' bedroom. It smelled nice when he walked into the room. He looked around and noticed the large, tall bed and a dresser with a big round mirror. On one wall, Granddad Bailey kept his guns on a mounted rack – a couple of shotguns, a rifle, and a revolver. The large target pistol caught Terry's eye, and he went right to it. "This looks just like the six-shooters the cowboys use in the movies!" Terry thought. Without much other thought, he removed the gun from the rack and started toward the door.

"Boy, lay the gun on the bed. Don't drop it," Granddad commanded firmly from the door by which he happened to be passing. Terry turned immediately and placed the pistol on top of the bedspread.

"I wasn't going to shoot it! I was just going to show it to Richard Lane," Terry said in a quivering voice. He recognized from granddad's tone that he was in trouble.

"You can't be messing with guns, and you should not be in here," Granddad said. Hearing the interaction, Terry's Mother stepped in the room and saw Terry at the edge of the bed with the pistol.

She screamed, "Oh no! Don't never touch a gun!"

She became flushed in the face and starting down in a faint when granddad reached for her arm and pulled her up.

He helped her out of the room, at the same time yelling back to Terry, "Come on out of there right now and close the door!" Stunned by his mother's reaction, Terry did as he was directed.

Terry had never seen his mother react in this way. He knew that he had done something terrible. He hadn't intended to shoot the gun. He had just wanted to see it closer and to show it to his cousin Richard Lane. Sobbing on the sofa in the living room, Vergie called to Doug who had been on the porch smoking, "Doug get in here!"

When Doug understood what happened, he knew it reminded Vergie about her mother and brother's death almost 11 years before. In her mind, she could see a flash of memory of her brother and mother being shot. It was too real for her to see her son with a gun. Doug embraced Vergie and reassured her that it would be all right. Terry was really frightened to see his parents like this.

"Boy, you should never touch a gun without me being there. You know that. You ain't allowed to touch my shotgun."

Terry responded, "Yes dad, I know."

"You are going to get a whipping for this."

"Doug don't whip him. You are mad. I am upset. We can't punish the kids for things that happened in the past," Vergie said quietly as her sobs subsided and she used a tissue to wipe away her tears.

On the way back to Covel that day, very little was said. Terry could not understand why his mother was so upset. He had messed up many times, but she never cried or got so red in the face. She had never told him about his Grandmother Terry or his Uncle Donald's deaths. And she never would talk to him or anyone about the tragedy.

Forged by Coal

On another Sunday in Rock, Terry and his cousins were engaged in a game of Follow-the-Leader. They explored outside the house until it started to rain, forcing the following and the exploring inside the house. Terry led the group up the stairs to the hallway on the second floor. He had seen granddad go into the attic through a small door at the back of the house on this floor. Wouldn't it be fun for the cousins to see inside the attic?

Terry turned the knob and lead the cousins into the attic. Terry found a light switch beside the door. The light revealed some boxes and a few other dusty items. Vickie started opening the large box next to the door when the last of the cousins entered. , Terry for a reason that he would not be able to figure out, closed the door.

Click!

"I don't like it in here. It's hot and smells," Cousin Arthur complained.

"Ok, let's go." Terry pushed on the door, but it would not open. The spring knob had locked the door from the outside.

"We are locked in!" Vickie screamed as Arthur tried unsuccessfully to push against the door.

The children screamed, cried and banged on the door to get the attention of the adults downstairs. Eventually, they came charging up the stairs to see what had happened. Arthur's dad, Melvin, opened the door, exclaiming, "What on earth are you all doing in here? Don't you have any sense?"

Vickie and Arthur, simultaneously chimed in "Terry brought us up here!"

Doug, who was at the bottom of the steps, spoke, "Terry, get down here. What are you doing? You know better than to get in the attic." Doug's face was red with embarrassment that his oldest had managed to lock himself, his younger brother and four young cousins in the attic.

Terry may have missed his dad's wrath on most occasions, but he wasn't so lucky that day. Doug took Terry by the arm and dragged him outside where he gave Terry the last belt-whipping he would ever receive. It was also the last day Terry would ever lead his cousins in an exploring adventure.

* * *

One year, Vergie's oldest brother, Kenneth Terry—known to her children as Uncle Kenneth—came to visit with his girlfriend, Jessie. They had travelled to Covel by bus from Bluefield since Kenneth did not drive. The bus ran twice a day between Mullens and Bluefield. The bus ride wasn't but a few minutes longer than a car ride. Kenneth was a middle-aged bachelor and often explained that he was "just waiting for the right one". Jessie was older than Vergie. The brothers would say she wore lots of "powder", and you could smell her perfume anywhere in the room.

Kenneth had served in the army during World War II. He was in Germany with the occupation force when his mother and brother died. Probably because he was single, his discharge was delayed. Soldiers with dependents were discharged first.

Terry and Rick thought it was fun to have company even though the boys had to give up their room for the guests and sleep in the living room.

"Doug, let's go to the carnival!" Kenneth suggested. "I will pay the admission. You drive us down there. What do you say?"

Every year, the traveling carnival visited the coalfields of Appalachia, providing an escape from the miners' labor and the day-to-day life of the coal camp community. The carnival had a midway of amusement rides for kids and adults, exotic food, games of skill and chance, carousels with full-sized horses, lions, giraffes, thrill acts and freak shows.

The Baileys always spent at least one evening or a Saturday at the carnival when it was visiting Wyoming County, so Doug agreed. "We thought we would go. The boys really enjoy the rides."

Four full-sized adults and two boys, ages 12 and 7, piled into Doug's new '57 Plymouth. Terry, Jessie, and Kenneth sat in the back and Rick sat between mom and dad in the front. Doug pushed the "R" button to back the car out of the driveway, remarking, "These push buttons don't work like they should. I think they have got some work to do to get this right."

It was just getting dusk when Doug parked. The carnival always drew a good crowd.

"Doug, you, and Vergie go on and have some fun. Jessie and I will keep an eye on the boys." Kenneth offered.

"Oh, they will be ok. We will meet them back at ticket booth at 8:30," Doug responded.

"I have my Timex on, and we will be here at 8:30." Terry held up his wrist as he grabbed Rick's arm to pull him toward the rides.

Vergie stopped them before they could get very far. "Here's some money for rides and remember don't get cotton candy, candied apples, or popcorn until you finish riding. You will get that stuff all over you."

Kenneth pulled a couple of bills from his wallet and handed one to each of the boys. "Here's a two-dollar bill for each of you. Don't spend it all in one place." He laughed at his own joke.

The boys ran toward the twirling swings. Kenneth and Jessie walked slowly after them. Doug took Vergie's hand and said, "Let's go down the midway and see if they have anything we ain't seen."

As they walked down the midway, it appeared about the same as years past. But the fortune teller's tent caught Vergie's eye. "Doug let's get our fortune told. I have never done that."

Doug shrugged, "I don't believe in that stuff, do you?"

"It will be fun, let's see what she has to say."

They approached the entrance just as a couple was coming out of the tent. The couple looked at each other with puzzled expressions, and Doug and Vergie overheard them say, "Do you think she could be right?" The sign at the entrance promised that "Madam Cleo Can See Your Future." Doug gave the barker two dollars for the reading. Doug smiled as they sat down at the round table. A crystal ball the size of a bowling ball sat in the center. Behind it sat Madam Cleo wearing a bright multicolor dress—part evening gown, part peasant dress. She topped it with a red and blue headscarf.

Doug and Vergie watched Madam Cleo slip into a slight trance. She started to mumble quietly, her voice becoming clearer as she told Doug and Vergie about their past: "Some wonderful times, the love of each but also you share tragedy and disappointment." Doug thought this could be said about any married couple as Madam Cleo continued a list of general statements. Then she paused, and reaching for Vergie's left

239

hand, she said, "Let me see your palm, madam. I see lines in your hand that show you have had pain; some more is to come." She looked at Doug and nodded to a sign pinned to the canvas above the table:

PALM READING $5.00

Finding himself caught up in the moment and not wanting to break Madam Cleo's concentration, Doug opened his wallet and dropped a Lincoln on the table.

She continued, "I see that you will bear four children. You and your husband will have much joy. You will have grandchildren that will bring you happiness, both granddaughters and grandsons." The fortune teller continued with some general financial advice and travel plans, but Vergie and Doug were already distracted. After the reading, the couple left the tent. Doug expressed his skepticism, "She could mumble a lot, but she didn't really tell us anything. And she got the number of kids wrong."

Vergie replied, "Yeah, almost anyone could guess we had kids and they will have kids when they grow up. It's about time to meet the kids, Kenneth, and Jessie"

The boys arrived back at the designated meeting point on time and ready for the return home. They were out of money and had sugar on their sleeves where they had wiped their mouths after eating caramel apples.

"We rode almost everything! We didn't do the merry-go-round. Not fast like the other rides," Rick said. The boys were tired and didn't say much on the way back to Covel.

The adults talked about a possible strike by the coal miners. Rumors were circulating. Kenneth worked as a lineman on the repair crew for the Norfolk and Western Railroad. If a coal strike came, it would probably cut back on overtime for the railroad workers. The union had a contract with all the coal companies that dictated the working conditions and salaries for coal miners, but that contract was set to expire at the end of the year. The miners were interested in keeping their health benefits, increasing wages, and building the pension fund, but according to the union leaders, the coal companies were not giving much during negotiations. "They want to cut out company doctors," Doug declared. "I don't think we can let them do that. There will be a strike if necessary."

"Have you heard that N&W is trying to buy the Virginian Railway?" Doug asked.

"We hear about mergers all the time. I know they would like to have Virginian out. More money for them." Kenneth quipped. "But I don't see how it would work. Virginian's got electric and N&W only uses diesel. I don't want to work on electrical lines. Too high off ground and too much current. Would they just close a line? In some places like Princeton and Roanoke, they run side by side."

Doug added, "Only Virginian serves our mines in this county. They would have to continue their use."

"Let's just hope they settle the contract before a strike and that N & W forgets about getting the Virginian," Vergie chimed in.

Harry Carrico, the owner of the Wyoming Theater in Mullens, had built the local drive-in theater around 1951 on route 10 near Bud, another coal camp about four miles toward Mullens, coming from Covel. Playing double features of movies that had already left the traditional indoor theaters, it became a very popular venue for the Baileys and the miners. Terry and Rick particularly liked westerns, especially Hondo with John Wayne and Riding Shotgun with Randolph Scott. But the movie that both boys would always remember seeing at the drive-in was The Ten Commandments with Charlton Heston as Moses. The family marveled at the great special effects of the Red Sea parting.

The drive-in's concession stand building stood in the middle of the parking area. For refreshments, the family usually got popcorn and "pop", as they referred to soft drinks. The length of two movies plus the cartoon and coming attractions required at least one visit to the restrooms.

The concession building's roof also served as a stage for live entertainment, such as bands performing with singers. On one of the live entertainment nights, The Foggy Mountain Boys performed, featuring Lester Flatt and Earl Scruggs. The group had not yet achieved the national fame that would come in the next decade when they found commercial success with theme songs for the popular television series The Beverly Hillbillies and the movie Deliverance. That evening, the group conducted a local talent search, inviting audience-goers onto the concession stand stage to sing with them. Rick participated by singing "The Ballad of Davy Crocket" with Flatt and Scruggs. He wore a "coonskin cap" on his head during his premier performance. His family and the capacity crowd enjoyed the performance, and Rick came to be noted as a young talent in the region. As a teenager, Rick would be the vocalist for a group that played high school dances. The group named "The Rejects" would end when the boys graduated from high school.

Covel had a community swimming hole thanks to the coal company. Mack Lambert who could operate a bulldozer was allowed to dam up the main branch of the Gooney Otter Creek. Rock was hauled in to add re-enforcement to the dirt dam to provide for a swimming area in a creek that usually was too shallow for swimming. Terry was allowed to go up the "holler" to swim provided that older kids were going to be present.

Returning from the swimming hole on the Gooney Otter Creek, Terry, Daniel, David, and Arlene Fine.

The swimming hole.

Chapter 22 –Death. Do the Right Thing. A Strike.

The week after the carnival, Terry attended his Boy Scout Troop meeting where G.C. Cecil, the Assistant Scoutmaster, conducted the meeting. Alvin Belcher, the Church's Pastor came down the steps to the basement and asked G.C. and his younger brother Rickey—a member of the troop—to come out with him.

Pastor Belcher came back after a few minutes and said to the troop members, "Boys, I have some sad news, G. C. and Rickey's dad, George, was killed in a mining accident just a couple hours ago. It seems like he was riding in the front mine cart on the way out of the mines when a fully loaded mine cart came back in the mines and mashed into their mine cart. It tore up the rigs bad. A couple other miners are in the hospital. So, let's bow our heads and pray for G.C., Rickey, their family and the other miners that were hurt."

After a long minute, the boys raised their heads, and the meeting ended shortly thereafter. Terry and some of the other Covel boys rode their bikes back up the road toward home. When Terry got home, he told his mother about Mr. Cecil.

Vergie replied, "I just heard about it from Lucille. She had come from the store where the word was out. Very tragic. I am going up to the Cecil house and see who is with Gracie. I think probably Jenny Jones or Beulah Hurst are there."

Vergie walked up the front road to the Cecil home. She saw that Jenny and Beulah were both there and Janice, the Cecil's daughter, had just come in. She was a newly graduated nurse who had started work at the Princeton Hospital. Jenny

Jones had called her about her father's death and Janice had come home straightaway.

Three days later a funeral was held at the Baptist Church for George C. Cecil, Sr. The church was so packed that an overflow crowd stood outside. Someone had raised the windows so that they could hear the service. Terry and the other Scouts attended in their uniforms to show respect for their Scout leader, G. C., and their fellow Scout, Rickey. Both Cecil Brothers along with their sister, Janice and their other brother, Verland came out of the church with the casket. Other miners served as pall bearers. They stood three on each side carrying the dark wood casket to the waiting hearse, operated by the Fogelson Funeral Home in Mullens.

Vergie and Doug had decided to go to the burial at Roselawn Memorial Gardens in Princeton. This was the first time Terry and Rick had experienced a funeral procession. The looked backward and forward at the long line of cars with their headlights on. A Wyoming County Sheriff's Deputy led the group to the top of the mountain where a Mercer County Deputy's car joined the procession for the remainder of the trip to the cemetery in Princeton.

As the procession of cars entered the expansive, newly opened cemetery, Doug said, "You know, I think Wally sold them their plots. He told me a bunch of folks in Covel had gotten burial plots. I am pretty sure they got them from him." Wally was the salesmen of the family. He and his wife, Faye, had gotten jobs with Roselawn Memorial Gardens. While church and country cemeteries depended on volunteers to maintain them and usually did not have much cost associated with the burials, this was a new, perpetual care, for-profit cemetery. Wally was a traveling salesman peddling pre-need plots on a monthly payment plan. Faye worked in the office as the bookkeeper.

"They have marked where the gardens are going. There is the "Last Supper" on the right. That's where our plots are." Vergie stated referring to the four plots that Wally had sold them. This section of the cemetery would include a large sculpture based on Leonarda DaVinci painting, "The Last Supper." After the purchase, Vergie had wondered why they needed four plots. The boys would marry, and they would want to be buried with their wives. Nevertheless, they would pay off the cost of four plots within the next two years.

The procession of cars reached from the Garden of the Good Shepherd around half of the circle and down the hill almost to the entrance, probably close to 80 vehicles. After a brief prayer and a graveside message, the family laid flowers on the casket, which sat suspended above the grave opening. Somberly, the mourners made their way through the receiving line to express their condolences to the Cecil family. Gracie and Janice thanked each one for coming by. The men didn't say much as their heads were lowered with lips almost trembling. The Cecil men were like most of the males in the coal camps, they felt deeply but had a difficult time expressing their emotions. In many cases it wasn't expected that men would have an outward expression of how they felt especially in sorrow.

Later, Gracie confided in Vergie that she was glad that Verland was working in a foundry up in Connecticut and G.C. had taken a job as the custodian at the elementary school in Covel. I just hope Rickey doesn't go in the mines either. Over the years, each of her boys found their way into the mines, against Gracie's wishes. Verland, anxious to return to his home state, took a mining job. Rickey attended Nashville Technical College for automobile technician training and worked for a short while in the automotive field but eventually went into the mines.

G. C. worked at the Covel Elementary School as the custodian, but his job only extended through the school months and a couple of weeks in the summer. One summer, he took a temporary job with a strip-mining operation. Strip mining is done by removing large amounts of rock and dirt with heavy construction equipment. There are no mines to enter. The coal seams are near the surface and can be loaded directly onto trucks to be taken to the tipple for processing.

During that summer employment, G. C. was riding on a Caterpillar tractor as it traveled below the base of the cut away from the hill. Just as he jumped off the tractor one day, a large boulder came off the ridge of the hill. The boulder rolled down the embankment, crushing G.C. and stealing a second loved one from his family.

Once again, the Scouts donned their uniforms and attended an even larger funeral. The trip to Roselawn Memorial Gardens was repeated. This time, it seemed much sadder for a man in his twenties who had just come back from Scout Camp. The people of Covel would miss G.C. As Terry changed out of his uniform, he remembered the scout lessons that G. C. had taught him and the other boys of Troop 140. He had a clear recollection of the first time he recited the Scout Oath in front of the troop with G.C. and Scoutmaster Curtis Helmandollar standing with him.

Death. Do the Right Thing. A Strike

On my honor, I will do my best
To do my duty to God and my country
 and to obey the Scout Law;
To help other people at all times
To keep myself physically strong, mentally awake
and morally straight

. * * *

As Terry grew up in Covel and before he graduated from high school there would be three additional miners to lose their lives while on the job. The men were Holland McBride who was the father of Terry's classmate Wade, Carl Marsh, the father of David, a fellow scout and friend who later photographed Terry's wedding, and Sid Smith, the father of good friends of Terry's brother, Rickey.

. * * *

Scout Troop 140 faced more tragedy later that year. In the fall, two of its members, Billy Lusk, and Freddy Taylor, got their parents' permission to go hunting on a Saturday. With shotguns in tow, they hiked up Herndon Mountain, following along the community antenna wire. At the top of the mountain, they walked across an open field that someone had farmed over the past summer. On the other side of the field, as they made their way toward the wooded area, they spied a couple of rabbits. But the rabbits ran deeper into the woods before the boys could raise their guns.

After an unsuccessful couple of hours searching for prey, Billy and Freddy started back. They decided to save distance by taking a route down the steeper part of the hillside. Crossing the field, they had to climb a wire fence. As Billy pulled through with his shotgun in one hand and the other hand on the fence, the gun recoiled. As the gun fired, it was only four feet from Freddy. Blood erupted as the pellets from the 20 gauge struck the side of Freddy's face and head.

He fell from the impact at the edge of the field. Billy, dropped his gun and reached over to Freddy. As he saw the blood flowing from the side of Freddy's face, Billy turned and began to run down the hill to get help for his friend.

Terry was playing with Jerry and Wade in the school yard as the ambulance and sheriff's car came to a stop at the company store. The boys ran across the road to see what was happening. They overheard the ambulance driver saying, "We need some help in finding this boy that was shot on the mountain."

"Don't know what you're talking about," a store clerk shot back.

About that time, Roger—Freddy's older brother by about 18 months—came running down the road, shouting, "Come on up the holler!" Billy had run home and told his mother what had happened. She, in turn, ran to Freddy's Mother, and they had called for an ambulance

The deputy and the two men with the ambulance needed a guide to find the right spot on the hill. No vehicle could reach the place where Freddy had fallen, so they would have to carry the boy out on a stretcher. Terry, Wade and Jerry piped up at that point, "We know the place. We can show you."

The boys lead the way up the hillside with the men behind carrying a stretcher, a medical bag and an oxygen tank. Wade walked in front of Terry and almost stumbled over Freddy. "Oh no!" Wade breathlessly yelled as his foot landed in blood. Freddy was dead.

"Probably died as soon as he was shot," The ambulance driver stated, shaking his head. The two men from the ambulance placed Freddy on the stretcher. The deputy picked up the two shot guns and unloaded them. The party made their way back down the hillside, with Terry carrying the oxygen tank and Wade carrying the medical bag.

Freddy's Mother remained silent throughout the service. At the wake the evening before, all she could muster to the women that came to her was, "They can't open the casket, I can't see my boy."

The boys of Covel would rarely talk about the accident, although Scouts served as pall bearers for Freddy's final services. The boys really did not know how to deal with the tragic accident that affected their friends. It seemed hard for the boys to figure it out and so no one would bring up the sad situation. Eventually, Billy left Covel to stay with his older brother who lived in Tennessee. He visited home on the holidays, but he never again lived at his parents' home.

* * *

Later that year, just before Terry's twelfth birthday, he started his first newspaper route for the Raleigh Register—an afternoon paper produced in Beckley, West Virginia. The position would last through the summer. Ben Murphy, the route manager for the paper, brought the bundle of newspapers to Covel each day to be delivered. Terry noticed that the Raleigh Register wasn't as popular as the morning paper from Bluefield, The Bluefield Daily Telegraph. He figured people liked to get their paper before breakfast and knew that many of the folks living in Covel had come from or had relatives in the Bluefield area.

Ben Murphy told Terry about a contest where he could win prizes if he increased circulation. Terry went in earnest to each of the 68 homes to recruit customers. He did gain some customers, and he expanded his route around the hill and to Garwood, about a half mile east on Route 10. Ben

Murphy was pleased by the results of his effort and to have additional customers. Terry didn't win the grand prize, but Ben Murphy did give him a trucker's wallet with a chain to keep the $1.80 in subscription fees he collected from his customers each month.

When his stint with the Raleigh Register came to an end, the local postmaster, Mrs. Akers, asked Terry if he would like to deliver the Bluefield Daily Telegraph. Terry knew the route had twice as many customers and that he would not have to go all the way to Garwood. Most importantly, since it was a morning route, he knew that it would not interfere with his position as manager of the high school's basketball team which required him to stay after school.

Mrs. Akers recommended that the paper offer Terry the Covel paper route. There had been complaints that the folks delivering the route were not delivering it in a timely fashion. On some occasions, people had received their paper after noon. Mrs. Akers wrote a letter to the paper complaining about the service. Since she was the postmaster and represented some of the other concerned customers, the paper was happy to take her recommendation. So, for almost five years, Terry got up by 6 a.m. went to the highway bus stop building to pick up his bundle of daily newspapers. Over the years, he expanded his total number of customers and delivered to, at one point, sixty of the 68 homes.

Terry's encounters on his paper route were generally mundane, but there were a few exceptions. During one of his morning routes, Terry overheard two miners talking while they waited for a ride. They were smoking as they leaned against the cinder block wall of the small building. The younger man said, "I tried to talk to Gerald, and he just cussed me out. We ask Brother Carl Marsh to talk with him. You know, there ain't no better man than Carl. He leads the Christian life and knows the way, but Gerald just almost hit Carl when Carl told him that he should not be beating up his wife."

The older miner responded, "Well Gerald should have listened. It ain't right to hit a woman. Especially your wife, mother of your kids. His wife is young. They got married when he was in the army. "

"Well, I guess he knows not to hit her anymore. But his arm should be ok in a couple of months." The miner smirked.

Terry discovered that some of the miners on Gerald's shift had decided to explain to Gerald the right way to treat his woman. The miners' wives had probably let their husbands know what was going on. This was part of doing the right thing, code of the coal camps.

. * * *

One Sunday morning, Terry was loading up his two canvas delivery bags with the paper when he noticed a very drunk older miner standing at the bus stop building with an equally drunk woman. Terry recognized the man from the camp and knew that the woman was not his wife. Since Sunday's paper was much thicker than the other days of the week, and there were three bundles to be opened, it was taking Terry longer than usual to get the papers ready for delivery.

"Boy, you want to see this lady naked?" The man slurred loudly. Terry just shook his head and rushed to get the bundles opened and in the bags.

"Look, I will hold her down and you can go at her," the man continued and moved toward the woman who remained silent.

Terry, very red-faced mumbled, "No, I have to get these papers out."

"Augh, come on have some fun. You afraid?"

Terry was afraid, but he answered, "I have to go, and I won't say anything to anybody about you all being here." With that, he picked up his delivery bags and the last bundle and rushed away from the building to his bike.

"That's right, you ain't seen nothing. You could have seen something, but you didn't. Ha!" The man roared in his drunken state as he sat on the concrete floor. Terry was relieved to be on his way. He never did tell anyone about the encounter.

Terry almost saw another younger woman naked. While collecting for the paper, one of the prettiest girls in the camp, Nora "Shibo" Davis, a high school senior, answered the door wrapped in a towel. At age of 13, Terry was quite nervous. She nonchalantly told Terry her folks had gone to Mullens, and she didn't have any money to pay the paper bill.

"That...that's okay," Terry stammered as he walked backwards down the steps away from the porch. I will come back." For some reason, this encounter was more interesting and not as scary as the one at the bus stop.

* * *

Terry was collecting the newspaper from Mrs. Akers one morning when she introduced him to the idea of postage stamp collecting. Terry was at the new post office building, which had been built to replace the burned company store. He was entering the combination on Box 68 when Mrs. Askers exclaimed "Terry, look at the new stamps coming out this year!" He had mentioned to her that he recently sent a box top from a Cheerios cereal box plus twenty-five cents to the H.E.

Harris Stamp Company in Boston Massachusetts in exchange for a small sack of used foreign and U.S. stamps. She was enthusiastic about the postal service and was glad to share her enthusiasm with someone who was interested.

Mrs. Akers explained how the first day of issue of new stamps occurred. She shared the postal announcement and would explain how to get the new first day cover. This sparked Terry's lifelong interest in stamp collecting and postal operations.

Mail arrived at the fourth class Covel post office twice a day by railroad. Verland Cecil had the job of taking the outgoing mail bag to the rail drop off and attaching the bags to the mail crane so that the railway personnel could collect the bags as the train travelled by without stopping. Incoming mail bags for the camp were tossed onto to the ground for Verland to pick up. A morning eastbound train and an afternoon westbound provided delivery of the mail. By the end of 1959, the train delivery had stopped, and truck delivery began twice a day.

* * *

Mrs. Akers' husband, George, had retired from the mines. He was the only man in the camp that didn't go to work each day. Instead, he kept busy with chores and maintaining the post office building. He cleaned out litter from the creek in front of his house. George had been in the army and had fought in World War I. He had been to France and was probably one of the very few in the community that had ever been to Europe. He didn't say much about the war or even about going to Paris.

The custodian at Herndon High, Mr. Whitt, had also been in World War I. He had suffered from a mustard gas attack. He did tell the boys, "Those French gals were pretty wild."

. * * *

When there was regular work in the mines, a miner did make good money. For labor, coal mining paid the best. There were slow downs when orders for coal dropped off. Then there was the possibility of a strike when it was contract renewal time.

A lengthy strike occurred in the coal industry in 1959. The companies wanted to cease providing medical services and start funding an insurance program. The miners were not sure about the change, and they also wanted improved wages and pension benefits. When the company did not readily agree to the union's terms, the miners went on strike. During the strike, the miners received some funds from the union's strike fund but nothing comparable to their wages.

As a result of this strike, Doug lost his 1957 Plymouth to a repossession by the finance company. Doug answered the knock at the door, and the middle-aged man in a dark green work shirt and pants stated somberly, "Mr. Bailey, I am here to get your car since you haven't made payments now for four months. Do you want to drive it out of town and let us take it on the highway, so nobody sees us take it away?"

"Nay, everybody knows we aren't working, and others' have been picked up. Here's my keys and I will get my wife's," Doug replied. "I don't care to see it go. That car has been in service for the transmission a couple times, and I still don't think it's right." Doug handed the man both set of keys.

It had been Doug's first new car. It was a fancy ride with a sharp white paint job and red trim and sleek fins that were new for the 1957 model. He would miss it. Their inaugural trip with the car had been to take Terry, David Marsh, and Wade McBride to Scout Camp in Virginia. The trunk was big enough to hold all their gear.

As Doug and his friend, Carl, watched the Plymouth disappear up the road, Doug quietly lamented the fact that he had already made half the payments on the car.

Carl said, "Doug, I think I know where you can get a car that will be a good one. My wife's father died last month, and he had a Dodge that he didn't drive out of the county the last three or four years. It's a 1950 but runs like a new one."

"Might as well take a look at it," Doug replied, turning away from the flashy Chrysler.

Carl was right about the Dodge. It ran well and wasn't worn-looking at all. "My wife and her sister were his only kids. His son was killed in Korea. So, I think we can let you have it for a reasonable price," Carl offered. They came to an agreement, and Doug drove away. They still had the Dodge when it came time for Terry to learn to drive. In fact, it became his first car.

After almost nine months, the strike came to an end. With his regular wages restored, Doug bought a fully equipped Ford Fairlane 500 with only one previous owner. It was white with grey and gold trim. He kept his Dodge as his work car, using it to travel to and from the tipple every day. It was a manual transmission while the Ford was an automatic transmission and suited Vergie. Doug never bought another new Chrysler product. He would say, "I've been burned once, don't need to get burned again." He was referring to the transmission problems he had with the 57 Plymouth. He stayed in the Ford and Chevrolet family of automobiles.

Forged by Coal

Chapter 23 – Do you want to buy a house?

In 1920, the Covel Coal Company opened the mine and built the town of Covel, including the houses, company store, roads, and bridges, and they helped the community to construct churches. From the start, the company had administered the housing. By 1958, American Coal Company owned Covel and had little interest in continuing as landlord and administrator of a community. Housing demand had dramatically decreased as the total workforce declined due to mining automation.

"I hear the company is going to sell the houses," Mrs. Akers said in a matter-of-fact tone as Vergie purchased a booklet of postage stamps. The rate had gone up the month before increasing the cost of a stamp to four cents.

Vergie replied, "I have heard that before, but I don't see how they can make people buy the houses. I don't think I would want the one we are in."

"What they are going to do—according to what George heard from Mr. Hill—is they are going to sell the whole place to a company. Then that company is going to sell them individually."

"I don't think it's right to make someone have to move or buy a place," Vergie said, disgusted.

It wasn't but a couple of weeks before an article appeared in the weekly newspaper, *The Mullens Advocate*, announcing that American Coal had sold their houses to Lilly Land Company of Princeton. The Lilly Land name was well known in the southern counties of West Virginia. Jackson Lilly, the company's founder, had developed most of the housing that wasn't owned by the coal companies in Mercer, Wyoming, and Raleigh counties.

After the article, Lilly Land sent a letter to all the renters. The letter gave instructions on how to pay the rent to Lilly Land or how to buy the house. Renters had first choice and were given 60 days to decide if they wanted their house. If they decided not to purchase the house, it would be offered for sale on the open market. Up to this point, the rent had been paid to the company directly out of the miners' pay, but the new owners explained that the practice would stop on July 1. They expected rent to be paid by the middle of the month and included a couple of pre-addressed envelopes. There were no postage stamps on the envelopes.

As the miners' families made their decisions in the spring and summer of 1958, work crews hired by Lilly Land Company replaced all the black tarpaper roof coverings with multi-toned asphalt shingles, which started to brighten each home. Then all the white houses were repainted with bright colors. Families who planned to purchase their house and placed a deposit down could choose the color. The colors were pastel hues of blue, yellow, and pink or beige.

While the work was happening, Terry, Darrell and David Jones stood on the railroad tracks near the end of the railroad trestle looking down into the camp. "Looks sort of like an Easter basket with colored eggs," Terry remarked, noting the green of the spring growth against the freshly painted houses.

"Doug, I don't want this place. I never have liked being next to the creek. There is a lot of cracks in the plaster and the hall floor is not level," Vergie exclaimed.

"Somebody else will probably buy it since they are offering the payment plan. It figures out to about $47 a month. It's a lot higher than rent, but you own the place in five years."

"I wonder if Geneva and Carl are going to buy their house." Vergie was referring to the Underwoods' house across the road from theirs. "Geneva said they might go to Bud. It would be closer to her folks. If they aren't going to buy their place, let's get it."

Vergie did check with Geneva who said that they had not made up their mind but would let Vergie and Doug know what they decided. "We got some time to think it over," Geneva reminded Vergie.

When the 60-day period was almost up, Geneva came over to the Baileys' front porch and told Vergie, "It looks like we have a house in Bud and are going there. If you want our place, you should let them know before we tell them we are moving."

As soon as Doug got in from work, Vergie told him what Geneva had said. With a big grin, he said, "Go ahead and let them know we will buy the house. They have a storage building too. I know we can put a bathroom in. Let's do it."

The Baileys were buying a house. Like most of the miners, this was their first house purchase. Now each property would be owned privately, and the company would no longer be responsible for the living conditions or the state of the community. The quality of the community's structures and the dwellings was dependent on the personal engagement of the residents who had purchased their homes.

The Underwoods asked for a couple of months' extension to move out. Vergie was anxious to move into her new home, but she understood that the Underwoods wanted to move after Christmas, and they agreed that the Underwoods could stay through December. It felt fitting for the Baileys to complete the Christmas holidays in the present house, and they would look forward to starting 1959 in their new home just across the road. On a cold but clear day in January, the Baileys – mom, dad, and two sons—with their neighbors' help, moved into their very first home of their own.

Lilly Land had offered to sell the houses to the miners, but that did not include the Black miners. There were only about a half a dozen Black families up the holler in what everyone, including the Black families, called the colored section. At one time there had been twenty houses with Black families. The one lane bridge crossing the upper branch of the Gooney Otter Creek had marked the division between the white and the "colored" part of the camp. This included the Washington family who knew that they would have to move out for new white owners. That was the way it was in West Virginia and all of the southern states at the time. Terry had often been in what was called the "colored school" and knew of the Black kids up the holler, but he never did know what happened to the Black kids once the homes were sold. He just knew the families had moved and had paid their newspaper bill before they left. Terry did not recall hearing any conversation by his parents or other adults about the end of the "colored" section of the camp. He would later just assume that was the way it was. You did not have whites and blacks buying homes in the same area.

Most of the white miners purchased their houses. It was the first step to disentangling their personal lives from the coal company. Up until that point, miners and their families were not accustomed to having checking accounts. Money orders issued at the post office were the usual method of payment if cash was not used. This included paying the house payment to Lilly Land, the car payment, and the Sears bill. The miners' wives generally took care of handling payments, and this was true for the Bailey family. "Doug, we should get a checking account at the bank in Mullens. It would save us on money order fees. I can write the checks and Terry can mail them. Saves me from going to the post office," Vergie explained.

"Go ahead. You are going to the People's Bank in Mullens?" Doug inquired.

"Yes, they have a drive-up, so you don't even have to park to deposit your money."

Banking was more convenient, cost less than postal money orders and was probably a better way to manage payments. Vergie was to discover how one miner's wife was diverting the house payment using postal money orders.

Vergie visited Lucille at her home across the street. They were having a cup of coffee in the kitchen when Lucille asked Vergie, "Did you hear about Sue Shrewsbury running off and keeping their house payments?" Vergie shook her head to indicate no, and Lucille continued, "She was getting money orders from Mrs. Akers here at the post office for the house payments, but instead of sending it to Lilly Land, she was taking it down to Herndon or Bud, putting her own name on it and cashing it."

"Why was she doing that?" Vergie asked.

"Looks like she was saving up the money to run off. You know she had been married before, and her girl isn't Larry's. The boy is his." Lucille continued, "It turns out she left with the girl yesterday when Larry was at work. She kept the girl home and sent the boy to school. When he got home, no one was there. That must be awful for the boy. Larry knew something was wrong, because he had seen a letter from Lilly Land about not making payments. Larry and Sue had words."

"I can't imagine how he must feel. Where did she go?" Vergie inquired.

"Somebody said that she has family out west—maybe Arizona—and that's where she was headed. It's a long drive." Nobody in the camp ever did learn anything about Sue and her daughter. Folks did not want to ask Larry, and he did not offer up any more information. Separation and divorce were very rare in the mining camps.

Chapter 24 – Easter 1959, End and Beginning

Spring came, and Vergie was excited that Doug was planning the bathroom for their new home. He had worked it out with some of his buddies. A tank for septic would be delivered from Beckley along with the pipes required for the drain field. The drain field would take most of the yard on one side of the house. Some folks who had houses on the side of the road next to the creek had run a pipe into the creek for drainage. This wasn't practical for Doug since he would have to run the pipes under the road and get permission to go through another lot. His plan was to have it dug up and set in his lot before the April rain.

Vergie stood on the porch watching the men unload the septic tank. She had felt a little lightheaded during morning and thought it would go away after her breakfast coffee, but she was still feeling "unsettled". She wondered if she may be entering the early stages of menopause, but at thirty-two, surely she was too young to be thinking this way.

As she went back into the house, it occurred to her, "Could I be pregnant?" She started rethinking her symptoms. It had been almost eight years since Rick was born. Could it be that she was going to have another child?

Over the next couple of weeks, Vergie continued having signs of pregnancy, and she became more certain that she was going to have her fourth child. Vergie decided to break the news on the day the bathroom was completed, just after Doug had tested the toilet, "Doug, you remember the fortune teller at the carnival?"

"Yea, she was full of it."

"Well, I think she may be right about one thing. I am pretty sure I am expecting our fourth baby." Vergie continues.

"Nay, are you sure?"

"I think so."

There were a few seconds of silence and then Doug grinned and hugged his wife of fourteen years and said, "It is going to be ok." "Doug, I know it is.", she responded with a slight sigh, thinking what was ahead in pregnancy.

Easter fell on the last Sunday in March that year. As usual, the Baileys piled into the Ford Fairlane 500 and crossed the mountain to attend services at the Rock Methodist Church. They left in time to attend Sunday school followed by the service. Terry and Rick were looking forward to the Sunday school class since they would be egg hunting and there would be Easter candy. Terry would be a teenager the following month, so this might be the last year for him to participate in the egg hunt, which was divided into two age brackets: seven and under and eight and above.

After the Sunday service, the sons and daughters of Lake and Cora met for the early dinner at the Bailey homeplace at Rock. Terry and Rick enjoyed the Easter ham, deviled eggs, and sweet potatoes. Of course, their favorites were the pecan and apple pies.

About midafternoon, Doug's family was the first to leave since they planned to go on to Aunt Mildred's and Uncle Nat's. Easter was even more special to the Terry sisters because. Aunt Carrie and Uncle Larry were visiting from New Jersey. Ruth, the oldest cousin, and Harry and their children were in from Norfolk, Virginia where Harry worked painting Lincoln Continentals at the Ford plant. He took pride in working in the luxury car factory.

As each guest arrived, Mildred explained, "Papa is feeling poorly. He has not had much to eat the last few days. He says he is very tired." Each of the daughters and sons-in-law engaged Papa Terry in a short conversation. He appeared more listless than usual. He did not play with the younger kids, but he did enjoy talking to his oldest grandson, Lowell, Helen, and George Davis oldest. Or as Lowell would say, the two liked to "shoot the bull" with Papa Terry. Lowell was 23 and had married his wife, Peggy, three years before. Papa Terry liked to barter, and he loved to share tales of his best trades in detail, especially reveling in the trades where he negotiated some "boot"—a little cash—with the trade.

Vergie and Doug had decided not to tell folks that they might be expecting another member of the family. Vergie reasoned to Doug, "I think it is too early. We haven't seen Carrie and Larry for a while. I would like to know how they are doing. I wish Clarence would come in too." Clarence had stayed in New Jersey and was recently married.

Carrie and Larry's son Lawrence James—Jimmy for short—had lost his battle with leukemia in 1949. He died in the Children's Hospital in Philadelphia. He was a year older than Terry. They had played together at Mildred's as toddlers.

"Vergie, you all should plan to come up to see us this summer when Doug gets his vacation. We had such a good time when you came in 56," Carrie urged.

"We will see. I hope there is no strike, and we are well," Vergie replied.

Terry and Rick joined in again and had the Easter Egg Hunt with cousins, first and second ones, from their mother's side of the family. Louise and Ruth, Mildred and Nat's daughters had children that were close to the age of Terry and Rick as second cousins.

The eggs for the hunt had come from Mildred and Nat's chickens. Mildred had saved them for a few days to have enough for coloring after they had been hard boiled. The colors were produced by dissolving a Paas dye tablet in a vinegar solution. In a way it was a waste. None of the kids would eat the hard-boiled eggs. They liked to hunt for them but preferred to eat the chocolate variety.

Driving home at twilight, Vergie told Doug, "I am glad I didn't tell anyone. If I am feeling all right, we ought to go to New Jersey for vacation."

Doug replied, "We will see."

A couple of days into the week, Vergie was feeling better. She flipped the page over on the Coca-Cola calendar—a gift her brother-in-law Junior Bailey had given all the family members last Christmas. Each month featured an attractive model dressed in a seasonal outfit holding a Coke bottle.

It was April 1st. April Fools' Day. Even before lunch at Covel Elementary, Rick had tired of the old gag: "Your shoes untied, April Fools'!" He busied himself developing new jokes to entertain his fellow second graders. "Anybody lose their milk money?" he asked, thinking he'd hit on something funny and original. "April Fools', I didn't find any!"

Terry's fellow seventh graders were not into the childish April Fools' jokes. Instead, one of the girls, Geneva, did wink at Terry and other boys. She would then hand them a note with APRIL FOOLS printed on it. This seemed to amuse the girls but escaped Terry and his pals.

Thursday night, Vergie could not sleep. She finally got up and sat in the living room for a while, hoping to doze off.

Doug rolled over to his right in bed and could tell instantly that Vergie was not there. He moved to his left to get up to check on her. "You all, right?", came from a sleepy Doug.

"Yes, I just can't sleep." She followed him back to bed and did fall halfway asleep when the alarm went off for Doug to get ready for work. "I can pack my lunch and get breakfast if you want to sleep," Doug told his wife.

"No, I have to get the boys off to school. Terry has already gone out for his paper route."

Vergie had packed Doug's lunch and was cracking eggs for breakfast when the phone rang. Vergie wondered who could this be wanting to talk so early?

"Doug, can you answer the phone?" He picked up the receiver from the phone in the living room. When he heard Mildred's voice on the other end of the line, Doug knew it was bad news. Mildred and Nat didn't make long distance calls.

"Papa died last night," Mildred delivered the news in her matter-of-fact style. "I am making arrangements. The service will be on Monday so everybody can get here."

Doug answered softly, "I will tell Vergie and we will call you back." He hung up the phone.

Doug came into the kitchen and was looking slightly down and almost in a whisper he said, "Vergie, Papa Terry passed last night."

Vergie sighed, "He has not been doing well for a while." She paused as her eyes filled with tears.

Doug hugged her and whispered, "So sorry, Vergie, so sorry."

Vergie sobbed, "I will call Mildred."

Doug interjected, "Not yet. She is calling others and will have more details after she talks to the funeral home. She thinks Monday for the service."

Vergie told Doug to go on to work. He would be off the following day and Monday. She would be okay. She needed some time to talk with Mil and would let the boys know after school when she had more information about the service.

Just as his dad pulled out to leave for work, Terry returned home from his paper route. "Must be running late," Terry thought. Terry took off his newspaper bag and heard his mother calling Rick to get up for school. "Breakfast is ready!" She exclaimed.

Vergie did not say much to her boys as they ate breakfast. Terry looked over the paper quickly to jot down a headline for his West Virginia history class. Students could receive extra credit each week for turning in the headline of a news story that took place in West Virginia or had impact on the state. It was due by Friday.

Rick and Terry left for school. They walked together to the elementary school where Terry waited for the bus with the other high school students while Rick met up with David Jones on the playground. It was only a little over a mile to Herndon High, but the school provided a bus for kids in Covel. In a couple of years, a new building for the high school would be built even closer to Covel. It would be above the elementary school below the Basin Road.

Just before noon, Vergie sat at the family's new gossip bench where the phone was on the small desktop. She called her sister. The line was busy, but she was able to get through on the second try a couple of minutes later. "What happened?" Vergie asked.

Mildred began speaking rapidly because she knew it was a long-distance call. "Papa wasn't feeling good and complaining of hurt in his chest. He went to bed before 7. You know that is early for him. I could feel that he wasn't doing well. That's why I called Lowell, and he and Peggy came over. Lowell talked with Papa until he passed about 10:30. I don't think he was in a lot of pain, and Lowell's talking seemed to help him think about other things. You know, he always liked talking with Lowell, his first grandchild. I thought he might have something he wanted to tell him here at the end. If he did, Lowell didn't say."

After a silent pause of four or five seconds and Vergie said "Mil, you know it has been 13 years since mother and Donald died. I went to their funeral expecting Terry. This time I will be going to Papa's funeral expecting another baby. It is hard for me to realize how the circle came around."

Mil was stunned and almost at a loss for a response, except to ask. "Are you all, right?

"I don't know. I feel like it is a fog, and I am just walking through it."

Mil thought for a moment before saying with wonder, "Another nephew or niece will be coming on Sundays. You know God has a way of making things better. One passes and another comes into the world."

"I sort of wish we had told Papa Sunday, but he probably knows now." Vergie slowly spoke into the phone. After a short pause, the sisters ended their call.

The day seem to be suspended as Vergie cleaned up the kitchen and made the beds. She sat quietly in the living room remembering her childhood with her three brothers and four sisters. Her memory was clearer about her mother. Her dad seems to be in the background of her thoughts. She did not eat lunch and she kept the television turned off. Usually, she would watch Guiding Light but today that did not occur to her.

Rick was home before Terry. He could tell that his mother was not feeling good. She did not say much to him except to stay in the yard or the house until Terry gets home. When Terry arrived, he turned on the TV set in the living room to catch the remainder of American Bandstand. He knew the kids would talk about the guests and the new songs at school tomorrow.

Vergie called from the kitchen to tell the boys to turn off the TV and to come see her. From the tone, the boys knew to follow up immediately. She told them of Papa Terry's passing. Rick and Terry seemed to understand. At the very least, they had an innate sense that they should not do anything to upset their mother and that they should be quiet and calm. To them, Papa Terry was always there on Sundays at Mildred's and had spent the one Christmas at their house. He never engaged the grandchildren in conversation or play the way Granddad Bailey did. He was not as active as Granddad Bailey, either who spent his days maintaining the home place, farming, working with the beagles and hunting.

Carrie and Larry Teel had left on the Monday morning after Easter. They had stayed in a motel in Princeton for a couple of reasons. First, Carrie wanted to visit with her college friends who had remained in the area. Second, Larry liked to have his afternoon cocktail, and he knew Mildred did not approve of drinking alcohol. They were back at work on Tuesday in New Jersey.

Carrie taught Home Economics at Hunterdon High School. Larry worked for the New Jersey Highway

Department as a signal light technician. He also owned a part-time business selling, installing, repairing Mercury Marine outboard motors. The store and shop were adjacent to their home in Lambertville. Since the Delaware River served as the city limit boundary and the state's boundary with Pennsylvania, boating was a big part of the local leisure culture.

On Friday morning, the phone rang just as Carrie came out of the bathroom. Mildred broke the news about their father. "Larry has left for work. I will talk with him. We probably will leave this evening and drive part of the way and be there early tomorrow afternoon."

Mildred had arranged for Papa Terry's wake to be held at the Mercer Funeral Home Chapel in Princeton. Visitation was much more formal than it had been for Laura and Donald's wake almost 13 years before in the Littlesburg home. There was a continuous flow of people expressing sympathies, and many of the people had also been at that wake.

The funeral the next day was another blur to Vergie. She sat deep in thought, remembering the earlier funeral of her mother and brother. She still had many unanswered questions and thoughts about the events of November 19, 1945. With the death of her father, she thought there would be no more answers, no more ways to search out the truth about the tragic deaths of her mother and brother.

This time, all the children were present. Kenneth lived in Bluefield. Clarence also lived in New Jersey with his wife, Viola. Mildred still lived in her Littlesburg home. The rest of the sisters—Vergie, Marie, and Helen—lived in local coal camps with their husbands and a total of 9 grandchildren.

Mildred and Helen's children had married. There were 5 great grandchildren.

As they walked down the hill from the Sandlick Cemetery, Vergie held her husband's arm, and the boys ambled ahead of them. Vergie and Doug remained silent, but they did nod their heads as they encountered their friends and relatives. They could not help but think of the burial of Laura and Donald almost 13 years before.

As they had done for most Sundays and holidays, the Baileys went to Mildred and Nat's after the burial. The neighbors had brought plenty of food. The usual condolences were shared. Robert Gilley, Marie's husband, spoke to the group of men smoking off the back porch. "Mildred waited on him, hand, and foot. He hadn't done much in years. Hard to figure how he could just sit around. Not to speak bad of the dead," he finished his remark with a slight smirk.

Edward Paris Terry 1958
1889 - 1959

Traveling home to Covel, the Bailey foursome was quiet. Terry and Rick were on their best behavior, knowing instinctively that this was a time not to bother their parents or each other. In the quiet, the boys could hear their mom and dad talking under their breath.

"Should we tell the boys?" Doug asked his wife a little louder.

"Maybe tomorrow."

That had Terry's attention. "Tell us what?"

Vergie sighed, straightened her back and said, "How would you fellows like a little sister or brother?"

Without hesitation Terry spoke for him and Rick, "We have enough. Don't need anymore. Where would they sleep?"

Doug sighed, "Hmm."

Vergie tried again, "Well let's think about it. It could be fun with another new member of the family. Show them how to play games. Let's see how it would be, ok?"

A few days later, Vergie made it clearer to Rick and Terry that she was going to have a baby. After a few thoughtful seconds, Rick said with a grin, "I will not be the youngest. The baby will be the kid now."

Terry sighed a little and said, "It will be fun to have a sister or brother. We will have to get some new things especially if it's a girl."

On Friday, April 10, 1959, Terry celebrated his 13th birthday. The teen years were starting and maybe Terry was beginning to understand the interaction of the family and his role as the oldest child.

Forged by Coal

Chapter 25 -Three Sons and a New Decade

School was out. The summer of 1959 lay ahead. Terry was grateful to get up later to deliver the newspapers, but there came a complaint from Mr. George Akers about how late the paper was coming—sometimes as late as 9:30 am. Terry didn't understand the problem. Mr. Akers was retired from work, and Terry figured that he could take all day to read the paper.

Mr. Akers was always running errands or doing a project. He even kept the creek in front of his house cleared of litter. His wife was the postmaster who had mentored Terry into his stamp collecting hobby. Terry did not want to disappoint Mrs. Akers but he was not as concerned about her husband.

Terry still collected the subscription payment for the Bluefield Daily Telegraph once a month. He usually had something else to sell while he was collecting. He figured out early on that while folks had their wallets out to pay for the newspaper, they might buy something else. His sideline paid off as he added to his savings for college. He sold greeting cards, household products and even punch boards.

The punch boards were popular. For a dollar, you could select a "punch" on a card, usually a name. A tab over the name was removed and a number was revealed. Your name would be written on the back of the card beside of the number revealed. After all the punch/names were sold, the winning number was revealed by punching out the larger tab on the card. If you were the winner, you won a prize like a fishing rod and reel set or a set of pans. Terry got to keep half of the collected money, or he could collect the same prize.

Usually, Terry kept the money and only ordered one prize for the winner.

Cloverine brand salve was one of the items he peddled. The salve was promoted as a treatment for many skin problems and as a first aid cream. The tin of petroleum jelly-based salve cost only fifty cents, and the company offered an 8x10 color photo free with each purchase. The photo typically depicted a historic figure or place. That summer, Terry was down to his last two cans of salve and two photos, both of which showed the current president: Dwight Eisenhower. Finally, Wimpy Pedneau bought the two cans of salve. "You can keep or burn that picture of Ike," Wimpy said with a grin. Wimpy's name was Richard, but everyone called him by his nickname.

West Virginia had been a Republican strong state until the depression. The slow economy had affected the mines and the party in power got the blame. Wimpy and most of the miners switched to voting for Democrats. The Republican Party was resurging as the end of the 1950s. West Virginia was one of only a few states that did not go for Eisenhower in 1952 but did support him in 1956. The state would enter the national stage in the next presidential election through its primary election in May of 1960. Senators Hubert Humphrey and John Kennedy would campaign to see who could win a state that had a small percentage of Catholics since no Catholic had ever been elected president. Kennedy was Catholic. Terry would even have a small part in the campaign for president in Covel on the primary election day as a campaign assistant.

Politics were discussed when most of the county's coal miners had their weekly ritual of going to town on Saturday

278

mornings. The men would hang out on the street and talk sports or mine and union business. Doug would get a bag of candy at the Mullens G. C. Murphy's Five and Dime store. The store displayed the candy in glass cases and sold it by weight. Doug liked the zagnut and bit-o-honey varieties. His teeth, like many other miners, were not strong and healthy. He had already had a few pulled and assumed he would get them all out in the next couple of years. Dentures were common for many miners and their spouses as they headed toward middle age.

As a result, Vergie insisted on dental health for her children. She took them for check-ups and cleanings and required brushing before bedtime. "You should keep your teeth for as long as possible," she told her boys.

While the men would hang out on the street by the parking meters, their wives would be doing the shopping. Groceries were the biggest purchases while clothing was the next category. Mullens offered stores were better variety and in most cases better prices than the company store.

Mullens, West Virginia early 1950s. Howard Avenue, the town's
main street.   Bobby Davis Collection

Vergie had purchased a few clothing items for the baby
that would be arriving, but she knew that she would be
receiving a number of items at her baby shower.

The women of Covel threw a baby shower for Vergie.
Most of the women had finished having children, and they
were pleased that Vergie was having another youngster to be
raised in Covel. Ginny Jones, Maude Milam, Lucille Dudley,
and Eunice Lusk coordinated the effort. Principal Tom Caves
let them use one of the rooms at the elementary school for the
event. Almost every woman in the camp came or sent a gift.
Vergie had attended many showers over the last nine years in
Covel. It was payback time and the women, all mothers except
Marie Pedneau. and Gertrude Caves. The women were sure
to include receipts with any gift that was clearly meant for a

boy or a girl so that Vergie could exchange it after the baby arrived and the sex was known. Most of the gifts had come from stores in Mullens with a few exceptions of items that had been purchased in Beckley or Bluefield.

* * *

1959 was wrapping up with the traditional Thanksgiving celebration at the Bailey Homeplace in Rock. As customary the family butchered two hogs. Grandfather Bailey and his sons were all experienced in this annual ritual. The roaring outside fire for boiling water for the hog skinning and cleaning provided light and heat for the early morning work.

Vergie was glad to be there. It was the first holiday without her dad but being with her unchanged extended family comforted her. The Baileys and Terrys celebrated the holidays as usual. Life was continuing.

At Rock and at Littlesburg, the family members all asked Vergie how she was doing. Her answer was always the same, "The baby is due within weeks and should arrive before Christmas." She was tired but felt better and perhaps was clearer in her thoughts than any time since April and her father's passing.

Terry and Rick were excited for Christmas. Both had given their Christmas list to Santa early. Terry was less sure that Santa existed, but he did not want to spoil it for Rick. For that matter, he didn't want to take any chances for himself, just in case. Both boys were thrilled that this year's Christmas vacation was a full two weeks. The last day of school before the break would be Friday, December 18, and school would reopen on Monday, January 3, 1960. It sounded so different. The boys had lived in the 1950's for most of their short lives.

1960 sounded like the future. Somehow the boys had a feeling that things were going to change faster in the 1960s.

On Friday, December 18th, Terry took the school bus home. There were no basketball practices scheduled until after Christmas. Terry was one of the new managers of the team. He and his co-manager, Estil Elliott, were a good pair to take care of the basketballs, uniforms, and equipment. Terry had exercised with the team and did some limited routines with the basketball passing the ball to each of the players for a running basket shot. He wasn't much of a player, but he liked spending time with the team. Ken Blankenship, a senior, was training Terry to keep the score book, a pastime that seemed like fun to a math nerd like Terry. He was thinking about becoming a math and science teacher, so he relished the number crunching required in scoring a basketball game.

When Terry arrived home, his mother greeted him and Rick." Remember boys the Milams are coming over after dinner. We are having sandwiches because you will have plenty of snacks all evening. Also, I will not have to clean up the kitchen before they come over."

Doug, Vergie, and the boys hosted Bill and Maude Milam for cards and board games. The Milams had three children, Gay and her two brothers, Billy and Johnny. Gay was Terry's age; Johnny was Rickey's age and Billy was in between Terry and Rickey. With the television on in the background the kids sat on the floor playing monopoly. Terry was the banker. The adults played 500 Rummy at the kitchen table—wives versus husbands.

After the Milams left, Vergie told Doug, "I am very sleepy. Let's get everyone to bed."

"Good idea, I'm ready for some shuteye." Doug replied. After brushing their teeth with the new Pepsodent toothpaste, the boys hit the bed in their bedroom while their parents turned in. About 3 am, Vergie woke up with the familiar pain she had experienced three times before. Labor was starting, and Madam Cleo's prediction was about to come true.

"Doug, I think we should go to the hospital but no rush," Vergie nudged Doug awake.

Doug got out of bed and dressed in his new flannel shirt and new pants that Vergie had given him for his birthday just four days earlier. He pulled the suitcase out from under the bed. "You need to pack anything else?" he inquired. Vergie had packed the suitcase with a new gown and under garments that she had purchased in Mullens at Cook's Department Store.

"Get my toothbrush, and I will put my cosmetics bag in there too," Vergie replied.

She wanted to be sure she had her products from Avon. The new sales representative, Shirley McKinney from Herndon, had delivered them earlier in the week. Shirley had been widowed about two years before when her husband was killed in a mining accident. Most people thought she would remarry since she was just in her late 20s, but she wanted to be independent and raise her two sons. She also wanted to finish her high school diploma. She had dropped out to have her first child and to be married when she was in the eleventh grade.

Doug took his sons to the Repasses across the road. Vergie had planned weeks before with the Repass clan for Terry and Rick to stay with them. Doug helped his wife out to the car and placed the suitcase in the back seat. "We only have ten miles to go this time," Doug told Vergie. They were headed to Mullens to the newly opened Wyoming General Hospital. This baby would be born in Wyoming County while Terry, Pamela and Rickey had been born in their parents' birth county, Mercer.

On Saturday, December 19, 1959, the Baileys had their third son and fourth child. The new arrival was named Jeffery Kevin Bailey. Vergie would later tell her girlfriends and sisters that this was her easiest delivery. She was ready and her new son was ready.

Terry and Rick were excited to visit the hospital later that day. They raised up on their tip toes to look through the glass in the maternity ward to see their brother. Dr. Ward Wylie, the hospital's director and founder walked down the hall and stopped to congratulate the father and brothers. "Everything going well?" The doctor asked.

"Doc, she did good. They are both fine. Dr. Penn says there is no sign of polio. You know, like this one," Doug rested his hand on Rick's small shoulder.

"That's good Mr. Bailey. We are glad to have Wyoming General here so that folks don't have to travel an hour to get to a hospital either in Beckley or Bluefield."

"We are glad too, Doc. I am thankful. This is making a difference to be this close. I think Vergie and the boy will get to come home Tuesday according to Doc Penn."

Doug had called his folks in Rock to tell them the news. He had caught his dad just as he was headed out to feed the chickens. "Dad, you got another grandson. We have named him Jeffery. Vergie and he are doing fine." Doug spoke in a loud a voice because he knew it was long distance and his dad had just gotten hearing aids. The hearing aids were built into the earpieces of his eyeglasses.

"Doug that's good to hear. Jeffery is his name, you say? Guess he will have a new cousin too. Wally just called; they had a boy just this morning. Two grandkids, ha! Wally's named theirs Lynn. They will get to grow up together. We look forward to having all of you here in the new year.

On Sunday, Doug and his sons spent most of the day at the hospital visiting with the new member of the family through the maternity ward window. There was a steady flow of visitors that afternoon, including neighbors from Covel and Marie Gilley and her family from Piedmont.

Terry and Rick were excited to have their new brother at home. They brought their coal camp playmates into the house to introduce them to Jeff. Rick told the guys, "He will grow up fast. We will have him playing cowboy and Indians in no time." Terry was given more of a caregiving role for Rick while their mother was recovering from the delivery and caring for Jeff. At almost 14, Terry was considered old enough to be responsible for his younger brothers.

* * *

As Terry collected the newspaper fees at the end of December, most of his customers asked about his new brother. Terry proudly produced a black and white Polaroid® picture to show his customers. His dad had decided to get an early Christmas present for the family and bought the new camera that could develop photos in 60 seconds. Doug had already used six rolls of film snapping family photos and learning about his new camera. He took pride in producing the photos and coating the image with the sticky substance from the sponge applicator that came with the film.

285

Doug Bailey takes a Polaroid® of his three sons, Terry, Rickey, and Jeffery on Christmas morning 1960.

* * *

Wimpy Pedneau, recently retired after the Virginian Railroad was purchased by Norfolk & Western, paid Terry with a two-dollar bill. "Keep the change," Wimpy said loudly. Wimpy probably had a hearing problem from working on the railroad line around the noise of the trains and maintenance equipment.

"What are you doing this election day, Terry?" Wimpy asked.

"School's out for voting, so I guess I am not doing anything," came Terry's reply.

"Would you like to earn another two-dollar bill that day?" Wimpy asked.

"Sure, what do I need to do?" Terry replied. Wimpy then explained that the Democratic Party had two candidates in the presidential primary election in May: Senator Hubert Humphrey and Senator John Kennedy.

"Dr. Ward Wylie is heading up Senator Kennedy's campaign in the state. He asked me if I wanted to support Kennedy. I don't really care, but he offered to pay me to work the polls here at Covel. So, I need someone to hand out campaign material while I talk Kennedy up. You want to do it?"

"I can do it," Terry quickly agreed. "Is Kennedy the one that's going to win?"

"Nay, he ain't got much chance. Everybody knows the Humphrey name and besides, Kennedy is Catholic. There won't be much support for him, but Wylie has money to spend on his campaign, so we might as well take some of it."

Terry pondered for a moment and then said, "I don't know about this. If we are going to work for a man, we ought to expect him to win."

"Maybe you are right. We can stay positive and push. Who knows, he might pull it off. Doc Wylie is a popular guy, and if they campaign hard and talk to enough miners, he might win it."

"I will ask my folks, and if it's okay with them, I will work for you and Kennedy on election day. We might get Covel to go for Kennedy," Terry's grin mimicked his dad's expression when Doug was pleased with something.

Button worn on West Virginia primary election day by
Terry in May 1960.

* * *

On New Year's Eve 1959, the Baileys joined the Milams
for their celebration to welcome 1960. Jeff slept through the
evening but was the first to wake up, around 2:00 am. As
Vergie rocked Jeff back to sleep, she was thought about the
years ahead. This year, she and Doug would be married 15
years. When she married, she had not given much thought
about the future. She was not worried about where she and
Doug would be living as long as they were together. She really
had not thought about how many children she wanted—only
that she wanted them. Now she was proud of her three sons.
But she also wondered about Pamela and what it would have
been like to have a ten-year-old daughter.

That night, in the first hours of the 1960s, she thought
about the future. Terry and Rickey would graduate from high
school, and she wanted them to go to college. Jeffery would
not even be in high school by 1970. She also thought about
the past. She could see the changes within the community.
Covel was now owned by individuals, not the coal company.
They were buying their house, not renting from the coal

company. When she and Doug first saw the camp, American Coal was mining coal at an operation called Covel, and now they were out of business. The company store had little business and probably would be closed. They no longer had scrip. There were no Black folks in the camp. She wondered what happened to them. There was no Virginian Railroad. It had been purchased by Norfolk & Western. There was talk of school consolidation, merging the elementary school with Herndon Elementary School. Doug had put in a bathroom which was the best thing that had ever happened for the house. There had been a lot of change in ten years.

* * *

As Jeff dozed off and Vergie became drowsy, her final thought for New Year's morning 1960, was, "What will the future bring to the Baileys of Covel and the thousands of coal miners and their families living in the coal camps of Appalachia? Then she thought of one of her favorite songs by Doris Day, Que Será Será. "Whatever will be will be", she hummed as her eyes closed.

- END -

A generation continues.

Forged by Coal

Forged by Coal

EPILOGUE

A Follow Up

Appalachia

You live in a company house. You go to a company school.
You work for this company according to the company rules.
You all drink company water and all use company lights.
The company preacher teaches us. What the company thinks
is right. (1)

Carl Sandburg
Poet Laureate of the U.S. 1964

The coal camps depicted in this work were situated in
West Virginia, in the heart of Appalachia—country rich in
bituminous coal. Coal became King in West Virginia before
1900. Before the Industrial Revolution expanded the need for
coal, aka black gold, few people lived in the hollows and
mountain ridges of southern West Virginia. The folks living in
West Virginia's Appalachia up until the 1890s were mostly
subsistence farmers with very limited income, living primarily
off the land. That changed as the demand for coal increased
and logging began. The mineral rights were purchased or
sometimes stolen from the local people by unscrupulous
speculators. The region's rich mineral resources and virgin
timber presented an opportunity for railroad operators to
expand into the area.

For a period of sixty years, hundreds of coal mines were
opened throughout southern West Virginia. Pre-automation

mining operations were labor intensive. Men dug and loaded the coal by hand, which required a large labor force. The available local labor was insufficient to meet the growing demand, so the coal companies recruited men from outside the Appalachian region and from other countries. Some immigrants to the United States were recruited to become coal miners by labor agents stationed at ports of entry. These agents often deceived new recruits by exaggerating the wonderful conditions for working and living in the Appalachia coal region. Other immigrants followed friends and relatives to the coal camps. Many came from the mining regions of Great Britain and Ireland. By 1930, immigrants made up the largest percentage of the workforce in the mines. There was also an increase in Black workers who found better opportunity in the mines than in the field work of the deep south.

To support the mining operations and the influx of workers, the coal companies built, and operated Company towns commonly known as "coal camps", which became as numerous as the coal mines. The locations of the coal camps were dictated by the location of the coal deposits. In most cases in West Virginia, these deposits were remote and frequently without accessible roads. By necessity, the coal companies had to provide housing and by extension, the fundamental services required by a miner and his family. They provided miners and their families a place to live, a place to buy goods and services, a place to worship, a place to go to school, as well as opportunities for personal and recreational activities. Covel, like most coal camps, had a segregated housing section for the Black miners, which included a separate church and school. (1)

Epilogue

The region remained isolated up until 1960, known to very few people outside of the corporate coal mine owners, railroad operators and the mine laborers and their families. Before the Interstate Highway System, traveling to this area by automobile was an effort.

The region received little national attention up until 1960, with the notable exception of visits by First Lady Eleanor Roosevelt (2). During the Democratic primary of 1960, Vice President Hubert Humphrey and Senator John Kennedy battled to win delegates to the Democrat National Convention. West Virginia became a proving ground to test whether a Catholic candidate—Kennedy—could win in a predominantly Protestant state. Film crews from national media outlets followed the candidates as they campaigned in Appalachia. The evening network news and television special programs broadcast into America's living rooms the poverty and living conditions of the residents of Appalachia. It was the first time the modern medium of television focused its lens on the economic and cultural aspects of the coal miners' lives in Appalachia.

Senator John F. Kennedy, far left, with state Senator Dr. Ward Wylie, center and Franklin D. Roosevelt Jr., April 26, 1960, in Mullens. Kennedy was the first presidential candidate to visit Wyoming County, West Virginia. He traveled from Bluefield to Mullens via state route 10 and probably is the closest any presidential candidate has ever been to Covel. File Photo Register-Herald, Beckley, WV. Used by permission.

This new attention prompted politicians and sociologists to focus on the area. "If...new leadership, and new understanding can restore prosperity to the coal industry— and I believe it can—then I am here to tell you that prosperity is on the way..." John F. Kennedy remarked in a campaign speech on April 18, 1960, in Morgantown. Later in the speech, he continued, "And we must act now to meet this challenge if coal is to be in the future – as it has been in the past – the foundation of American strength and the source of American plenty." (3)

Despite the sentiments of Kennedy's speech, job provided by mining began to decline dramatically. In 1965, author Mary K Bowman wrote: "... Suffice it to say that the operators mechanized the mines each machine replacing several men. They also put up for sale the low-cost company houses. The net result of the many acts of consolidation and improvement of mining methods which eliminated men is that a greatly reduced work force of skilled men get out a greater amount of cleaner coal than ever before. Thousands of miners lost their jobs permanently, and all who could do so left the state..." (4)

The mines where Douglas Bailey worked—the Covel mine at Deerfield and the Itmann mine—have all closed, as have all the mines that existed along Route 10 when the Bailey sons were growing up in Wyoming county: Herndon, Monticello, Bud, Alpoca, and New Richmond. In 1950, there were 44 coal operations in the county, but by 2020 there were only three.

To this day, there continues to be a steady flow of studies, projects, books, video documentaries and oratory about coal mining and invigorating the economy of Appalachia.

* * *

"We love clean, beautiful West Virginia coal. And you know, that's indestructible stuff. In times of war, in times of conflict, you can blow up those windmills, they fall down real quick. You can blow up pipelines, they go like this. You can do a lot of things to those solar panels, but you know what you can't hurt? Coal. You can do whatever you want to coal. Very important." Donald Trump, August 21, 2018, speaking at a rally in Charleston, West Virginia. (5)

* * *

The U.S. Census for 1950 reported a population of 37,540 for Wyoming County, the setting of this book. Today the population is estimated at 20,798. The state of West Virginia has the distinction among the United States of having fewer people in 2020 than it had in 1950. Where are the plans and strategies to revive the economy of this area of Appalachia? From John Kennedy to Donald Trump, the people of Appalachia have listened to and supported candidates that have failed, to-date, to deliver a future for the region that does not depend on coal mining.

Jefferson Never Slept in this Monticello

Early photo of Monticello coal camp. Used with permission of the WV State Archives.

When the Monticello coal camp was first constructed by Monticello Smokeless Coal Company, it was referred to as Monticarlo. By the time the Baileys moved there in 1949, it was called Monticello. As a Regional News Services (RNS) reporter for the daily Raleigh Register newspaper, I wrote an

Epilogue

article entitled "Monticello Bows to Progress". In my research for that 1965 article, I verified the community's name. The article detailed the end of the coal camp known as Monticello. The company replaced the camp with a new coal preparation plant. A copy of the article is reprinted here.

Covel

At one of the two West Virginia highway signs identifying Covel. The Covel Post Office located in the shadow of the Virginian Railway trestle. August 2021. Photos by Scott Bailey

Covel, West Virginia is my childhood community. I grew up there with the guidance of my parents, Lowell Douglas and Vergie Ellen Terry, and with my brothers, Richard Keith and Jeffery Kevin. In 1930, Covel was one of nearly 500 coal company towns in West Virginia. The community is located 11 miles west of Mullens on state route 10 at coordinates: 37°29′19″N 81°19′24″W. Both branches of the Gooney Creek flow through the camp creating a natural boundary for the community.

The Gooney Otter Creek flows for a total distance of seven miles, starting from the mountain near Clarks Gap, running by the original Covel coal mine operation and through the camp, merging with its left branch in the camp before dumping into Barkers Creek, about three miles west of Covel.

A railroad trestle with a span of 720 feet still towers 150 feet above the community. It is the second largest on the former Virginian Line; however, no trains currently travel the rails towering above the former camp, and there has been no mining of coal in the Covel "holler" for more than 85 years.

~ Bobby Davis Collection

A new Virginian class EL-1A electric locomotive number 113 has twenty six assorted freight cars in tow as the train crosses the Covel Bridge, milepost 366. With no white flags showing on the front of the locomotive, the train is scheduled freight number 64. When the 113 was built in March 1926 by Alco ~ Westinghouse, it could produce 2,375 horsepower. More sleuthing suggests a window for the date: The first car in the train is a "Billboard Reefer," meaning it carried advertising for its owner. In 1934, such advertising was outlawed by the

My parents purchased their home in 1958, indicated by the arrow. The coal railroad cars parked on the siding are waiting to be filled from the mines. The photo above is probably from the early 1930s. Text description by Aubrey Wiley, author, historian, and a friend of mine from my days in Lynchburg, Virginia.

Flood of 1961
The second house on the right is our home. Flooding in the spring from the Gooney Otter Creek would occur almost annually. The woman is Francis Jones, our neighbor.

From the Francis Jones Collection

Epilogue

I took the photo below in the early 1960s. An additional room was added to our house. The house purchased is under the right arrow. The left arrow marks the house where we lived when last renting from the coal company. Neither house is standing today.

Covel Elementary School, (White) three rooms, grades 1 through 6. The school has been demolished. Manufactured homes are on the site today.   Photo taken about 1960.

Forged by Coal

Scale model of the Covel School for Blacks and the Black Church built
by Bobby Davis. The buildings were adjacent to each other and used a
shared parking lot. They were located at the upper end of the community
closest to the mining operations. Both were demolished for the building
materials in the early 1960s. After the individual sale of homes including
those occupied by Blacks there were no Black residents in the community
Photo by Bobby Davis

Covel was built by J.T. Morris in 1915 as a mining camp
for the labor force of their new coal operation. The coal camp
was originally named Morco probably for **Mo**rris **Co**al. The
mines and tipple operation were at the head of the hollow with
a rail spur line to transport the coal from the tipple to the main
Virginian line.

Camps were built close to the mining operations so that
the miners could walk to their work Covel had two schools,
one for the white students and one for Black students. And
there were two separate churches, separated also by race.

The company-owned and operated store served
everyone. The store stocked groceries, clothing, cookware,
basic furniture, hardware, and the items a miner needed to

perform his work, such as picks, shovels, blasting caps, explosives and lanterns. Eventually union contracts required coal companies to furnish the equipment and materials necessary to mine the coal and the company store discontinued stocking the mining supplies.

The mining operation, along with the coal camp, were sold in 1919 to Major William P. Tams. Tams was considered a unique owner of coal mine operations in the bituminous coal fields. He earned an engineering degree from Virginia Polytechnical Institute and came to the area in 1904. Four years later he started his own coal company, Gulf Smokeless Coal Co and built the coal camp called Tams in neighboring Raleigh County. Unlike most fellow coal barons, he resided in a modest house in his coal camp like the miners. He was very progressive in establishing the first bath houses for miners in West Virginia. The Tams coal camp also had the first movie theater in the county and a recreation center that included an indoor swimming pool. (6)

"Major" William Purviance Tams, Jr. (May 19, 1883 – August 3, 1977) second owner of the Covel coal camp.
File photo Register-Herald, Beckley, WV

Fifty cents script value issued by Tams' company, Covel Smokeless Coal Company.   From Terry's collection of script.

Upon purchasing the mining operation in Wyoming County, Tams selected the company name of Covel Smokeless Coal Company and changed the camp's name to Covel. Tams may have been attempting to secure favor with a major coal broker, Borden Covel who lived in Boston. Tams and Covel were prominent, influential leaders in the coal industry.

The mines at Covel operated from 1915 until 1937. When we moved to Covel in late 1949, it was owned by the American Coal Company, which operated mines in Deerfield and Itmann. Miners working at these locations rented houses at Covel. In 1957, J.H. Lilly Land Company purchased all the houses in the camp. The houses were sold individually to the miners on an installment plan. Lilly Land provided a payoff of the remaining balance in event of death of the miner.

The classified advertisement from the Beckley Post Herald for the houses is on the next page.

At the time of the housing sale by American Coal, every house but two was occupied by a miner or company employee's family. In 2022 there were only two coal miners living in the community.

The company store closed in 1963. The only remaining commercial entity in the community is a post office. Covel was assigned the zip code 24719 when the postal service added the zip code system in 1963. Strong lobbying efforts have avoided the possibility of closing the post office at least twice during the last decade.

2020 Photo of Covel taken from Route 10 by Bobby Davis

The spirit of community cooperation still thrives in Covel. The Baptist church serves as the focal point for community involvement, not only for religion but service to people. The community operates a food bank that serves the county, much of southern West Virginia, and bordering southwest Virginia. In 2020, the food bank received a generous gift from an anonymous donor to purchase a shell building which was placed on the foundation of the last company store building to serve as a warehouse.

Epilogue

The Scout House, built by the coal company as a warehouse, was used as a Scout meeting place until the troop was disbanded, serves as a community center for socials and dinners.

I attended meetings at the Scout House and remained a Scout until I was 17, earning the rank of Life Scout. I earned the required number of merit badges for Eagle Scout; however, I never developed an Eagle Project, having become more focused on high school activities like many other teenage Scouts. Scouting provided me the opportunity to also serve as a patrol leader, scribe, and eventually senior patrol leader. These scouting positions provided me with experience that would contribute to my professional career in education for 45 years. I am thankful for the opportunity and the Scout leaders that helped me.

* * *

As of this writing, 76 individuals call Covel their home. Covel's residents, like most of their fellow West Virginians, have a love for their state. The anthem for those who call the area home is John Denver's "Take Me Home Country Roads." Nestled at the foot of a mountain with an elevation of 3200 feet above sea level and accessible only by a two-lane state road, the residents take heart in hearing:

"Country roads, take me home
To the place I belong
West Virginia, mountain mama
Take me home, country roads" *(7)*

Bailey Family

Lake Erie Bailey   **Cora Lee Foster Bailey**

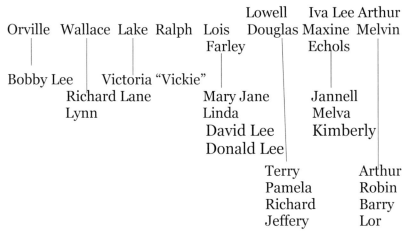

Lowell   Iva Lee Arthur
Orville Wallace Lake Ralph Lois   Douglas Maxine Melvin
Farley   Echols

Bobby Lee   Victoria "Vickie"
Richard Lane   Mary Jane   Jannell
Lynn   Linda   Melva
David Lee   Kimberly
Donald Lee

Terry   Arthur
Pamela   Robin
Richard   Barry
Jeffery   Lor

Lake and Lee Bailey
Daughters – Maxine and Lois
Sons – Melvin, Douglas, Junior, Wallace, Orville
Photo at 50th Wedding Anniversary 1965

Terry Family

Edward Paris Terry   Laura Belle Hedrick Terry

Nellie
Kenneth Mildred Helen Marie Carrie Vergie Clarence Donald
Tabor   Davis Gilley Teel   Bailey

Ruth   Lawrence James
Louise

Lowell   Donnie Jo   Terry
(Sigmon)   Lindell Robert Lane Pamela
Carmen   Lois   Iris   Richard
Andra   Connie   Joyce   Jeffery
Vickie   (Stella)
Laura   India "Mitzi"
Todd   Jackie
Greg   Mark
Tammy

Terry Sisters – Carrie, Mildred, Vergie, Helen, and Marie.1985

*These families helped shape the life and times portrayed
in Forged by Coal: A Family's Story.*

The following sources were used in writing the epilogue.

(1) National Park Service. (n.d.) Retrieved from https://www.nps.gov/neri/planyourvisit/african-american-life-in-a-coal-camp-nuttallburg.htm

(2) Griffith, Amanda "Eleanor Roosevelt." e-WV: The West Virginia Encyclopedia. 08 December 2015. Web. 24 January 2020. Retrieved from: https://www.wvencyclopedia.org/articles/129

(3) Papers of John F. Kennedy. Pre-Presidential Papers. Presidential Campaign Files, 1960. Speeches and the Press. Speeches, Statements, and Sections, 1958-1960. Natural resources: Coal by Wire. Retrieved from: https://www.jfklibrary.org/asseT viewer/archives/JFKCAMP1960/1031/JFKCAMP1960-1031-008?image_identifier=JFKCAMP1960-1031-008-p0001

(4) Mary Keller Bowman, Reference Book of Wyoming County History: McClain, 1965

(5)President Donald Trump, August 21, 2018 speaking at a rally in Charleston, West Virginia. (Rolling Stone, August 22, 2018, "Trump's Love of Coal will Never Not be Absurd.") Retrieved from: https://www.rollingstone.com/politics/politics-news/trump-coal-west-virginia-714322/

(6) Sullivan, Ken "William Purviance Tams Jr.." e-WV: The West Virginia Encyclopedia. 09 December 2015. Web. 22 January 2022. Retrieved from:https://www.wvencyclopedia.org/articles/684

(7) Danoff, Bill & Denver, John & Nivert, Taffy (1971). Take me home, country roads.

ACKNOWLEDGMENTS

I am fortunate to have the encouragement and support of my wife, Ann, in writing *Forged by Coal*. She suggested that I approach her daughter, Martha Helen Ware to edit this work. I am grateful beyond measure to Martha as she spent untold hours with the manuscript and made this work possible.

My son, Scott, and daughter, Terry Lynn, made suggestions, encouraged me, and have always had a love and respect for their family heritage.

Clarence Terry, my uncle, who shared his memories of childhood and the impact of the tragedy of his mother and brother's deaths. Our last conversation was a month before his death in April 2021. He was 90.

Lowell Davis, my first cousin and son of Helen Terry and George Davis recounted the story of attending our grandmother and uncle's funeral in 1945 at age 8 ½ and was with our Papa Terry when he died in 1959. Lowell died at age 84 on January 5, 2022.

Marie and Robert Gilley, my mother's sister, they shared memories of their and my parents early married life. They helped me to relieve memories of my childhood at Mildred and Nat's. They raised three children in the Piedmont coal camp just a few miles from Covel. After 68 years of marriage, they died in 2008 six months apart.

-   Continued   -

Margaret Pugh, the oldest living former resident of Covel (age 99 at this writing) made her home there from 1929 to 1946. She went to church and school in the camp, married there, and had her first child at home in a Covel company house. She shared with me the firsthand experience of what life was like during the pinnacle of coal company operations. Her father and her husband mined coal in the Covel mines. Her father was the first Black motorman in the mining operations.

Verland Cecil shared accounts of his experiences as a coal camp kid and as a second-generation coal miner and the loss of his father and oldest brother in mining accidents. Verland died at age 84 as the result of an automobile accident in February 2021.

Bobby Davis shared his knowledge of the history of Covel as well as insight into the current community which is pulling together for the good of its neighbors throughout southern West Virginia and beyond.

To my extended family, friends and especially those individuals mentioned in this book, you have provided me with precious memories. Each person's life is touched by so many other lives. It is a wonderful life.

ABOUT THE AUTHOR

Terry Douglas Bailey was born, grew-up, and was educated in the coalfields of West Virginia. Some of his childhood experiences are presented in *Forged by Coal*. He graduated from Concord University, Athens, West Virginia and earned a masters and a doctorate from the University of Virginia. He retired after a 45-year distinguished career in public education as a teacher, librarian, supervisor, principal, and superintendent. He was named Virginia Media Educator of the Year 1988 and Vermont Vocational Director of the Year 2003. Terry lives with his wife Ann and their dog, PT, "Prince Terry" in Greenville, South Carolina. He enjoys his seven grandchildren, ages 6 to 16 that he entertains with magic tricks. He can be reached at terrydbailey@gmail.com.

The author at 7 with Blinky by the coal house in Covel.

Forged by Coal
A Family's Story

Terry   Jeff   Rick   04/2018

BAILEY BROTHERS

Terry left West Virginia after college. He worked in public education for 45 years. He retired in 2014 and lives with his wife, Ann in Greenville, South Carolina

Jeff graduated from Bluefield State College in Mining Engineering Technology and worked in the coal mines for 16 years before returning to college to become a Physical Therapist Assistant in 1996. He lives in Mullens, West Virginia with his wife, Liz.

Rick graduated from Bluefield State College in electrical engineering. He worked in mining for 42 years and lived in Mullens, West Virginia, He retired in 2014 and lives with his wife, Jamie in Palm Bay, Florida.

Coal work of Doug, Rick, and Jeff Bailey total 101 years.